International Business Development

Ludwig Martin
Editor

International Business Development

A Concise Textbook Focusing on
International B-to-B Contexts

 **Springer** Gabler

Editor
Ludwig Martin
Pforzheim University
Pforzheim, Germany

ISBN 978-3-658-33220-4   ISBN 978-3-658-33221-1   (eBook)
https://doi.org/10.1007/978-3-658-33221-1

Die Deutsche Nationalbibliothek verzeichnet diese Publikation in der Deutschen Nationalbibliografie; detaillierte bibliografische Daten sind im Internet über http://dnb.d-nb.de abrufbar.

Planung/Lektorat: Ulrike Loercher
This Springer Gabler imprint is published by the registered company Springer Fachmedien Wiesbaden GmbH part of Springer Nature.
The registered company address is: Abraham-Lincoln-Str. 46, 65189 Wiesbaden, Germany

Foreword

Theories, terminology, common approaches and current topics in international business development, in one concise book. This was the aim of this book from the onset. The task was to pair the content with suitable authors, who understand the audience and are experienced in the field of international business development.

To this end we brought together authors from different continents and diverse educational and professional backgrounds to collaborate on a well-rounded book on international business development. A thank you to all authors for your efforts and bearing with me as the editor of this book. Through your contributions it is possible to give advanced business students as well as practitioners some well-founded, practice-grounded insights on the topic of international business development. A further thanks to the reviewers involved, who ensured the quality of the contributions. The input of Gabriella Loveday in editing and improving the use of the English language in the texts shall not go unnoticed. Thank you all. Thank you also to the families and friends for supporting the authors.

The assembly of the contributions tries to mimic the process of a business taking its product abroad. This covers the full range from developing products for an international market to strategic considerations, setting up supply chains and sales channels—combined with a close look into the social responsibility of business in a globalized multicultural world. A particular feature of this book is the focus on Business to Business contexts as ample textbooks mainly look into Business to Consumer type of interactions and settings. With this book a shift in focus is hence encouraged.

This book provides students and practitioners with basic concepts used in the field of international management. It is a good resource for anyone tasked with developing business interests on an international level.

January 2021

Prof. Dr. Ludwig Martin
Professor for International Management in Engineering
Pforzheim University, Germany

Contents

Contributors

Rafael Correa is a lecturer of English for Engineers at Pforzheim University. With a background in environmental law and cross-cultural competencies, he has assisted European and North-American companies in navigating Brazil's legal system and settling into the Brazilian market.

Michele Elio De Tullio is an attorney at law and trademark attorney admitted in Italy and EU. He is the founder and managing Partner of De Tullio & Partners (Rome, Italy). He is author of publications on Intellectual Property and frequent lecturer in Italian Universities of law. He is an active member of main IP Associations with leadership roles, and expert in working groups set up by EUIPO and European Commission.

Jorge Del Castillo is Professor of International Business at Universidad Esan in Lima, Peru as well as a consultant on governmental affairs. He has had previous experiences at the United Nations' Organization for International Migration and at the Inter-American Development Bank. He has also experience in international education and training courses design when managing international law enforcement programs in South America. He is currently working on comparative international education policies and its influences on Peruvian college degree students.

Marcel Fortwingel is a scientific assistant at the Fraunhofer Institute for Industrial Engineering IAO. The focus of his work is on frugal innovation research, start-up eco-systems and human factors in research and development. Marcel Fortwingel is also co-founder of the Stuttgart-based food startup Kernique and works as a freelance learning coach. He has a master's degree in Sociology (M.A.) with focus on empirical research and a bachelor's degree (B.A.) in English & American Studies.

Hector Gomez Macfarland holds an Electronic and Telecommunications Engineering degree, as well as Master and Philosophy Doctorate degrees, in business management and Marketing, respectively. He joins vast experience in academia and industry. He works in academia for the last 25 years. He is a Professor of Marketing in the School of Business and Technology at Huston Tillotson University in Austin, TX (USA), and the Tec de Monterrey (Mexico). As a visiting academic he regularly teaches at Pforzheim

University (Germany). Additionally, Dr Gomez Macfarland is an international high technology entrepreneur, corporate executive, and independent consultant. Dr Gomez Macfarland has a broad international network in industry as well as in the scholarly world.

Henning Hinderer is Professor of Business Administration and Technical Sales at Pforzheim University. He holds a doctoral degree in engineering/technology management from the University of Stuttgart since 2005. He is a full-time professor at Pforzheim University, having served in various positions and is the program director BSc Engineering and Management/Innovation and Design. His main research interests are strategic management, innovation, and ecosystems in mobility. He also has a sound business experience in business consulting mainly in the area of innovation and process management.

Katharina Kilian-Yasin is Professor of International Business for Engineers at Pforzheim University, Germany, and serves as the university's Ethics Officer. She also works as an intercultural consultant and trainer with a regional focus on the Middle East and North Africa. Prior to her university appointment, she worked in the printing machines industry and served as a diplomat to the German Federal Foreign Office. Her research interests include critical perspectives in international and cross-cultural management, CSR, organizational learning, and international HRM.

Ansgar Kühn is Professor of Operations Management at Pforzheim University. He holds a doctoral degree in industrial science and technology of University Henri Poincaré I, in Nancy, France since 2001. He is a full-time professor at Pforzheim University, having served in various positions, and is the program director M.Sc. Engineering and Management. His main research interests are strategic management, operations and project management. Prior to being appointed professor at Pforzheim University he gained profound business experience in international companies in wood products and chemical industry.

Jasmin Mahadevan is Professor at Pforzheim University, Pforzheim, Germany. Drawing from a multi-ethnic, multi-cultural and multi-lingual background, she has experienced international and cross-cultural management as a practitioner, as a researcher, and as an academic. An editorial board member and frequent guest-editor of several academic journals, Jasmin Mahadevan holds an executive position at the *European Academy of Management*, and her work has appeared in numerous journals, books and handbooks. She is the author of the *Very Short, Fairly Interesting and Reasonably Cheap Book about Cross-Cultural Management* (Sage 2017), and the main editor of *Cases in Critical Cross-Cultural Management* (Taylor und Francis 2020).

Ludwig Martin is Professor of International Management in Engineering at Pforzheim University (Germany) and serves on management boards of consulting firms in Germany and South Africa. He holds a doctoral degree (PhD) from the University of Cape Town.

His work as an academic and as a consultant has provided much exposure to international networks in industry and academia alike. Ludwig Martin has published extensively. As a consultant he engages in various development projects, with a particular focus on projects on the African continent.

Maria Giorgia Mazzilli is an attorney at law and associate with De Tullio & Partners. She has a LLM at the College of Europe in European Legal Studies and working experience in IP Law acquired at the EUIPO and the EPO.

Moritz Peter is Professor of Procurement Management at Pforzheim University (Germany). Prior to this appointment he served as vice-president, head of campus, program director and professor at the International School of Management (ISM). Moritz Peter gained first hand practical experience working in the finance and procurement department of Mercedes Benz Cars & Vans for five years before switching to Porsche Consulting.

Claudio Pousa is Professor of Marketing and Research Methods at Lakehead University (Canada). He holds a doctoral degree in Business Administration, as well as Masters in Strategic Management, Electrical Engineering and Mechanical Engineering. He has a sound business experience as a consultant in sales management in Latin America, and has published extensively on topics of coaching salespeople, leading sales forces and salesperson relationship behaviours.

Philipp Rathgeber is Professor of Brand Management & Entrepreneurship at the International School of Management (ISM). He is also the Co-Founder and CEO of the beauty brand ELIXR. He previously spent 7 years at McKinsey & Company where he advised clients in the consumer goods industry.

Tobias Reichert is a graduate student of Management at NOVA School of Business and Economics, Lisbon, Portugal, with strategy as a focus field of study. Tobias Reichert holds a B.Sc. in International Engineering and Management from Pforzheim University, Pforzheim, Germany, with a specialization in International Management. His research interests involve strategy as organizational activity, as related to strategy-as-practice, and international and cross-cultural management. In his previous work, Tobias Reichert has focussed on identifying and facilitating successful strategizing in the increasingly relevant context of Global Virtual Teams.

Astrid Wiedersich Avena is an attorney at Law with 16 years of experience and Senior Associate at De Tullio & Partners. She attained an LLM in Intellectual Property Law at Queen Mary University of London and has sound expertise in advising both Italian and foreign companies on trademark, copyright, design, IT and commercial matters as well as on domain name and geographical indications issues.

Liza Wohlfart is a senior scientist and industry consultant at the Fraunhofer Institute for Industrial Engineering IAO and head of the Center for Frugal Products and

Manufacturing Systems at S-TEC, the Stuttgart Technology and Innovation Campus. The focus of Liza Wohlfart's work is on frugal innovation, strategic management and human factors in research and development. Her work experience includes national and international projects with partners from e.g. Brasil, Australia, Russia, and Malaysia. Liza Wohlfart has been involved in Frugal Innovation research and consulting since 2008. She has a master's degree (Magistra Artium M.A.) in Economics, English and French.

International Business Development in Context—History, Trends and Realities

Ludwig Martin

1 From trade to International Business

International trade has a long history. Entrepreneurs and people in power have always strived to gain access to goods they deemed important and desirable. Many cities such as Augsburg in Germany, Timbuktu in Mali, Cape Town in South Africa or New York City in the US developed along trade routes. And many cases of gaining individual wealth through engaging in trade are reported upon. This is particularly true for the early colonial era (e.g. Groenewald 2009).

International trade and globalization started many centuries ago. The absence of a universally accepted definition of "globalization" entails that there is no distinct date as to when globalization started. Some authors assert that "*globalization comes and goes*" (Meyer 2017). The Romans conquered the Mediterranean and areas beyond, and with their army came Roman traders. The Muslim conquest of the Iberian Peninsula brought spices and goods to Spain. Empires and religions developed and supported international trade. The foundation of the Hanseatic league (1356) or the founding date of the Amsterdam Bourse (1602) certainly mark important first steps of intensified international trade as precursors of globalization. At this point in history a particular capitalist mode set in too. The Amsterdam Bourse is worth a particular note: This was a place where investors and not only kings or queens could get a share in the world's fortunes. Transport has been cited as a driving force behind globalization (Hoffmann and Kumar 2010). The Dutch East India Company (VOC) is a good example. The 'retourship' used for the Dutch ventures to the East were purpose built to carry large quantities of products

L. Martin (✉)
Pforzheim University, Pforzheim, Germany
e-mail: ludwig.martin@hs-pforzheim.de

L. Martin (ed.), *International Business Development*,
https://doi.org/10.1007/978-3-658-33221-1_1

home to the Netherlands. Further, the 'oorlogsjacht', known for its versatility in use (military or trade), contributed to the business edge of the VOC (Parthesius 2010).

Globalization came and went in the course of history. New imperialism started with the second phase of colonialization in the nineteenth century. Of particular interest to European powers were the African continent as well as the Far East territories including the Pacific. In this era, international business was marked by securing access to resources and the heavy-handed governance of colonies, marked by brutal practices of exploitation. Furthermore, trade was almost a one-way street: Goods were taken from the colonies and sent for consumption to Europe. World War I did not change many of the realities in the colonies, only some of the colonial masters changed. And throughout most of the twentieth century no real change came. After World War II the world developed into two spheres: A western (capitalist) and an eastern (communist) sphere. Trade developed further mainly within these spheres. The advancements of telecommunication, the introduction of common standards (within their spheres), trade liberalisation (within their spheres) and increased shipping capacity allowed globalization to take a further step (Hoffmann and Kumar 2010). As Zielonka (2018) rightly points out, it was the fall of communism that paved the way for neo-liberal economics in Europe and in other regions of the world. Globalization and international trade found its new strength towards the end of the twentieth century through this tremendous shift in geopolitics. The integration of many formally national economies into a global economy, through free trade and free flow of capital, in contrast to mere international trade describing the exchange of goods between nations, are key features of modern globalization. Globalization also describes the changes in societies and economies due to "*increased trade and cultural exchange*" (Ibrahim 2013).

Since the global financial and economic crises of 2008, globalization has come into the spotlight again. This time, however, the light is shone upon globalization by activists, showing the flip-side of the coin. All trade is good in neo-liberal thinking and will advance all parties involved. The role and the power of the national state however changed (Cerny 1994). Examples of states sliding into bankruptcy and individuals being dispossessed have highlighted the ugly face of globalized financial markets and poorly practised free trade. Some authors argue that protectionist agendas and the rise of nationalists is a result of the financial crises of 2008 (Meyer 2018; Zielonka 2018). Raising barriers for trade through tariffs and import taxes as well as political parties portraying their own nation above others, and at times opting out of existing multinational frameworks, are seen as challenges for international trade.

The critique of anti-globalization activists must certainly be taken into consideration. Free unregulated capitalist markets have led to exploitation and unethical, only just legal, behaviour of some actors. The willingness of humans to pay for the achievements of the twentieth century in terms of every day comfort and luxury has created markets. Mobility, power supply, entertainment and travels are some of the markets which have grown significantly in the past decades. Value chains feeding these industries experienced an upsurge in demand. In particular, industrialized nations have flourished.

However, this leap in living standards and economic activity has its downside. Through the increase in demand for energy, the consumption of fossil fuels has led to global warming and climate change. In particular, countries and economies in the Global South as well as some Asian countries are the first who have to bear the direct effects of climate change. Yet, these nations often still lag behind in living standards of industrialized nations.

2   Trends

International business plays a particular role in the context of international economic and overall development. The business relations of international companies are often valuable links between nations. Political relations are often flanked by industrial interests with regard to topics such as ease of doing business, investments or trade barriers. International business has the ability to create job opportunities in less industrialized nations as well as securing jobs in industrialized countries. However, a balance will need to be struck between free international trade and addressing global issues as well as host country particularities. The responsible use of natural resources, often located in less industrialized nations, and land use patterns needs to be addressed. Sustainable development, as proclaimed to be a common goal for all nations by the United Nations, is an increasingly important aspect to consider in all international business development activities. The United Nations introduced the Nations Sustainable Development Goals (SDGs) in 2015, together with measurable indicators to assess the advances in achieving these goals. International trade has a fundamental role in achieving the SDGs (UN, n.d).

The SDGs set by the UN have started to have an impact on some business strategies. The use of natural resources is one of the many topics on the agenda of shareholders of companies around the world. Related to this is the emergence of the concept of dematerialization. This is a concept which stems from industrial ecology. It implies that fewer materials should be used in the production of goods since this will save natural resources. It is advocated as a *"prerequisite for environmental sustainability"* (Bringezu 2003). The circular economy is a closely linked approach. Such changes will require innovative product development approaches since the development process of products will already need to consider the use of resources. However, this is only partly a shift in thinking. Materials have always been a cost factor in the production of goods. Lowering the use (consumption) of materials can result in material cost savings. Yet, such savings in materials might result in the use of substitution materials to balance out usability and durability of some products. Product developers will have to better understand the material flows and resources used in their production process. This understanding will enable developers to create products which will require fewer resources. However, customers will still demand the same level of quality of products provided. Therefore, unless customers do not lower their expectation it is up to the companies providing these products to look at product efficiency: less input with the same output.

In particular, customers in less developed markets will be critical of re-engineered products. The perception of lower quality might prevail. This concern about product quality encounters another macro-level challenge. Many nations of the Global South found their independence from colonial rule only half a century ago. In many nations, the call for decolonization exists and gets louder. This is possibly also as a result of the financial crisis of 2008. Stakeholders in these markets became more aware of their existing dependencies on the former colonizers. Decolonization entails a call for more independence in a socio-economic sense. The advocates of decolonization call for a complete revision of social systems and thinking since many existing systems are still based on colonial paradigms. This drive for decolonization is aimed at many aspects of daily lives. Dismantling *"European values and making ways for local philosophy"* (Nordling 2018) and ultimately changing the way economies work are the aims of this movement. Decolonization is a form of full emancipation of markets in parts of the Global South. This move to decolonize impacts how products are designed. In response internationalization approaches of companies will need to change. Some governments have set protectionist local content rules as well. This demonstrates an additional degree of complexity. As a result of the long overdue growth in confidence of societies in the Global South, international relations and international business strategies will have to change as well.

In the past decades western companies were the leaders in many economic activities. China, partly due to its sheer size and manpower available, took on a particular role. It served as a market as well as production site for many western companies. However, more and more inventions from nations less developed have made their way into industrialized countries. The term reverse innovation was initially coined to describe innovation efforts by western companies in their research and development business units in less developed countries. Products are invented in less developed markets and find their way into industrialized economies (von Zedtwitz et al. 2014). Nowadays, this process of reverse innovation is not bound to activities by western companies only. In the past few years, more and more examples of foreign companies inventing products or services and exporting these to developed economies can be found (Martin 2018). International business is becoming a true two-way street, and the notion of *reverse* innovation may be obsolete. Some theories taught in business schools might therefore have to be updated in this regard. The original idea of Vernon (1966) on the international product life cycle, which has been revised several times before (e.g. Rao and Krishna 1984), is one of these theories.

Further trends in international business will impact future research, teaching and practices of international business development. Digitalization has already set in. Global supply chains are managed with the aid of information processed in the digital world. However, the current use of digital abilities is still way beyond its full potential. Industry 4.0, the term to describe the digital transformation within industry, will impact global production and material flows even more. This will enable companies to reconsider their positions with regards to production as well as offerings and will potentially make companies even more flexible in reacting to contextual changes at their production sites or markets. However, the vulnerability of companies may increase too. In an even more connected world any disruption, for instance through cyber-crime or other global events, will have a stronger impact. On the other side, the flexibility created through digitalization might assist in circumventing or reacting to such disruptions.

Politics has always impacted business activity. Yet the world is very differently structured in its differing parts. Some industrial nations follow the call of populists and raise trade barriers. In other parts of the world, new free trade (e.g. African Continental Free Trade Agreement or the Regional Comprehensive Economic Partnership) and bi-lateral agreements are signed. A trend towards a fragmentation of the arena for businesses seems to be developing. This will influence future decisions on international markets and production sites. Considerations on sourcing and marketing might therefore have to take such fragmentation into account.

3   Realities

Having outlined the past as well as some emerging trends, the current realities have to be addressed as well. In order to do so, some observations on real companies are shared. Subsequently these observations are mirrored against two leading ideas in the field of international business development. It will be shown how these two leading ideas can be combined. Both ideas are used in some of the subsequent chapters.

Table 1 indicates some core data on various randomly selected companies. The companies selected are set in different industrial sectors and countries. At a glance the numbers show that international business is real. The larger share of the revenue generated is created outside the companies' country of origin. Further, their workforce is truly international. Apart from two of the randomly listed companies, the majority of staff is employed abroad. The industrial sector and type of product offering reveals some insights as well. The two companies with a strong home-base workforce, both project-driven companies, earn the larger part of their income abroad. Furthermore, the data shown seems to suggest that with company size the proportion of staff working abroad is rising too. Internationalization is not only about exporting goods. Exporting is often at the beginning of internationalization of companies. As markets and companies develop, the need of customers abroad will require further services, faster delivery times etc., prompting companies to establish presences abroad. Cost considerations further drive companies to establish production sites in countries where the overall costs to deliver products to the customers are more advantageous.

It is interesting for researchers to follow the development paths of companies like the ones listed in Table 1. Researchers try to verify theoretical models and concepts using "real" settings. Furthermore, researchers try to develop existing as well as new approaches based on observations made. Igor Ansoff was one of these researchers. Ansoff used his work in industry to develop his ideas on corporate strategy (Puyt et al. 2020). In his seminal article "Strategies for Diversification", Ansoff (1957) described

Table 1 Revenue, Employees and R&D of selected companies (based on 2019 annual reports)

Company	Caterpillar Inc	B. Braun SE	Krones AG	Renault S.A	Robert Bosch GmbH	Royal Haskoning DHV
Home country	USA	GER	GER	FRA	GER	NLD
Sector	construction equipment	medical	automation	automotive	industrial technology / consumer goods / mix	engineering consulting
Type	B-to-B	B-to-B	B-to-B	B-to-C	B-to-B/C	B-to-B
Total revenue	53,800 m USD	7471 m Eur	3959	55,537 m Eur	77,721 m Eur	650 m EUR
Revenue abroad	31,204 m USD	6263 m Eur	3491 m EUR	41,956 m EUR	62,019 m Eur	323 m EUR
Revenue abroad in %	58%	84%	88%	76%	80%	50%
Total employees	103,400	64,585	17,353	179,565	398,150	5150
Employees abroad	58,700	48,757	6620	131,587	265,489	2125
Employees abroad in % of total	57%	75%	38%	73%	67%	41%
Expense on R&D of total revenue	3.2%	4.9%	4.9%	5.7%	7.9%	not clear

four strategic paths companies can take in order to develop their business (Fig. 1). It takes two dimensions into consideration: markets as well as products. Companies have a choice about which strategy to opt for accordingly. Market penetration implies an increase of sales in a market companies are already set in (MP, Fig. 1). Market development is the strategy where one uses the existing (possibly modified) product and develops the market for an alternative use of the product (MD, Fig. 1). Product development is the strategy to remain in a market, yet developing other products for this market (PD, Fig. 1). Lastly the strategy diversification seeks to find other markets in combination with new products (D, Fig. 1).

This depiction of possible strategic paths is known as the Ansoff matrix. This model combines the market and the product view and helps when trying to formulate or understand some of the international business development strategies of companies. However, the aim of Ansoff was not to develop a base for international business strategies, but Ansoff looked at strategy development in general. Furthermore, this model does not assist in decision making about shifting production sites to locations abroad. The Ansoff matrix, however, assists in narrowing down strategic approaches for companies in a traditional product-based view on international business development. New entrants to markets, who are in the focus of this book, will mostly be concerned about market development (MD) and diversification (D). Simply put, these strategies are new market strategies.

According to Vernon (1966) the above-mentioned international project life cycle (IPLC), as well as its subsequent variations, is an important model to grasp when looking at internationalization. It is common to all variations of this model that the product takes centre stage. The product life cycle consists of four phases: Introduction, growth, maturity, decline (Fig. 2). Combining the Ansoff matrix with IPLC, it would become clear which strategic approach fits to which product phase. In the first stage, the product is developed and established in the home market. This is driven by a strategy of product development. In the second phase of growth, companies seek to gain market share.

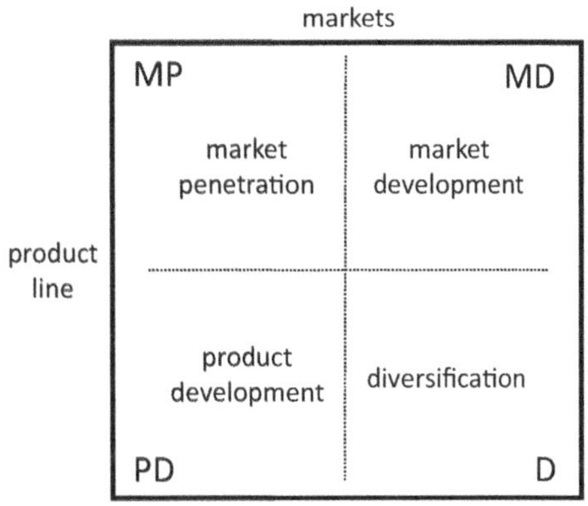

Fig. 1 Product-market strategies (according to Ansoff 1957)

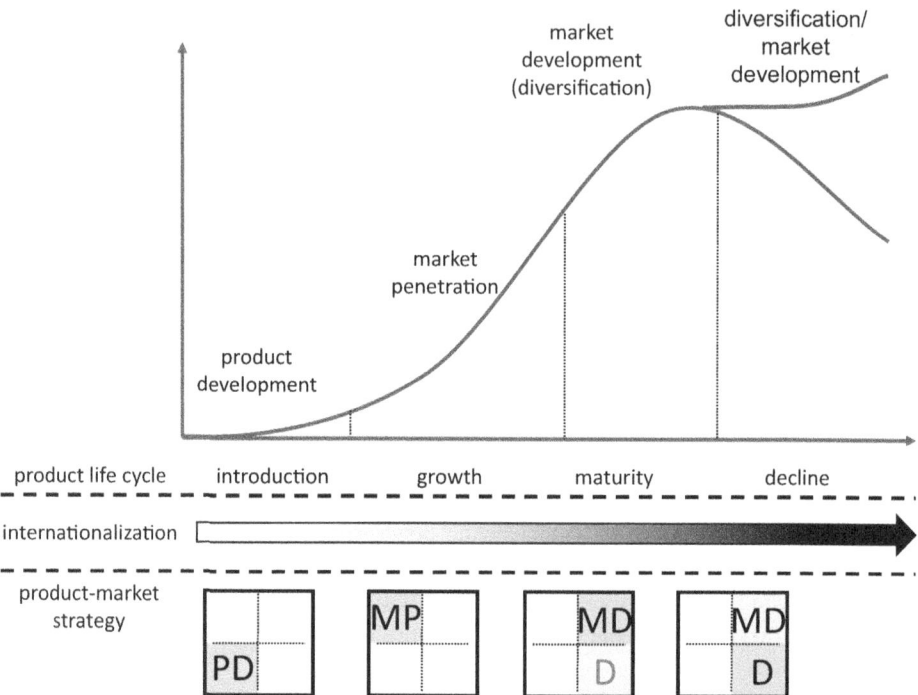

Fig. 2 Product life cycle modified according to Vernon (1966); linked product-market strategies according to Ansoff (1957)

A strategy of market penetration is likely to be at the forefront in this phase. In the maturation phase, as it becomes more difficult to sell the product due to competitors' offerings, market development is a likely strategy companies follow. At this phase of the product life cycle, markets in other countries become more important to companies. So, companies are well advised to consider the next step at this phase already. In the decline phase of the product, less demand might occur as a result of replacement of the product by other products. To avoid such decline, diversification or market development abroad is the obvious choice of strategy to follow. The life cycle of the product could therefore be re-vitalized—albeit in another location. It can even be argued, that new product life cycles are started in the markets abroad. The IPLC links consideration of location (markets) as well as the production sites of the product. Thus, the gradual change in the internationalization of the company can partly to be seen as a result of the product life cycle (Fig. 2).

In the international development of most of the companies listed in Table 1, diversification and market development were part of their journeys to their current status. Exporting products, followed by establishing business units abroad and shifting parts of the production abroad are part of the wider product life cycle thinking as well. Strategic paths of companies change and develop together with the changes in the type of interaction with markets abroad. Further, product development for particular markets, based on experiences and understanding of demand as well as market penetration will be added to the array of strategies followed by companies engaged internationally. This is possibly the final point of companies in terms of product-market strategies with regards to internationalization. However, in order to get to this point international business development is required.

Critique of and exceptions to the product life cycle model exist. For instance, born global companies establish their presence in many markets simultaneously. Such companies are mostly found in the realm of the digital world. Other critique pertains to the inability of the model to predict the duration of the phases. Furthermore, the base assumption that products will be successful can be questioned as well. Nevertheless, the model helps in framing many observations and is therefore a useful tool to understand some international business development paths of companies.

4   Outline

This book aims to combine current thoughts and new ideas on international business development. Taking a traditional approach on the internationalization process of products according to Vernon (1966), and linking these to the base business development strategies as postulated by Ansoff (1957), the book follows the thread of how a product enters an international market. Companies and products are, however, deeply linked. And products are not produced outside of a context. This context is highlighted and elaborated upon throughout the various chapters. A further focus of this book is the Business to Business market (B-to-B). This has some implications for the reader as well. The vast majority of business or marketing books focuses on Business to Consumer (B-to-C) type of interactions. A great part of the theories developed in this sphere have their relevance in B-to-B contexts as well. Yet, products and final interactions with customers are vastly differently structured in a B-to-B context compared to B-to-C contexts. Custom-making of products, regulated procurement routes of customers, and binding customers over long periods are some of the features which differ to B-to-C interactions. The book will follow the route from the creation of products to embedding them in target markets with B-to-B in mind.

Research and Development (R&D) is key to ensure that products remain interesting and up to date in their value proposition to customers. Product development is one strategy for business growth. When this is combined with covering new markets, companies follow a strategy of diversification (Ansoff 1957). The ratio of spending on R&D to total revenues differs depending on the industry sector, compare Table 1. However, R&D remains important in all sectors. The power to innovate and create products which customers in a globalized world will seek is of great importance. Chapter "Product Development for International Markets: Tools for Excelling in Frugal Engineering" of this book will present particular methods which can be deployed in product development processes, with a special emphasis on frugal innovation. This is an important area to consider. The products of frugal innovation are in a sense tailor-made to the actual needs of customers, in that additional features are left out and resources are spared. Sustainable development of products is often associated with frugal innovation. The topic of sustainability will further rise in discussions on international business development in general. Globalized capitalism and its feature of growing businesses on an international level is bound to hit an ecological boundary. Taking the same approaches as in the past decades will deplete natural resources (Altvater 2015). General economic growth will not be possible anymore. Within these new boundaries the innovative drive of individuals and companies will however continue to result in offerings that will contribute to the satisfaction of human needs.

The protection of business ideas and product inventions becomes important in a globalized world, amplified by the internet and social media, with its instant distribution of information. During the history of industrialization particular industrial sectors appeared to have simultaneous thrust towards inventions by its differing players. A prime example is the development of the first car. Carl Benz applied for his patent No 37435 (vehicle powered by a gas engine) in 1886. Not even 100 km further, Gottlieb Daimler independently worked on a similar idea (Daimler 2016); granted with patent No 36423 in the same year as Benz did. Simonton (2004) postulated that four factors contribute to creativity: chance, logic, genius and Zeitgeist. When looking at simultaneous inventions, Zeitgeist seems to be the overarching common denominator. The recent approach to vaccine development based on messenger RNA (mRNA) taken simultaneously by biopharmaceutical companies is such a case and evident through the registration of patents (Martin and Lowery 2020). This mRNA approach required the Zeitgeist of using mRNA mechanisms in health treatment. The other factors postulated by Simonton certainly play a role as well. However, any invention needs to be protected. It is a common agreement that the inventor should have the first right to reap the benefits of his or her invention. The legal aspects when taking products onto an international stage need careful consideration. Patent systems have been established to protect the rights of inventors in the various markets. Chapter "Legal Aspects of Launching Products Internationally" will discuss these legal aspects regarding inventions and the subsequent protection of rights.

Often product offerings of companies may not be directly linked to human needs, but will contribute towards addressing these needs. Chapter "Ecosystem Evaluations in Business Development" of this book will show how internationalization of companies, their product offering and their settings within the industrial environment can be evaluated. The complexities of ecosystems surrounding companies and their products is exemplified in a need-driven ecosystem (NDE) approach. The core argument of this approach is that all economic activity is aimed towards addressing human needs. Hence, the success of a company will be determined by their ability to position themselves within the value chain towards offerings satisfying such needs.

Companies developing their business on an international level, or considering to do so, however, need to weigh up the opportunities presented. Developing business is always associated with risks but also with the potential of benefits. Typically, the product is the key to other markets. Chapter "Assessing International Markets" introduces the basic product life cycle model according to Vernon (1966) and addresses market assessments. A thorough assessment of international markets needs to be conducted prior to launching any activities abroad. Common approaches for market assessments are discussed. The key to such an assessment is twofold. It is essential to assess the external market; however, a critical review of a company's own products as well as resources available to successfully enter a market is required as well. The overall market-company fit is therefore an important aspect in such an assessment.

In order to develop business activities abroad and coupled with the question of protection of intellectual rights or inventions, macro-economic and political aspects need to be thought of too. Chapter "Political Coverage for International Ventures" offers some insight on how governments foster their companies. Governments use various tools to protect business interests abroad. The enforcement of rights for particular denomination of origin labels as well as the assistance of governments when companies are reaching abroad through export or investment guarantees are two prominent examples for such political coverage. Companies are well advised to investigate possibilities to use such coverage when going abroad as it reduces risks.

Venturing abroad and developing business internationally may take on various forms. The development efforts of target markets are often viewed as projects and precede the establishment of routine processes to work in those markets. Sales offices need to be set up, supplier networks need to be established etc. In order to do so companies are well advised to already use local resources. Often an entrenchment in local networks assists in reducing risks, since local market knowledge is of importance. Project management concepts and standards for a common framework of such endeavours need to be agreed upon and used in such international development steps. Chapter "Project Management Standards" provides a solid overview on existing standards and current trends in the project management field—with a particular reference to internationalization projects.

As companies shift their products abroad, many activities are shifted too. Embedded in a value chain of activities the importance of reliable suppliers as well as evaluations of the potential for vertical diversification (Ansoff 1957) may be considered. Chapter "Sourcing Strategies and Trends: Global Versus Local" provides insights into the development of international supply chains. The authors offer an overview of many options companies may be faced with when considering the input side of a company's economic activity. A trend towards regionalisation of global supply chains can be observed. Companies are well-advised to establish agile procurement regimes, combined with the power of real-time computing and the benefits of digitalization.

The various considerations on the supply chain, and how to sustain a venture abroad are important to be done upfront, prior to the decision to engage in internationalization. These considerations are closely coupled with the differing possible modes of market entry. The commitment to a particular international market can be measured by the level of investment too. However, setting up a presence abroad is often guided by an invisible blueprint. Companies develop their own culture and ways on how to engage in markets.

Chapter "Establishing Local Business Units" reviews some important aspects to consider when establishing business units abroad. Organizational aspects, including company culture, staffing as well as financial considerations, including foreign exchange matters, are covered in this chapter.

Focusing throughout this book on international business development from a product point of view, the art of selling a product is an important aspect to study. With business to business (B-to-B) outnumbering business to consumer (B-to-C) sales a focus is set on the former type of market engagement. Chapter "B-To-B Sales Approaches" introduces various sales approaches. Embedded in the wider context of the typical procurement processes of customers and using an understanding of existing sales approaches, a new model of sales approach linked to the product life cycle is introduced. The product life cycle model by Vernon (1966), or rather its variation, is an important model at use here.

Further important aspects to internationalization of business activities are less traditional and are important emerging themes in internationalization. Digitalization and modern communication channels, in particular in B-to-B communication, need to be considered. Using the base of Chapter "B-To-B Sales Approaches" on B-2-B sales approaches, Chapter "Digital Communication in B-To-B Sales" offers a solid insight into digital communication in this market. Communication is key to sales but also to customer relations management (CRM) in general. Hence Chapter "Digital Communication in B-To-B Sales" uses a five-staged sales approach to present an in-depth overview of existing communication channels. Particular characteristics of communication channels are discussed. Companies can assess the usefulness of the channels for their own endeavours through this characterization—particularly considering the aspect of remoteness in international business development.

As discussed above, in many companies the development of supply chains, market reach and operations in general are aspects of internationalization. Economic activity is almost not possible without touching on international aspects. The local plumber uses pipes produced in one part of the world, the pipe manufacturer uses moulding machines from another part of the world, and the supply chain upstream continues further. Each actor within such value chains is seeking an optimum position with regards to costs and benefits. Production sites are shifted to countries where a better cost–benefit position and arbitrage is expected. Suppliers are selected on price (and quality). Chapter "Corporate Social Responsibility in International Supply Chains" critically looks into the context of these business practices and how consumers expect certain standards. Companies have become corporate citizens and have to carry social responsibilities too. Corporate social responsibility (CSR) orientated supply chain management practices have shown their value in reducing risks. The authors of Chapter "Corporate Social Responsibility in International Supply Chains" show the benefits of responsible engagement in international markets. Such a CSR-oriented approach has rightly so become an international standard.

International business development has a very personal human face too. People of different backgrounds work on product development, market surveys or sales approaches. People have different skills sets and professional knowledge but more importantly, in an international context, people have different cultural backgrounds. Chapter "Cross-Cultural Strategizing for Successful Customer Relationship Management" introduces cross-cultural strategies in CRM. Individuals engaging in cross-cultural business activities undergo learning curves. Reflection on encounters with other individuals from different cultural backgrounds will inform future strategies of interaction. Forecasting the expected behaviour of the business partner, based on these reflections, will ease further encounters.

Each chapter provides the interested reader with some practical exercises. The previously described concepts and approaches form the basis for many of the exercises. The application of some of the theoretical concepts in a "real" setting allows the reader to further contextualize and internalize the concepts presented in this book.

5 Conclusion

The face of international business activities is changing. But it has always been changing. International business has always relied on international trade. In order to develop international business, particular macro-economic and political factors need to be set correctly. However, within this setting ample opportunities exist for companies to develop a global footprint. Such an expansion of reach will need to consider particular aspects in future years. Sustainability, climate change, emancipation of nations (and markets) need to be considered in order for companies to become true corporate global citizens. Business opportunities present themselves, while others have to be created. Companies need to set strategies to sustainably harvest these opportunities.

Using the international product life cycle as a base model, strategies can be developed taking the phase of development of products into consideration. When following the set strategic paths, various aspects of international business development need to be considered. The following chapters offer some insights into approaches for the tasks ahead.

Exercise 1-A

The International Product Life Cycle is a useful tool for determining the stage of a product within the market and hence using it as a basis for decisions pertaining to its (international) future. How can you determine which stage of the Product Life Cycle a product is currently in?

Exercise 1-B

A Swiss-based company produces special ferro-magnets for industrial use for the Swiss, Austrian and German market. The company is in the process of setting its strategy for the years to come. Using the product-market strategies as defined by Ansoff discuss available options to the company with regards to expanding their presence to countries such as the UK, Poland and Spain.

References

Altvater, E. (2015). Der Grundwiderspruch des 21. Jahrhunderts. *Atlas der Globalisierung*, pp. 16–19. LeMonde diplomatique/taz Verlag.

Ansoff, H. I. (1957). Strategies for diversification. *Harvard Business Review, 35*(5), 113–124.

Bringezu, S. (2003). Industrial ecology and material flow analysis. In D. Bourg & S. Erkman (Eds.), *Perspectives on industrial ecology* (pp. 20–34). Sheffield: Greenleaf.

Cerny, P. G. (1994). The dynamics of financial globalization: Technology, market structure, and policy response. *Policy Sciences, 27*, 319–342.

Daimler. (2016). Carl Benz's patent application on 29 January 1886. https://media.daimler.com/marsMediaSite/en/instance/Carl-Benzs-patent-application-on-29-January-1886-Birth-of-the-automobile-130-years-ago.xhtml. Accessed 5 December 2020.

Groenewald, G. (2009). An early modern entrepreneur: Hendrik Oostwald Eksteen and the creation of wealth in Dutch colonial Cape Town, 1702–1741. *Kronos, 35*(1), 7–31.

Hoffmann, J., & Kumar, S. (2010). Globalisation: The maritime nexus. In C. Th. Grammenos (ed.) *The Handbook of Maritime Economics and Business*, pp. 35-62. Routledge.

Ibrahim, A. A. (2013). The impact of globalization on Africa. *International Journal of Humanities and Social Sciences, 3*(15), 85–93.

Martin, L. (2018). Drivers of reverse innovation. *Proceedings of the IEEE International Conference of Engineering, Technology and Innovation (ICE/ITMC), Stuttgart, 17–20 June.* Piscataway: IEEE.

Martin, C., & Lowery, D. (2020). mRNA vaccines: Intellectual property landscape. *Nature Reviews Drug Discovery, 19*, 578.

Meyer, K. E. (2017). International business in an era of anti-globalization. *Multinational Business Review, 25*(2), 78–90.

Nordling, L. (2018). South African science faces its future. *Nature, 554*, 159–162.

Parthesius, R. (2010). *Dutch ships in tropical waters: The development of the Dutch East India Company (VOC) shipping network in Asia 1595–1660.* Amsterdam: Amsterdam University Press.

Puyt, R. W., Lie, F. B., De Graaf, F. J., & Wilderom, C. P. M. (2020). Origins of SWOT analysis. *Academy of Management Proceedings*, 1, July.

Rao, C. P., & Krishna, E. M. (1984). A review and reassessment of the IPLC concept. In J.D. Linquist (ed.) *Proceedings of the 1984 Academy of Marketing Science (AMS) Annual Conference*, Niagara Falls. 9–12 May 1984. Heidelberg: Springer Cham (reprint), pp. 122–125.

Simonton, D. K. (2004). *Creativity in science: Chance, logic, genius, and Zeitgeist.* Cambridge University Press.

UN. n.d. Topics—Trade. https://sdgs.un.org/topics/trade. Accessed 12 December 2020.

Vernon, R. (1966). International investment and international trade in the product cycle. *Quarterly Journal of Economics, 80*(2), 190–207.

Von Zedtwitz, M., Corsi, S., Soberg, P. V., & Frega, R. (2014). A typology of reverse innovation. *Journal of Production Innovation Management, 32*(1), 12–28.

Zielonka, J. (2018). *Counter-revolution: Liberal Europe in retreat.* New York: Oxford University Press.

Product Development for International Markets: Tools for Excelling in Frugal Engineering

Liza Wohlfart and Marcel Fortwingel

1   International Product Development

International product development has to consider various factors, such as legal regulations, environmental aspects and competitive situations. While market studies can help to deal with challenges related to these aspects, understanding the needs of target customers is trickier. The reason for this is diversity. End consumers across Europe, for example, differ with respect to language, cultural background, lifestyles, and economic status. Companies venturing into international product development have to achieve a good insight into the specifics of the customers they want to target.

In a broad sense, the term diversity describes differences between groups of people (Mazur 2010). In a narrower sense, diversity refers to identity-based differences between people (Bright et al. 2019). There are different approaches to categorize manifestations of diversity. One possibility for this is the division of diversity into a primary, secondary, and tertiary dimension: surface-level, deep-level and hidden diversity respectively (Bright et al. 2019), see Table 1.

The three dimensions can be distinguished by considering the obviousness of a diversity characteristic and its level of individual identity. The primary dimension comprises visual, obvious characteristics, such as age, gender, and disabilities, i.e. biological differences between people.

L. Wohlfart (✉) · M. Fortwingel
Fraunhofer Institute for Industrial Engineering IAO, Stuttgart, Germany
e-mail: Liza.Wohlfart@iao.fraunhofer.de

M. Fortwingel
e-mail: Marcel.Fortwingel@iat.uni-stuttgart.de

L. Martin (ed.), *International Business Development*,
https://doi.org/10.1007/978-3-658-33221-1_2

Table 1 Diversity dimensions (Rijamampiniani and Carmichel 2005; Bright et al. 2019)

Surface-level diversity	Deep-level diversity	Hidden diversity
Race	Religion	Beliefs
Ethnicity	Culture	Assumptions
Gender	Sexual orientation	Perceptions
Age	Thinking style	Attitudes
Disability	Geographic origin	Feelings
	Family status	Values
	Lifestyle	Group norms
	Economic status	
	Political orientation	
	Work experience	
	Education	
	Language	
	Nationality	

The secondary dimension includes less obvious characteristics below the visual surface, such as religion, nationality, and economic status that depend more on social issues than characteristics from the first dimension. The tertiary dimension, for example values, beliefs and feelings, is even harder to grasp and constitutes the core of individual identity (Mazur 2010).

The support of diversity in engineering teams is also important for the success of international product development projects. Studies show that there is a strong correlation between cultural diversity and innovation potentials; a diverse ethnical and cultural background of teams fosters the innovative power of companies (Stahl-Rolf et al. 2018).

2   Frugal Innovation

Frugal innovators reduce solutions (i.e. products and/or services) to the core of what is important for specific cost-sensitive customers. Success stories show that robust, high-quality designs that appeal to target groups are essential, despite the focus on a low price. This is not an easy task—but a very profitable one if done in the right way. Innovators that manage to capture relevant requirements and translate them into convincing concepts can get a strong grasp of price-sensitive consumer markets. Just consider the enormous increase of market share achieved by budget hotels compared to their high-end competitors. Numerous German high-end companies such as BSH and Daimler have introduced frugal innovations to emerging countries in recent years to profit from the growing global entry-level market (see case studies). Weyrauch and Herstatt (2017) have identified three main characteristics of frugal innovations based on a bibliographic analysis:

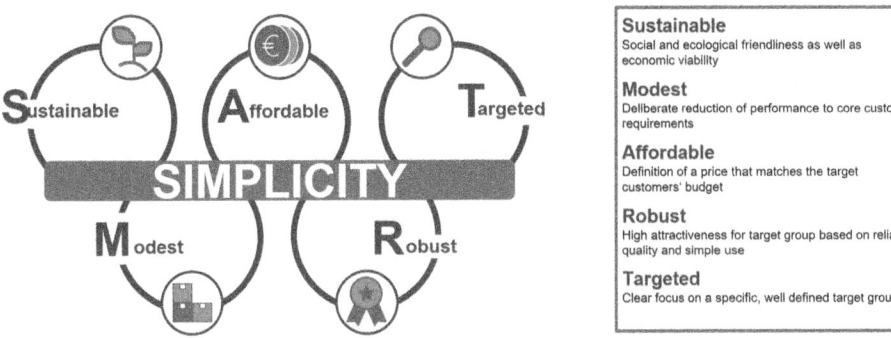

Sustainable
Social and ecological friendliness as well as economic viability

Modest
Deliberate reduction of performance to core customer requirements

Affordable
Definition of a price that matches the target customers' budget

Robust
High attractiveness for target group based on reliable quality and simple use

Targeted
Clear focus on a specific, well defined target group

Fig. 1 Frugal innovation definition (Fraunhofer IAO 2020a)

- substantial cost reductions,
- focus on core functionalities, and
- optimised performance levels.

Substantial cost reductions relate to initial cost or purchase price as well as the total cost of ownership. Focus on core functionalities means targeting aspects with high customer benefits and user-friendliness. Optimized performance levels ensure the fit of a solution to its intended purpose as well as the specific requirements of its environment. Roland Berger (2015 2017) similarly specified six principles as key to frugal innovation: functionality, robustness, user-friendliness, growth, affordability and locality. Fraunhofer IAO (2020a) has set up a definition based on an assessment of case studies that stresses the factors sustainability, modesty, affordability, robustness and targeting (Fig. 1).

Sustainability means paying respect to social and ecological issues while achieving a profitable business model. The **modest** design of frugal innovations deliberately reduces performance to the needs of specific users, thus achieving a high **affordability**. While focussing on core functionalities, successful solutions also ensure a high **robustness** in terms of reliability and ease of use. Frugal innovations do not compromise on quality but keep costs low by **targeting** the solution to the needs of a specific well-defined group of users.

Case study: BSH

In 2019, home appliance provider BSH introduced a new product to the Indian market—Bosch Modern Chulha (BSH 2020). People in India often cook on a campfire, because they cannot afford oil or gas, which is both inefficient and unhealthy. The Bosch Modern Chula is a wood stove that creates much less smoke, uses less wood, and cooks faster. In addition, it is much cheaper than existing high-quality offers. The stove helps BSH to make its brands known in emerging markets and to profit from their economic potential. BHS visited people in India at home who cook with wood during the product development process. In addition, the company did consumer test runs and interviews. ◄

3   Success Factors

Examples of frugal innovations, including failed ones, stress four main success factors for frugal engineering, see Fig. 2. It is important to keep a good eye on all of them to ensure the success of an initiative.

The first factor is **empathy**. It is important to get a good understanding for the pains and gains of the target group addressed by the solution, e.g. by means of interviews and observations. Designing suitable methods takes time and local insights. Many questions that seem obvious at first may prove to be obsolete once engineers meet potential end consumers. However, some projects suggest that a consulting of people with local expertise such as expats can provide first steps towards this understanding.

The second relevant success factor is **creativity**. Frugal innovations often profit from cross-industry inspirations, traditional techniques or new inventions. The Wonderbag cooking device, for example, imitates the old pot-in-a-blanket technique people use to simmer food or keep it warm (Wonderbag 2020).

Radicalness means making drastic decisions about needed functionalities. This is especially difficult for companies with an engineering mindset trained for high-end innovation. These companies find it easy to come up with ideas for additional features they could add to a product concept, while struggling with deciding on what to omit and what to do in a new, simpler way. Radicalness also means finding a good balance between price and quality: Some features may need a high performance level to please customers, others may have to be removed to save costs.

An excellent product concept may still fail due to a lack of **awareness** about critical surrounding factors that impact its ability to scale. A frugal innovation concept should always include the product and the business model. Factors such as insufficient delivery channels, unreliable local partners or a wrong sales pitch can put a stop to an otherwise successful initiative.

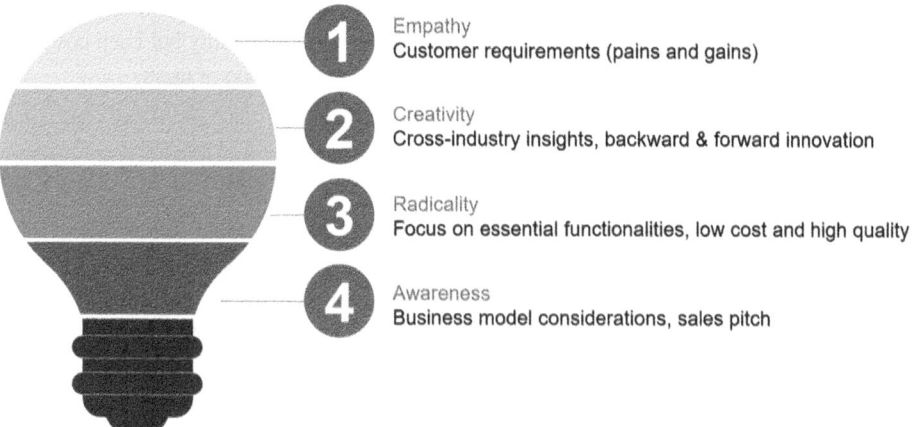

1 Empathy
  Customer requirements (pains and gains)

2 Creativity
  Cross-industry insights, backward & forward innovation

3 Radicality
  Focus on essential functionalities, low cost and high quality

4 Awareness
  Business model considerations, sales pitch

Fig. 2 Success factors of frugal engineering (Wohlfart et al. 2019)

4 Development of Frugal Innovations

There are two types of frugal innovators: Grassroots and corporate. Grassroots frugal innovators start with an idea to solve a problem they have or that exists in their immediate vicinity. They collaborate freely with different people, make fast decisions and test new ideas in a trial-and-error process. This enables them to develop products that are a good match to the needs they perceive. Their main motivation usually is social and/or environmental goals (Wohlfart et al. 2016).

Established companies, i.e. corporate frugal innovators, see frugal solutions as a way to extend their current business to new geographical markets and customer segments. They usually use a much more structured approach and more resources. Their innovation process starts with the identification of a profitable market opportunity for serving price-sensitive customers. Once they have found an attractive gap and developed their first product ideas, they have to analyse the market carefully to identify relevant features and to find a good balance between price and quality (Wohlfart et al. 2016).

The frugal engineering process and methods presented in the following aim at the specific needs of corporate frugal innovators and the success factors listed in the previous section, such as the development of a strong empathy for target customers and radicalness, when deciding about which features to include in a new product and which ones to omit.

4.1 Frugal Engineering Process

A mix of traditional and agile innovation methods has proven to be a suitable basis for the development of frugal products and services, see Fig. 3. Typical traditional innovation methods include value curves and the morphological box. The emergence of agile approaches such as scrum and design thinking has enabled a more flexible, customer-focused process, which is very much in line with the specific needs of frugal engineering, as the success factors highlighted above have shown.

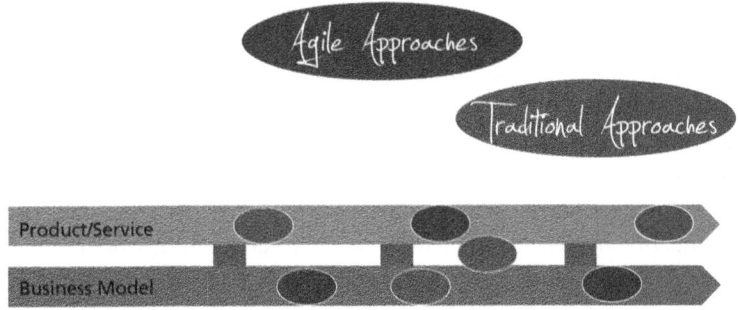

Fig. 3 Frugal engineering: selected methods

Frugal engineering should always consider the entire solution, the product or service as well as the business model. Successful approaches therefore include methods for business model design in the different solution development phases. The next sections will provide an insight into some of the methods that can support this process. A short overview is provided and details on each method are presented.

4.2   Frugal Innovation Methods Overview

Table 2 is an introduction to some innovation methods that are specifically interesting for frugal engineering. Some of them have been in use at Fraunhofer IAO's consulting and research projects from the start of the team's frugal innovation activities; others are recent additions. Overall, the toolbox is growing as the team aims at ensuring an optimum mix of methods for each specific application field.

The next section will give a short illustration of each method. The insight includes an indication on the specific relevance of each method for frugal innovation.

4.3   Value Curve

Value curves are diagrams that highlight the value of a certain product feature from the customers' perspective. Blue Ocean Strategy, the book of the method's authors W. Chan Kim and Renée Mauborgne, was published in 2005 (Blue Ocean 2020b). They stress that every effective strategy consists of three essential factors (MindTools 2020):

1. A clear focus
2. Divergence from the competition
3. A compelling tag line

Value curves specifically address the first two points in helping to set a clear focus, while considering the competitive landscape on the market. The method first ranks features of available products according to their value for customers and then designs a new product based on these features. Besides assigning a certain value to a feature, product developers can also delete or add a feature in the value curve to enhance the product's differentiation from the competition.

See Fig. 4 for an example from the hotel industry (Simon Associates 2020). The owner of a new hotel decided to set up an affordable concept that clearly differs from both luxury and budget hotels. While aiming at a low price, the hotel will put a strong focus on bed quality, hygiene and quietness to make sure that their offer is perceived as a high-quality service. Setting up the value curve starts with identifying the main competing factors (x-axis) for the current competition (budget and luxury hotels) such as availability of lounge areas, room size and quality of furniture. Then, their comparative

Table 2 Selected innovation methods

Method	Description
Value Curve	Value curves help to get a good understanding of the competitive situation on the market and features valued by customers. The method compares different available products based on the attractiveness of key characteristics for target customers. The visual overview allows an easy identification of features that would make a product specifically attractive for target customers, while providing an insight into the potential Unique Selling Point (USP) of the new offer. (Simon Associates 2020)
Kano Model	A Kano model classifies the features of a product according to three categories: basic needs, performance needs and delighters. The categories consider the customers' satisfaction with regard to the implementation of the features: What is the impact of the presence or absence of a feature on the customers' satisfaction? The method uses a standardized questionnaire that captures the preferences of target customers. Participants respond to two questions for each product feature, a positive and a negative one. The summary of the feedback enables the classification according to the three categories. (Sapio Research 2020)
Personas	Personas are fictitious target group representatives that help to streamline a product to the specific needs of this group. Methods such as market studies, interviews and observations can serve to develop a persona. Personas have a detailed profile that, for example, includes a name, a gender, an age, a profession and habits. They are, however, not real persons but rather abstracted, summarized prototypes, inspired by reality. Personas often serve for obtaining a better understanding of the goals of customer.
Conjoint Analysis	The conjoint analysis helps to uncover consumer preferences with regard to product features. The method breaks a product, service or business model concept down into its components and then tests different variations of these components with existing or potential target customers. The summary of the feedback highlights most relevant features. There are different ways of how the method can be done that vary in complexity. IT tools can support the process.
Morphological Box	The morphological box is a creativity technique developed by the Swiss astrophysicist Fritz Zwicky (Mulder 2017). It splits problems, or products, into components to allow the identification of suitable component combinations. The morphological box can be a good support for the establishment of a conjoint analysis.
BIEC Business Model Canvas	There are different methods aimed at business model design. The BIEC canvas includes eights elements clustered into five key dimensions. The systematic overview helps to detail relevant aspects of a business model, to identify and fill crucial gaps as well as to cross-check for consistency.
Price Sensitivity Meter	The price sensitivity meter by Dutch economist Peter van Westendorp is a method for determining consumer price preferences (5 Circles Research 2020). There are different variations of the method. The traditional one asks four price-related questions, aimed at identifying an acceptable price range. Newton, Miller and Smith add two new ones with a focus on the probability of a purchase. (Conjointly 2020a)

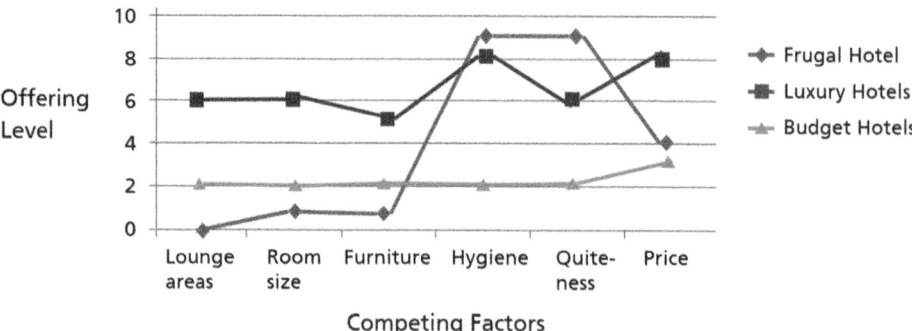

Fig. 4 Value curve for a frugal hotel (based on Simon Associates 2020; Blue Ocean 2020a)

performance is rated (y-axis). As a next step, the concept team sets up the curve of the new hotel.

Identifying the main competing factors is not an easy choice. They should not just include hard facts such as room size but all relevant factors from a customer's perspective. When listing the existing competition, it is useful to define categories such as luxury and budget. In any case, try to avoid having too many curves. Drawing the new curve then basically means answering four questions (Simon Associates 2020):

- Which factors can be eliminated as they offer little value?
- What will be reduced that is necessary but not really important?
- What will be raised that will add a lot of value to your offer?
- What will be added that creates a real competitive edge?

One major advantage of value curves is their simplicity. They do not consider complex factors such as brand identity but offer an easy and fast way to identify important features and to check market fit throughout the development process (MindTools 2020).

Relevance for frugal engineering: Identifying most essential, most valued features is crucial when developing a frugal innovation, since these products restrict themselves to the core of what customers want. In addition, product developers have to have a good understanding of the market to ensure that their innovation is at the perfect spot between sophisticated, expensive offers and cheap low-quality products.

4.4 Kano Model

The Kano model was created by the Japanese professor Noriaki Kano and serves to identify customer requirements product developers need to be aware of. It helps to explore and measure the basic needs of customers, as well as performance and excitement requirements. Instead of only evaluating a product in terms of its functionality, the Kano model also takes emotions into account. It uses a standardized questionnaire to measure participants' opinions. The participants respond to two questions for each product feature, a positive and a negative one:

- Positive: How do you feel if you have this feature?
- Negative: How do you feel if you do not have this feature?

The model then classifies attributes according to three categories (Sapio Research 2020):

- Threshold attributes (basics): features that customers expect
- Performance attributes (satisfiers): features that surpass basic requirements but are within the range of expectations
- Excitement attributes (delighters): on-top features that surprise customers in a positive way and add to the product's unique selling point. Often, these features relate to implicit needs of customers.

On the one hand, the Kano model can help to identify the features a product should have. On the other hand, it serves as a model for benchmarking it against other offers on the market (Rotar and Kozar 2017). The summary of the customer feedback helps to categorize features according to their level of satisfaction with respect to the degree of implementation (see Fig. 5).

Relevance for frugal engineering: The Kano model helps to categorize customer requirements with respect to relevance. An engineer's ability to identify basic features (i.e. features at the core of a product) and delighters (i.e. features making it special) is of specific importance for frugal innovation.

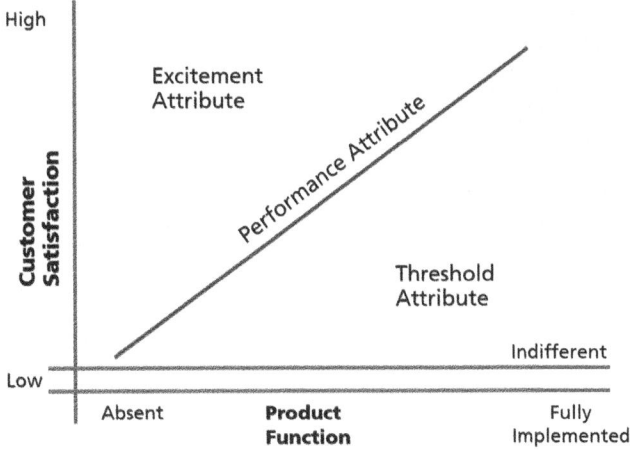

Fig. 5 Kano model (Sapio Research 2020)

4.5   Personas

Personas are fictional characters that represent users of a product in a stereotypical way. A new product can address different types of personas, while frugal innovations should have a very clear focus. Personas are not real persons but rather abstracted, summarized representatives, inspired by reality. Usually, market studies and qualitative methods such as interviews and observations serve to develop a persona. Interviews aimed at the development of personas often use open, indirect questions to gain knowledge about unconscious needs and desires of customers. Examples in the context of frugal innovation could include the following:

- When was the last time you struggled with the complexity of x?
- Which challenges did you face when dealing with x and why?
- Did you find any workarounds to simplify x?
- Which low-cost offers could you use?

In order to get a holistic overview of the user, personas aim primarily at emotional and psychological needs, challenges and wishes. Therefore, personas typically have a detailed profile that, for example, includes a name, a gender, an age, a profession and information about the persona's housing situation and living conditions (see Fig. 6). Important user aspects that should be included in the persona are motivations, challenges, goals, obstacles and also basic attitudes towards life. This not only expands the empathic skills on the part of the developers, but also sharpens their understanding for

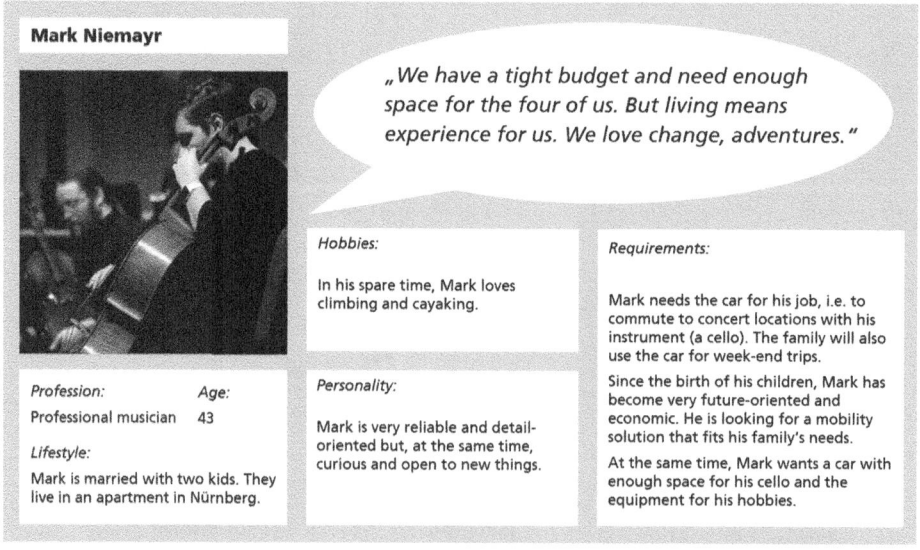

Fig. 6   Persona of a professional musician (own image; photo by Kael Bloom on Unsplash)

more implicit requirements of the target users that otherwise risk being ignored in the development process.

Relevance for frugal engineering: Since frugal innovations are tailored to a very specific target group, it is essential to know the motivations, needs and challenges of this group. An empathic approach to the target group and a focus on psychological and emotional aspects can help to gain a deep understanding of specific customer needs.

4.6   Conjoint Analysis

Conjoint analysis is a tool that helps to uncover consumers' preferences with regard to product features. This information can be used to identify relevant features, forecast market shares, assess customers' sensitivity to price, and predict their readiness to adopt new products (Conjointly 2020b). Important questions a conjoint analysis can answer include the following:

- Should a product include a specific feature?
- Which features should be combined for the product that is offered on the market?
- Which combinations are specifically relevant for different target groups?

An important difference to customer surveys is that a conjoint analysis presents different variations of a potential product to customers instead of asking them to simply decide for or against *one* product. A conjoint analysis starts by identifying key components of a product. It then creates so-called "choice sets", see Fig. 7, that consist of different

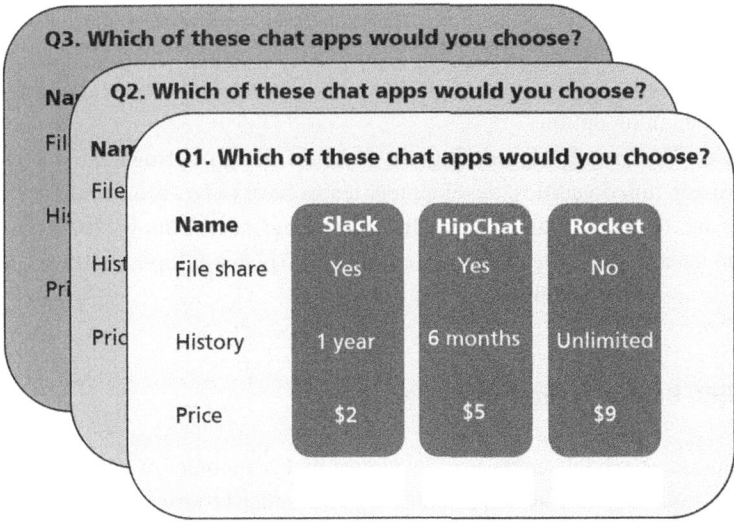

Fig. 7   Conjoint Analysis (Musallam 2020)

combinations of these components. The feedback of the customers on the choice sets helps to assess their preferences with regard to single components (Conjointly 2020b). Figure 7 presents the example of a conjoint analysis on a chat app that considers three attributes: file share, history and price. The proposed choice sets include different options with respect to these attributes. A customer survey results in a numerical value, the so-called "preference score", that measures the value of each component for participants (Conjointly 2020b).

Relevance for frugal engineering: A conjoint analysis can help product developers to prioritize product features and to identify combinations that excel both in attractiveness for customers and affordability. The method is specifically suitable when a product development team has set up a draft concept of the product and wants to test different alternatives before detailing this further.

4.7   Morphological Box

The morphological box is a creativity technique developed by the Swiss astrophysicist Fritz Zwicky in the 1960s (Mulder 2017). It aims at exploring all possible problems to a complex problem by dismantling it. It splits problems, or products, into components to allow the identification of suitable component combinations. In doing so, a product developer can make sure that he has identified and investigated all aspects that need to be considered (Mulder 2017). The morphological box can be a good support for the establishment of a conjoint analysis.

A morphological box is a visual matrix that breaks a problem or a product down into relevant categories and then lists options for each of the categories. Relevant categories ("dimensions") are listed in the first column, potential options ("conditions") in the rows (see Table 3). The combination of columns and rows creates the cells. Each cell describes one option (Mulder 2017). Table 3 shows the example of a morphological box for a bottle wrapping machine. New product concepts or solutions for a problem can be created by combining options.

Relevance for frugal engineering: In order to design a frugal innovation that is restricted to key functionalities, development teams have to be aware of different options concerning the features of a product. The morphological box allows them to detail the components of a product, develop a broad range of potential options for each of them and select fitting frugal combinations.

4.8   BIEC Business Model Canvas

The BIEC business model canvas was developed by Fraunhofer IAO. It is based on existing concepts such as the canvas presented by Alexander Osterwalder and Yves Pigneur (2010). The canvas offers a template for detailing relevant aspects of a business model,

Table 3 Morphological Box (Rochester Institute of Technology 2020)

System	Option 1	Option 2	Option 3	Option 4	Option 5
Wet label	Uniform layer of glue	Semi-automatic glue applicator	Auto glue applicator	Different adhesive	
Apply label	Tool assisted manual	Semi-automatic labeller	Manual combo labeller / glue app	Revised place mat with can-tered lines	Automatic labeller
Conform label	Tool assisted manual	Conform bottom with labeller	Leave as is		
Attach neckband	Ensure all operators have dispenser	Leave as is			
Stamp bottle	Pre-stamp by material handlers	Pre-stamp by machine	Pre-tamp with idle operators	Ensure all operators have their own stamp and stamp-pad	Leave as is
Place bottle back in box	Place bottle in tray	Leave as is			
Package and close box	Material handlers responsible	Idle operator responsible	Leave as is		
Transport box	Taped-off location to sig-nal complete tray/box	Flag used to signal com-plete tray/box	Re-work sta-tion design		
Inspection	New location for scale	Inspect before going in box	Tray inspection		

identifying and filling crucial gaps as well as cross-checking for consistency. The canvas outlines eight elements clustered into five categories (Fraunhofer IAO 2020b):

1. **Solution:** Product and/or service at the heart of the business model
2. **Customers:** Key customers of the solution
3. **Value creation**
   - *Activities*: Activities that have to be performed to run the business model
   - *Resources*: Internal resources that are needed (e.g. competences, infrastructure)
   - *Network*: Partners involved in the business model
4. **Finances:** Generated income, occurred costs
5. **External and internal factors:** External factors that have to be taken into account (e.g. trends, competitive landscape), internal factors that have an impact (e.g. strategies, existing portfolio)

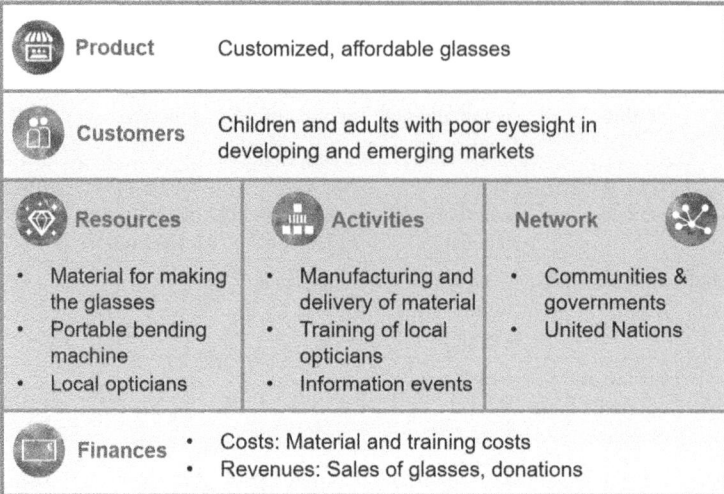

Fig. 8 BIEC business model canvas (Fraunhofer 2020b)

A business model canvas is suitable for different application purposes. It can foster the digital transformation in companies and help to discuss potential strategic directions of companies (Diehl 2019). Figure 8 presents the example of a BIEC canvas for the frugal innovation One Dollar Glasses.

Relevance for frugal engineering: Successful frugal innovations excel both in terms of products/ services and business model. Development teams sometimes neglect to sufficiently consider the latter in the design of a new product and then struggle to scale their concept later on.

4.9   Price Sensitivity Meter

Van Westendorp's price sensitivity meter uses open-ended questions that consider price and quality (5 Circles Research 2020). The method is not useful for luxury goods, where sales volumes increase with an increase of prices but valuable in frugal engineering contexts.

Typical questions are:

- Too expensive: At what price would the product be too expensive for you to consider?
- Expensive: At what price would you feel that the product is expensive but still worth considering?
- Cheap: At what price would you consider the product as a bargain?
- Too cheap: At what price would the product seem so inexpensive that you question its quality?

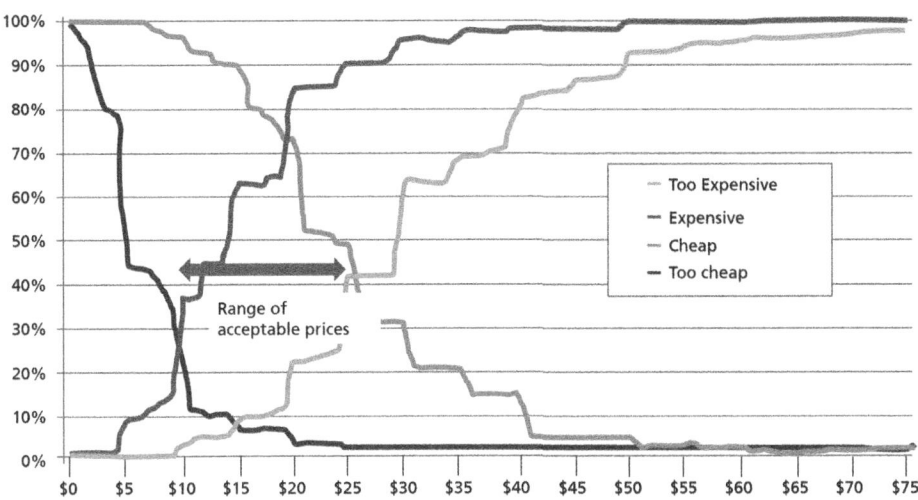

Fig. 9 Price sensitivity metre (5 Circles Research 2020)

A Likert scale response (very unlikely, unlikely, unsure, likely, very likely) can help to collect feedback. The cumulative responses of the participants are summarized in a graph, see Fig. 9. The most useful result usually is the so-called "Range of Acceptable Prices" (5 Circles Research 2020). Its lower bound is the intersection of too cheap and expensive, called the "Point of Marginal Cheapness". The upper bound is the intersection of too expensive and cheap, the so-called "Point of Marginal Expensiveness". In frugal engineering, a smaller, lower range could be more interesting. Additional optional questions focus on the likelihood of a purchase: How likely is it that you would purchase at the range of acceptable prices?

Relevance for Frugal Engineering: Identifying a suitable low price is of utmost importance when developing a frugal innovation. These products are usually not at the very low end of the price-range but a good quality product for a bargain price.

Case study: Daimler

In 2012, Daimler started a brand of commercial vehicles for India, BharatBenz (Daimler 2020). The price of the buses and trucks is just a fraction of that of the European portfolio. They excel in simplicity and robustness, while also offering several safety and comfort features such as air conditioning and driver drowsiness detection. Daimler put a lot of effort into understanding the specific needs of the drivers. They analysed street data and observed the driving behaviour of end users (Nesselhauf 2019) in real-life settings by taking part in the drivers' tours. ◄

Exercise 2-A

A French-based company produces vacuum cleaners. It wants to expand its reach to Brazil and Japan. Using the innovation method "Personas", please describe a typical end user for each country (Brazil: five-person family living in a wealthy neighbourhood; Japan: three-person family living in an apartment in Tokyo). Consider the differences in living conditions in doing so as well as cultural specifics.

Exercise 2-B

In line with the method "Kano Model", think about potential basic needs, performance needs and delighters of vacuum cleaners for each persona. Which similarities and differences do you anticipate?

References

Blue Ocean. (2020a). Strategy canvas. https://www.blueoceanstrategy.com/tools/strategy-canvas [11 November 2020].

Blue Ocean. (2020b). Our story. https://www.blueoceanstrategy.com/our-story [11 November 2020].

Bright, D. S. et al. (2019). Principles of management. OpenStax. https://openstax.org/details/books/principles-management [11 November 2020].

BSH. (2020). BSH presents: Bosch Modern Chulha. https://stories.bsh-group.com/en_DE/article/bsh-presents-bosch-modern-chulha-39397 [11 November 2020].

Circles Research. (2020). Van Westendorp pricing (the price sensitivity meter). https://www.5circles.com/van-westendorp-pricing-the-price-sensitivity-meter [11 November 2020].

Conjointly. (2020a). Van Westendorp's price sensitivity meter. https://conjointly.com/products/van-westendorp [11 November 2020].

Conjointly. (2020b). What is conjoint analysis? https://conjointly.com/guides/what-is-conjoint-analysis [11 November 2020].

Daimler. (2020). BharatBenz History. https://www.daimler-trucksasia.in/index.php/english/about-us/traditions/bharatbenz-history [11 November 2020].

Diehl, A. (2019). Business Model Canvas – Geschäftsmodelle visualisieren, strukturieren und diskutieren. https://digitaleneuordnung.de/blog/business-model-canvas-erklaerung [11 November 2020].

Five Circles. (2020). https://www.5circles.com/van-westendorp-pricing-the-price-sensitivity-meter [11 November 2020].

Fraunhofer IAO. (2020a). Frugal Innovation. https://www.engineering-produktion.iao.fraunhofer.de/de/%20produkte-und-loesungen/produktentwicklung/frugal-innovation.html [11 November 2020].

Fraunhofer IAO. (2020b). BIEC Canvas. https://biec.iao.fraunhofer.de/de/Toolbox/BIEC-Canvas.html [11 November 2020].

Kano Model. (2020). What is the Kano model? https://kanomodel.com [11 November 2020].

Mazur, B. (2010). Cultural diversity in organisational theory and practice. *Journal of Intercultural Management, 2*(2), 5–15.

Mindtools. (2020). The value curve model. Chart a new direction for your company. https://www.mindtools.com/pages/article/value-curve-model.htm. Accessed November 11, 2020.

Mulder, P. (2017). Morphological analysis. https://www.toolshero.com/creativity/morphological-analysis-fritz-zwicky [11 November 2020].

Musallam, N. (2020). Conjoint analysis: Optimize your product & pricing. https://sightx.io/conjoint-analysis-optimize-product-pricing [11 November 2020].

Nesselhauf, E. (2019). Frugal Engineering – Erfolgsmodell für die Lokalisierung von Trucks in Indien. InnoFrugal Germany. Stuttgart, 19 November 2019.

Osterwalder, A., & Pigneur, Y. (2010). *Business Model generation*. Wiley.

Rijamampinina, R., & Carmichael, T. (2005). A pragmatic and holistic approach to managing diversity. *Problems and Perspectives in Management, 1,* 109.

Rochester Institute of Technology RIT. (2020). Systems Design. https://edge.rit.edu/edge/P17709/public/Systems%20Design. Accessed November 11, 2020.

Roland Berger. 2015. Simply the best. Frugal products are not just for emerging markets: How to profit from servicing new customer needs. Roland Berger Strategy Consultants.

Roland Berger. (2017). Frugal: Simply a smart solution. Roland Berger Strategy Consultants.

Rotar, L. J., & Kozar, M. (2017). The use of the Kano model to enhance customer satisfaction. *Organizacija, 50*(4), 339–351.

Sapio Research. (2020). Kano analysis. https://sapioresearch.com/kano-analysis [11 November 2020].

Simon Associates. (2020). Strategic canvas. https://www.simonassociates.net/strategic-canvas [11 November 2020].

Stahl-Rolf, S., Holtmannspötter, D., Hutapea, L., Mecks, E., Pfaff, D., von Proff, S., & Reuß, K. (2018). The diversity factor – How cultural diversity impacts innovation in Germany. Bertelsmann Stiftung.

Weyrauch, T., & Herstatt, C. (2017). What is frugal innovation? Three defining criteria. *Journal of Frugal Innovation, 2* (1).

Wohlfart, L., Schneider, B., & Fortwingel, M. (2019). Is the future smart or simple – or maybe both? Taking a glimpse at the future of Frugal Innovation based on Scenario Technique. *Proceedings of the R&D Management Conference 2019.* Paris, 17–21 June 2019.

Wohlfart, L., Bünger, M., Lang-Koetz, C., & Wagner, F. (2016). Corporate and grassroot frugal innovation. A comparison of top-down and bottom-up strategies. *Technology Innovation Management Review, 6*(4), 5–17.

Wonderbag. (2020). Homepage. https://www.wonderbagworld.com [11 November 2020].

Legal Aspects of Launching Products Internationally

Michele Elio De Tullio, Astrid Wiedersich Avena and Maria Giorgia Mazzilli

1 Introduction

Taking products to international markets is a big challenge. This chapter will focus mainly on how intellectual property (IP) can be of help to support circulation of knowledge, information, and related goods in the context of following opportunities abroad. It will further highlight legal tools companies can deploy with regard to trademarks, patents, and licencing agreements. This will be clarified for local contexts and existing international systems for the protection of IP will be introduced.

1.1 The Role of Intellectual Property Rights

Knowledge and information are private goods in production, i.e. they cost "private" human and financial resources to be created, but are public goods in consumption since, once they are available, they may be used by the general public without reducing the enjoyment of the producer. One of the tools to make innovation sustainable for private entities is intellectual property. Intellectual property (IP) is an exclusivity right granted

M. E. De Tullio (✉) · A. Wiedersich Avena · M. Giorgia Mazzilli
De Tullio & Partners, Rome, Italy
e-mail: edt@detulliopartners.com

A. Wiedersich Avena
e-mail: astrid.wiedersich@detulliopartners.com

M. Giorgia Mazzilli
e-mail: mariagiorgia.mazzilli@detulliopartners.com

L. Martin (ed.), *International Business Development*,
https://doi.org/10.1007/978-3-658-33221-1_3

for a certain period of time to the holder as an "award" for the time, energies and financial resources invested in a creative effort as well as an incentive for the development of further knowledge, progress and innovation. Indeed, IP rights represent a fundamental tool for enterprises to earn a significant place on the market and to become principal actors in economic and social progress.

Companies which own IP rights can create new job opportunities, contribute to the growth of the gross domestic product (GDP) of their country and, ultimately, contribute to the progress of the economy at micro and macro scale. When those undertakings are also innovative, meaning that they are capable of embracing new technologies available on the market, they experience faster development and become more competitive at international level.

The European Commission, in its communication of 2019 on the intellectual property action plan, has shown that small and medium-sized enterprises using IP rights grow faster and are more resilient to economic crises (European Commission 2019). Well-calibrated and balanced IP strategies can build up a strong asset structure and boost industrial competitiveness, putting companies on track towards economic recovery from the crisis following the Covid-19 outbreak. Finally, by stimulating technological developments, IP can also play an important role in promoting a greener and digital economy.

1.2   Intellectual Property

Intellectual property rights (IPRs) are separated from the physical objects in which they are embodied (Bently and Sherman 2009, pp. 1–12). Indeed, the term intellectual property indicates a system of legal protection of intangible assets, to be construed as human creative/inventive activity, which attributes to the creator a series of moral and economic rights for the purpose of promoting and stimulating the latter's creative capacity.

These rights are outlined in Article 27 of the Universal Declaration of Human Rights, which provides for the right to benefit from the protection of moral and material interests resulting from authorship of scientific, literary, or artistic productions.

Intellectual property refers to creations of the mind and can be divided into two main categories: industrial property and copyright. Industrial property includes, *inter alia*, patents and utility models for inventions, trademarks, industrial designs, and geographical indications.

Copyright, on the other hand, covers literary works (such as novels and poems), films, music, drawings, paintings, photographs, software and architectural design as well as other creative works that are original and bear the author's expression. Rights related to copyright include those of performing artists in their performances, producers of phonograms in their recordings and broadcasters in their radio and television programs.

To understand the value of intellectual property in the current economic scenario, a valuable insight is given by the IP Contribution Study. The European Union Intellectual Property Office (EUIPO) and the European Patent Office (EPO) joined forces in 2013 to carry out the first "IP Contribution Study", a study that quantified the economic contribution made to the EU economy by IPR-intensive industries. This study has now been updated for the second time, demonstrating that in the period 2014–2016 IPR-intensive industries have become even more integral to GDP, employment, and trade in Europe. There are now 353 IPR-intensive industries in the EU economy, compared with the 342 identified in the previous (2016) study. Indeed, the study (EUIPO 2019a) provides an insight into the number of industries which can be considered as "intensive" in respect of more than one IP right (approximately two thirds). More particularly:

"The IPR-intensive industries generated 29.2% of all jobs in the EU during the period 2014–2016. On average over this period, they employed almost 63 million people in the EU. In addition, another 21 million jobs were generated in industries that supply goods and services to IPR-intensive industries. Taking indirect jobs into account, the total number of IPR-dependent jobs rises to 83.8 million (38.9%). Over the same period, IPR-intensive industries generated almost 45% of total economic activity (GDP) in the EU, worth €6.6 trillion. They also accounted for most of the EU's trade with the rest of the world and generated a trade surplus, thus helping to keep the EU's external trade broadly balanced. IPR-intensive industries pay significantly higher wages than other industries, with a wage premium of 47% over other industries. This is consistent with the fact that the value added per worker is higher in IPR-intensive industries than elsewhere in the economy. Among IPR-intensive industries, the economic weight of industries engaged in the development of climate change mitigation technologies (CCMTs) and those related to the Fourth Industrial Revolution (4IR) has increased in recent years. CCMT industries accounted for 2.5% of employment and 4.7% of GDP in the EU in 2014–2016, while the 4IR sectors made up 1.9% of employment and 3.9% of GDP during the same period."

1.3 International Trade and the Protection of Intellectual Property Rights

Recent years have been marked by an interesting translation from a manufacturing based-economy to a service-based economy, led by important improvements in digital technologies that increased the key role of intangible assets. The economy has gradually turned into a knowledge-based economy, where the value of goods, services and companies is partly defined by tangible assets and mostly defined by intangible assets based on all kinds of knowledge (Volkov and Garanina 2007).

As the law granted property rights over intangible assets, the question arose as to how to define the boundaries of these rights; in other words, how they could be defined and identified (Bently and Sherman 2009, pp. 1–4). The law had to identify specific parameters for each intellectual property right, like deposit schemes, duration, ownership, specific legal concepts, and typical legal requirements.

The first issue which arose with respect to international trade was that IPR are exclusive rights in the territory in which they are valid. It was evident that within the globalized market, the divergence between the different national IP rules was able to create fragmentation and unequal conditions of trade. Hence, in the light of the increasing of cross-border commercial exchanges, a first crucial aspect was to consider a harmonisation of IP legislation at international scale. The question arose as how the right holders could protect and enforce their rights into other jurisdictions as a consequence of international trade. Initially, these concerns were resolved by way of bilateral agreements: Two nations agree on allowing their respective nationals to claim protection in each of their jurisdictions. Afterwards, multilateral treaties were also adopted. First benchmark treaties are the 1886 Paris Convention for the Protection of Industrial Property and the 1886 Berne Convention for the Protection of Literary and Artistic Works, both administered by the World Intellectual Property Organization (WIPO). The two treaties differ in their subject matter: The Berne Convention focuses on literary and artistic creations i.e. works protected by copyright, while the Paris Convention focuses on industrial rights, e.g. patents, utility models, trademarks, industrial designs, and geographical indications. Both provide for minimum standards of protection for intellectual property rights and a possibility of signing special agreements to simplify administrative procedures.

The Paris Convention ensures several minimum standards which apply to all industrial property rights. Among them are the principle of priority right and the principle of national treatment. The first concerns the initial filing of the industrial property right: On the basis of a regular first application filed in one of the Contracting States, the applicant may, within a certain period of time (twelve months for patents and utility models and six months for trademarks and industrial designs), apply for protection in any of the other Contracting States. These subsequent applications will be regarded as if they had been filed on the same day as the first application. The advantage given to the applicants is to have several months to decide in which countries they wish to extend their business and IP protection without the risk of losing their rights.

The principle of national treatment is a rule of non-discrimination. It requires Contracting States to apply their own IP legislations to nationals of other member states: e.g. an Italian patent owner willing to apply for patent protection in the Netherlands, will be treated as a Dutch national. The innovative aspect of this principle consists in allowing countries to apply their own IP rules and, at the same time, meeting the demands for international protection; the downside is that this system lacks harmonization, which brings inconveniences for those willing to take their business to international markets.

The same principle of national treatment is also established by the Berne Convention: Works of an author of a Contracting State must be given the same protection in each of the other Contracting States as the latter grants to the works of its own nationals.

Furthermore, the Berne Convention establishes the principle of automatic protection, according to which, protection must not be conditional upon compliance with any formality, and the principle of independence of protection, which sets forth that protection of an artistic work in a Contracting State is independent of the existence of protection in the country of origin of the work.

International conventions have also tried to overcome inconveniences related to registration formalities. Of paramount importance are, *inter alia*, the Madrid System, the Patent Cooperation Treaty, and the Hague System.

In the field of trademarks, the legal basis is the Madrid Agreement, a multilateral treaty concerning the international registration of trademarks, concluded in 1891, as well as the Protocol relating to the Madrid Agreement of 1989. Under the Madrid system, trademark owners may file a single application for an international registration and pay one set of fees to apply for protection in up to 123 countries. A similar procedure for patents was developed later, in 1970, with the Patent Cooperation Treaty. As for the industrial designs, the legal basis is constituted by two international treaties concluded during the second part of the twentieth century, the Geneva Act of July 2, 1999 (the "1999 Act") and the Hague Act of November 28, 1960 (the "1960 Act"). The Hague system gives stakeholders the possibility of filing an international application for designs. The harmonization process and the revision of these treaties are still ongoing.

1.4   The TRIPS Agreement and Post-TRIPS Agreements: Towards Economic Goals and Beyond

The most comprehensive international intellectual property treaty is the Agreement on Trade-Related Aspects of Intellectual Property Rights (TRIPs) signed during the Uruguay Round of the General Agreement on Tariffs and Trade (GATT) in 1994. The TRIPs Agreement recognizes the threat to economic relations caused by the lack of harmonized IP rules in the context of international trade and covers a wide range of IP rights. Indeed, the appendix of the TRIPs agreements reads as follow:

"Members, desiring to reduce distortions and impediments to international trade, and taking into account the need to promote effective and adequate protection of intellectual property rights, and to ensure that measures and procedures to enforce intellectual property rights do not themselves become barriers to legitimate trade".

The TRIPs system has a twofold aim: it requires the minimum standards provided by the Paris and the Berne Conventions to be respected by all WTO (World Trade Organization) members operating in international free trade, and it implements further minimum standards for substantive provisions regarding the enforceability of IPRs and dispute settlements. The Agreement contains provisions on civil and administrative procedures and remedies, provisional measures, special requirements related to border measures and criminal procedures, which specify, in a certain amount of detail, the procedures and remedies that must be available so that right holders can effectively enforce their rights.

The TRIPs Agreement certainly does not represent the end of the road (Kur et al. 2019, pp. 31–37).

Several Post-TRIPs bilateral and plurilateral Agreements followed, targeting specific aspects of IPRs, fostering their protection and providing enforcement measures. The WIPO Copyright Treaty, which deals with the protection of works and the rights of their authors in the digital environment, and the WIPO Performances and Phonograms Treaty were both concluded in 1996 with the purpose to improve the Berne Convention and the TRIPS Agreement, and to take successfully into account the needs brought by the digital era and the information society.

Moreover, in the field of Copyright law, the Marrakesh Treaty entered into force in 2016 to facilitate access to published works for persons who are blind, visually impaired, or otherwise print disabled. The treaty is also directed towards the interest of developing as well as the least developed countries.

The Treaty, together with the most relevant international treaties, has had broad global support. That being said, the real challenge lies in the harmonization procedures set up by the contracting parties and on how they will incorporate these international norms into their legal system.

2   SME Growth at International Level Through IPRs

Small and medium enterprises (SMEs) and/or start-ups aiming at long-term growth should think how to strategically maximize their profit from their IP portfolio. Most high-tech SMEs are nowadays focused on new technologies related to the Internet of Things (IoT), i.e. the development of interoperable software pulling together thousands of devices, in order to deliver unique solutions applicable in different sectors. These new solutions can be used for internal purposes in order to reduce possible disclosures of trade secrets and comply with new upcoming standards aimed at protecting legitimate supply chains from counterfeiting, or for changing business models, with the aim of increasing quality of products and turnover as well as improving the global value chain. In doing this, SMEs have to face concerns mainly related to IPR issues at worldwide level, such as the protection of their own inventions and know-how as well as avoiding possible infringements of third parties' rights.

An undertaking wishing to export its business internationally and secure its intangible assets must tackle a number of strategic preliminary steps. First of all, before filing any application for registration of an IP right, a company should verify its intrinsic protectability. This is primarily an investigation on the compliance with the legal requirements established by law to register a patent, a trademark or an industrial design. Such requirements are discussed more in detail in the subsequent paragraphs.

The second step to be carried out is an availability search, which allows identifying whether similar trademark/design applications or equivalent patent applications have been filed by third parties in a certain territory. Those availability searches are carried out by specialized consultants or by means of free databases, such as the EUIPO's database for trademarks and designs (TMView-DesignView). Finally, in the preliminary phase, there is the need for an evaluation as to the territory where protection is being sought (e.g. the geographical market). This implies an analysis on the different application systems and, of course, of the potential commercialization of the goods and/or services for which the IP right protection is sought.

Small and medium-sized enterprises (SMEs) represent more than 99% of enterprises operating in the EU non-financial business sector. However, only 9% of SMEs own any registered Intellectual Property Rights (IPRs), reflecting the lack of awareness and barriers that SMEs experience when trying to protect their intangible assets (EUIPO 2019b). Copyrights and trade secrets, as IP rights which do not need any formal registration, have become very relevant rights and cheaper options for SMEs, since the budget needed to register IPRs is often considered a key issue for start-ups. SMEs also perceive complexity and high costs in enforcement of IPR in case of infringements: legal action appears too lengthy and expensive, and some are deterred from going to court for fear of revealing their trade secrets.

In such a context, it is crucial to identify and adequately support the specific segments of SMEs that would benefit from better use of IP. Companies should give particular attention to the nature of their inventions, their commercial potential, the possibility of independent creations by competitors as well as their ability of easily applying reverse engineering from the product developed (Bertelli 2020). More information should be given on the processes to register the different IP rights and the importance of establishing a business model and strategies that includes the protection of the company's intangible assets.

3   Patent Law and International Trade

The patent system has been responsible for constructing the most complete, systematic, and accessible record of humanity's technology. One of the added values of a patent system is to get new knowledge disclosed. This function of patents was well explained by Francis Gurry, former Director General of WIPO, during his speech of 2013 at the University of Melbourne (Gurry 2013, p. 3):

> *"A good example of this function of patents is the saxophone. The saxophone is the only instrument in the orchestra that was once patented. It was patented in 1846 in France by Adolphe Sax. Throughout the course of the next 70 or so years, another 14 patents were taken out in relation to the saxophone, some by Adolphe Sax and some by what we would now call "competitors". These led to the mouthpiece that we now know, the alto sax, other different varieties of sax, and an improved mechanism for the saxophone itself. Much of*

that technology has been in the public domain for well over 100 years now, and anyone can make or use the saxophone. It is interesting and instructive to compare that with the evolution of the violin. In Cremona, in Italy, in the seventeenth and eighteenth centuries, the technology for making violins was family based and secret. It was transmitted from genera-tion to generation in secrecy. The result is that nobody, to this day, knows how the very best violins that the world has ever heard – by Stradivari, Guarneri and others – were made. The secret of their manufacture has been lost in time and in the secrecy of families and the meth-ods by which they transmitted their knowledge".

Indeed, the inventor is granted with the exclusive right to exploit the invention for a cer-tain period of time in return for public disclosure. The invention becomes part of the public domain, and its main characteristics and specifications, detailed into the claims, are made available for the community.

Looking back at the historical background, the Venetian Statute of 1474 (Khachigian 2020, pp. 1135–1141) was one of the first innovation awards, aiming to enhance motiva-tion to innovate and social progress. It granted an exclusive privilege of 10-year terms to inventors of 'new and ingenious device(s)' in return for the inventor disclosing the nature of the invention to the Venetian General Welfare Board. This influenced the subsequent development of the entire European patent system and resulted in incentive theories such as the principle that a 'true and first inventor' should be granted a monopoly patent.

The industrialized world has profoundly changed the economic system in which busi-nesses operate. Patents became an asset not only for the big companies, but also for new-born enterprises (e.g. start-ups) and SMEs.

The first economic advantage for the enterprise willing to start/foster its business appears already at the stage of the filing of the patent application. Once the preliminary searches are conducted, namely, the identification of possible prior arts and an analysis on the existence of all legal requirements, it is recommended for the applicant to imme-diately file a patent application. In fact, the said application gives the applicant a first immediate return: it grants a right to claim a patent pending on a product and/or service, giving the applicant an immediate advantage over competitors.

Depending on which geographical market the patent owner wishes to place their invention, different territorial choices can be selected. An invention can be patented via the national route, via the European route, filing the application with the European Patent Office (Euro-direct route), or via the international route (PCT route) (Kur et al. 2019, pp. 107–113). A centralized system for granting patents at European level is provided via the European Patent Convention (EPC), establishing a unitary procedure before the European Patent Office.

As for the legal requirements which are needed to file a European patent application, the European Patent Convention establishes four basic criteria (so called, patentability criteria) which should be taken into consideration, in accordance with Article 52(1) of the EPC:

- there must be an "invention", belonging to any field of technology
- the invention must be "susceptible of industrial application"
- the invention must be "new"
- the invention must involve an "inventive step"

An invention shall be considered new when it does not form part of the "state of art", i.e. everything which has been made available to the public, by means of use, a written or oral description, before the date of filing of the relevant patent application. The inventive step involves an examination of the patent application from the point of view of an expert, a person skilled in the art. The EPO examination guidelines refer to the "person skilled in the art" as a practitioner in the relevant field of technology who is possessed of average knowledge and ability and is aware of what was common general knowledge in the art at the relevant date. Industrial applicability implies, instead, the possibility for the invention to be exploited in "any kind of industry, including agriculture".

In case the patent applicant seeks protection in countries others than those members of the EPC, it would be an option to file an international application first and enter into the national or European phase (Euro-PCT), once the international phase is concluded.

An "internationalization" of this phase is provided by an International Convention, the Patent Cooperation Treaty (PCT) concluded in 1970, amended in 1979 and modified in 1984 and in 2001. The procedure constitutes a standardization and simplification of the application phase (no patents can be granted by means of PCT). It represents a solution for filing a unique patent application having effect in each PCT contracting states (currently, 152 members are part of PCT), as it had been filed in each designated patent offices, choosing only one set of formalities. Consequently, the applicant does not need to worry either about the different time frames of the single national patent filing processes or about tailoring each application to comply with each country's patent laws. A PCT application constitutes a valuable option as it gives the applicants a practical advantage e.g. time to commercially explore the invention. Indeed, the substantive examination of the patent application will be postponed until 30 months from the priority day. The Patent Cooperation Treaty, in its Article 8(1), provides the possibility of claiming a right of priority for one or more earlier applications filed in any country party to the Paris Convention. The PCT procedure gives the applicant the possibility to retain the priority date from the first application by postponing the decision on if and where to further pursue the patent application for at least 30 months. The EPO has set up a time limit of 31 months for the entry into the "European phase". In other words, having a pending patent application gives the applicant time to find the best wording for the patent claims, or to choose the right markets in which to validate the patent. Furthermore, within this time, the applicant receives an international search report with an opinion on patentability which will be useful to carry out complete market research. Financially speaking, the filing of an international patent application is also advantageous as it automatically defers the cost of a possible national phase. The advantages of filing an international application may be summarized as follows:

- One set of formality requirements (official fees, language)
- Obtention of an international search (with a written opinion on novelty and inventive step)
- Delay of national proceedings
- Electronic filing
- Financial savings

Once the innovation is already developed and patent protection is granted, the granting of the patent application stimulates both the current innovator and third parties to create further innovations. At this point, the enforcement of patents provides protection against competition in the creation and distribution (or performance) of their innovations (Bertelli 2020).

Furthermore, it can be stated that practical advantages may also arise from harmonization on procedural and substantial aspects of patent systems. A system where patent protection is effective and harmonized attracts foreign investments, since foreign enterprises are willing to reveal their technologies, for example through the means of technology transfers. Based on the acquired technologies local innovators may build new ideas and accede to more advanced products, strengthening the innovation, social welfare, and the economy as a whole (Ezell and Cory 2019).

In such respect, harmonization procedures in patent legislation are provided by multilateral treaties. At European level, a step forward has been made through the Unitary Patent and the Agreement on the Unitary Patent Court 2013/C 175/01(UPC). The Unitary Patent will make it possible to obtain patent protection in 25 EU Member States by a single filing application through EPO, with a consistent simplification for the applicants. The UPC for the settlement of disputes relating to European patents is comprised of a court of first instance and a court of appeal, having jurisdiction for all the contracting states. The UPC aims to enhance legal certainty and reduce costs of parallel national proceedings.

4   Trademark Law and International Trade

Back in time, trademarks were used by public authorities for purposes of control and supervision. However, the scenario changed completely after the liberalisation of the markets. Nowadays, a trademark is a commercial source identifier, a sign that is capable of distinguishing the goods or services of one undertaking from those of others. Trademarks also became a mean of communication with consumers, conveying information about the history of the enterprise, its values, the quality of its goods and /or services. This has been defined as the *'psychological dimension'* of trademarks (Kur et al. 2019, pp. 182–185). As a result, their market power grew enormously. Many companies have built their reputation and expanded their business in many countries by means of trademarks. The emotional suggestion created in the consumers made it possible for those companies to be identified and recognized through their brands in the whole world.

In general, it is possible to distinguish several trademark categories:

- word marks which consist exclusively of words, letters and other standard typographic characters;
- figurative marks that consist exclusively of figurative elements;
- figurative marks containing word elements that combine verbal and figurative elements;
- shape marks consisting of a three-dimensional shape;
- position marks that protect the specific way in which the mark is placed on or affixed to the product;
- pattern marks where a set of elements are regularly repeated.

Some trademark systems grant protection to 'non-traditional' trademarks such as colours, motions, sounds, scents, and holograms. The lack of technological tools for the correct registration of such kind of marks, make their protection particularly difficult.

At European level, before the legal reform in 2015, only trademarks capable of being graphically represented could be registered. The new EU Regulation (Regulation of the European Union 2015/2424 amending the Community trademark regulation) removed the requirement of "graphical representation" and introduced the criteria of simple "representation", opening the way for a series of unconventional trademarks whose registration could be accepted as long as they were capable of distinguishing goods and services of the holders and as long as they were suitable to *"be represented in the manner that enables competent authorities and the general public to clearly and precisely identify the object entitled to the protection conferred upon their holder"* (Article 3 of the Directive of the European Union 2015/2436).

In other words, a trademark may be represented in any appropriate form, using the generally available technologies. However, it needs to be reproduced on the trademark register in a clear, easily accessible, intelligible, durable and objective manner, so as to enable the competent authorities and the public to clearly determine the subject matter of the protection afforded to its proprietor.

The first aspect to consider before filing a trademark is its inherent registrability, i.e. the respect of the requirements set forth by the law of the chosen territory where registration is sought.

From a general point of view, to be eligible for registration, a trade mark must be first of all distinctive: Consumers should be able to recognise a sign as an indication of origin capable of distinguishing a certain company in the marketplace. Particularly distinctive trademarks are sometimes referred to as "strong" trademarks. The stronger a trademark, the higher the likelihood of it receiving registration and the greater the protection provided by the courts. Furthermore, a trademark shall not be descriptive of the goods and services for which it is intended to be applied for. While distinctiveness implies the interest of consumers to be able to distinguish the commercial origin of goods and services, descriptiveness is a rule of free competition. Everything which is merely descriptive of the products or services for which the trademark seeks protection should remain available for the general use of all competitors. Moreover, trademarks should not be contrary to public policy or to accepted principles of morality.

The second aspect to consider before registration is that a prospective trademark is not infringing a prior third party right. In such a respect, availability searches are essential to reduce the risk of conflicts with third party owners of prior rights and to avoid the litigation costs of administrative opposition proceedings or legal actions. The World Intellectual Property Organization (WIPO) and national/regional IP offices make databases available to applicants wishing to check the availability of trademarks (WIPO's Global Brand Database and the abovementioned TMView). The results of an availability search within the selected classes of goods and services allow the trade mark owner to have an idea of the current *scenario* in the market, and to compare the novelty and the distinctiveness of the proposed sign with the previously registered marks.

A trademark holder can prevent others from using their trademark or a confusingly similar mark for the same or similar goods or services. In many countries, famous or well-known trademarks also enjoy protection against uses that disparage, dilute, or take unfair advantage of the reputation of such marks. For example, trademarks with a reputation which are registered in the European Union benefit from enhanced protection against unfair advantage taken of, or detriment caused to, their distinctive character or reputation – a protection which extends to dissimilar goods and services.

There are several international agreements on trademark protection. The main ones, adopted by the largest number of countries, are the Paris Convention for the Protection of Industrial Property (1883) and the TRIPS Agreement (1994), which set the main rules of harmonization among countries. For procedural issues, the main treaties are the Madrid Agreement concerning the International Registration of Marks (1891) and its Protocol (1989), which establishes the possibility to register international trademarks through a single procedure administered by WIPO, and the Nice Agreement concerning the International Classification of Goods and Services for the Purpose of Registration of Marks (1957).

At European level, the European Union Trademark Regulation (EUTMR 2017/1001) has created a unitary IP right throughout the entire European Union, while the EU Trademark Directive (TMD 2015/2436), implemented by the Member States, had the aim to harmonize national laws governing trademarks. More specifically, the EUTMR established a set of rules governing European Union trademarks which in return "*promote a harmonious development of economic activities and continued balanced expansion by completing an internal market which functions properly and offers conditions which are similar to those obtained in a national market'* (Preamble of the EUTMR). Businesses have hence the possibility to file a European Union Trade Mark (EUTM)—formerly known as the Community Trade Mark (CTM)—through the European Union Intellectual Property Office (EUIPO) in Alicante, which allows obtaining a single trademark registration covering all member countries of the European Union. A European trademark, hence, is meant to have equal effect throughout the European Union (*principle of unitary right and unitary character of a trademark*). A European mark can also coexist with a national mark. The latter, known as *principle of coexistence*, implies the equality of the rights, meaning that the European and the national trademark receive double protection and are mutually exclusive, in case of conflict.

As previously already mentioned, the registration of a trademark can also be made internationally, in case a company wishes to extend its business in extra European countries. In that case, the registration is made under the Madrid System: the application shall be filed within the WIPO International Bureau by the owner of a trade mark which is already validly registered in the country of origin, designating the countries of prospected protection. WIPO carries out a formal examination while the single national trademark offices will carry out a substantial examination, according to local applicable laws, and issue the statement of granting or refusal of the trademark application. The main advantage of the Madrid System is the centralized filing since it allows a single application to be filed with WIPO in one language (English, French or Spanish) through the payment of one set of fees, rather than filing different applications in each country where protection is sought.

Trademark protection enables companies to access new markets through licensing, franchising, and other contractual arrangements. This entails the possibility for SMEs to have an instrument to expand the manufacturing and distribution of products relying on brand reputation. In this context registering a trademark is strategic, since it grants the related right to stop others from using identical or confusingly similar marks to defend their IP rights against unauthorised use (in many countries, this is granted only by registered trademarks). In the absence of legal protection, all marketing and commercial efforts can otherwise easily be frustrated as other companies might register or use a similar sign for similar products.

5   Industrial Designs and International Trade

Industrial designs refer to the appearance of the whole or a part of a product resulting from its features; in particular, the lines, contours, colours, shape, texture and/or materials of the product itself and/or its ornamentation. To be eligible for protection, an industrial design must display aesthetic features which are not dictated solely by a technical function and are not anticipated by a known overall identical or similar design.

The TRIPS Agreement includes only two Articles (25 and 26) on the protection of industrial designs, setting the principle of a minimum standard of protection for new or original designs, which should be protected for at least 10 years against the unlawful manufacture and sale of products reproducing a protected design. As a consequence, the term of protection varies globally, ranging from 10 to 25 years: in the United States of America, the period of protection was recently increased from 10 to 15 years, whereas in the European Union it is possible to register a design and ask for protection for 5 years, renewable for up to 25 years.

Design protection benefits from harmonization at the levels of international filing thanks to the Hague Agreement (1925) concerning the international filing of industrial designs, as amended by the Geneva Act (1999), which allows for centralised filing for in the 65 countries that are currently parties to the Agreement. Moreover, the classification of goods is governed by the Locarno Agreement (1968). Industrial designs were also recognized to be fundamental tools for strengthening the European Union internal market; hence, they were regulated through the Design Directive 71/1998/EC (DD) and the Community Design Regulation (EC) No 6 /2002 (CDR). Both clearly follow the trademark system. Indeed, the CDR aims to establish a unitary right which has effect throughout the whole European Union while the Directive has the purpose of harmonizing the applicable laws of Member States. According to the CDR, it is possible to seek protection by means of a registered EU design, valid in all Member States, which grants protection for up to 25 years, and for a shorter term of three years for unregistered designs. Unregistered Community Design (UCD) arises automatically from the first disclosure in the EU, but merely prevents third parties from copying such UCDs.

A business seeking protection at EU level for industrial designs may thus opt for a Registered Design Right (RCD) which confers the right to prevent unauthorized copying and to prohibit the making, selling, importing or exporting of products incorporating or applying the design, or for an unregistered design right, with a three-year duration, without the necessity of any formal procedure. The latter implies a lower level of protection. For instance, industrial designs in the fashion industry are usually not registered, as they may represent a typical example of commercial short cycle products.

To be eligible for RCD registrations, designs must have both novelty and individual character. In other words, there should be no identical designs already available to the public and the impression produced by the design in the eyes of an informed user, not to a user of average attention, but a particularly observant one, should differ from other existing designs.

Due to the growing economic importance of designs in the modern economy, they have been earning more and more attention and are often brought into the conception phase of a product or a service. From a business perspective, the range of items eligible for design protection have changed in the current digital landscape. Graphical User Interfaces (GUIs) allow users to interact with electronic devices in many different sectors (such as smartphones, home appliances, medical devices, vehicles) through design elements such as icons and menus. In particular, Stigler (2014, p. 216) defines GUIs as a "*computer environment that allows a user to interact with the computer through visual elements such as icons, pull-down menus, pointers, pointing devices, buttons, scroll bars, windows, transitional animations, and dialog boxes*". In some jurisdictions, design rights are currently one of the most important tools for protecting GUIs. The United States Patent and Trademark Office Manual of Patent Examining Procedure (MPEP§1504.01(a)) explicitly states that designs for computer-generated icons embodied in articles of manufacture are protectable by design patents. At EU level, GUIs might be registered as designs reproducing the computer screens layouts, graphical menus, or icons of a computer program (*inter alia*, judgment of the Court of Justice of the European Union, in *Bezpecnostni softwarova alliance—Svaz softwarove ochrany v Ministerstvo kultury*, C- 393/09, §39–51).

Their increasing importance and value as strategic assets for companies, and the relevance of design rights for protecting the visual appearance of GUIs, is reflected by the strong growth in GUI design applications in recent years: as of 17 February 2018, the EUIPO register counted 22,903 community designs protecting graphical user interfaces or some of their elements.

6   Other IP Rights: Trade Secrets and Utility Models

Other IP rights which might be relevant for globally operating companies are trade secrets and utility models, which are strictly connected to patents.

Article 39 of the TRIPS Agreement requires member states of the WTO to ensure effective protection to "undisclosed information" as long as it is not generally known or readily accessible, develops "commercial value" from its secrecy, and has been the subject of "reasonable steps under the circumstances[1]" to be kept as a secret. In practice, as outlined by an OECD study carried out in 2014 (OECD 2014), the scope of protection and enforcement of trade secrets varies from country to country. At EU level, the adoption of the Trade Secrets Directive (EU) 2016/943 has aimed at harmonizing and strengthening laws among the member states with respect to the protection of trade secrets. Similarly, the US enacted the Defend Trade Secrets Act (18 U.S. Code § 1836.Civil proceedings) which for the first time provided a federal civil remedy for misappropriation.

Unlike registrable industrial property rights (patents, utility models, trademarks, and designs) trade secrets are typically protected without any procedural formalities. Trade

---

[1]In practice, "reasonable steps under the circumstances" requires that a company make at least a high level assessment of the categories of valuable information under its control, and that it then conduct some sort of risk analysis, in which it identifies the existing threats to information security and assesses the cost-effectiveness of measures to mitigate those threats. In practice, courts expect that organizations will establish policies and procedures designed to communicate the importance of confidentiality, use contractual protections as appropriate, limit access to those with a need to know, take and update the necessary cybersecurity measures and continuously adapt their efforts to the changing nature of their assets and the threats that they face.

secret protection is often preferred by start-ups and SMEs for processes that are difficult to reverse engineer, or that are not patentable but provide enterprises with a competitive advantage, or when patent protection appears to be too expensive.

If trade secrets are related to the moment of creation and development of a new invention, utility models are connected to the improvement of an existing invention.

More particularly, utility models consist of minor improvements of technical products or parts thereof. The wording 'utility' recalls their function, being to ease or to improve the use of an already existing invention (e.g. a new ergonomic handle for a working tool which already exists in the market). Minor improvements of existing products, which do not fulfil the patentability requirements, may have an important role in a local innovation system, granting an exclusive right which allows the right holder to prevent others from commercially using the protected invention, without their authorization, for a limited period of time.

The requirements of protection vary from country to country, which also means that there is no international utility model protection. However, most countries will protect utility models by means of their patent system, hence, following a procedure characterized by similar rules to those for patenting an invention.

In general, compared with patents, utility model systems require compliance with less stringent requirements (e.g. lower thresholds for the inventive step and the novelty criteria). The rights granted to the owner of a utility model consist of a limited exclusive right to prevent others from commercially exploiting the protected invention, that is usually between six and fifteen years from the filing date, depending on the country. The utility model system appeared to be very crucial for SME development in fast-growing economies e.g. in Brazil, China, India, and Russia. For instance, utility models accounted for nearly half of Chinese-issued patents in 2018 (Raffoul 2019).

7   The Exploitation of Intellectual Property Rights (Transfer, License and Assignment Agreements)

Considering the various legal means described, offered by international, European and national Conventions, companies may choose the most suitable IP right for a broader protection of their products and/or services also with a view of an expansion in further markets. According to the principle of interdependence of rights, it is possible for businesses to benefit from a multiple level of protection, through a system of simultaneous applications made for several IP rights, such as trademarks, patents, designs, and copyrights. The building up of an IP rights portfolio covering different aspects of a product plays a pivotal role in the commercial success of an undertaking for such reasons.

A correct strategy of exploitation would imply not only the direct utilization of IP rights (e.g. commercialization of products based on an invention or bearing a certain trademark) but also the signing of intellectual property private agreements to license or assign such rights to third parties. Indeed, intellectual property rights have emerged as new assets to be monetized into an additional source of income.

A license agreement is a contract by which the IP owner allows the use of its rights to a licensee upon certain terms and conditions. In particular, licenses may be set on an exclusive or non-exclusive basis or can be limited to a certain geographical territory and specific period of time. Generally, license agreements are concluded upon payment of a certain amount of money (fee), which can be fixed or variable, the latter depending on what is achieved by the licensee in terms of commercial exploitation (so called *royalties*). Despite the wide use of such types of this kind of agreement, which is the core business in some industries like entertainment and media, licenses may entail very complicated aspects such as the use of different IP rights in multiple jurisdictions whose laws have to be taken into consideration. Technology transfer agreements concern the licensing of technology and may be bilateral or multilateral (so-called 'patent pools'). In March 2014, the European Commission adopted a Technology Transfer Block Exemption Regulation (TTBER), clarifying how EU competition law applies to certain categories of licensing agreements and the criteria used to assess these agreements.

Different opportunities are also offered by merchandising, franchising, and assignment agreements. By means of merchandising agreements, the owner of an IP right grants a licensee the use of a certain trademark or image for purposes of distribution, selling and marketing of products which are generally different from those of its own business (e.g. for example toys depicting Disney cartoons). A franchising agreement (or commercial affiliation) serves instead for granting a range of intellectual property rights such as trademarks, patents, utility models, designs, copyrights, know-how to commercial affiliates distributed throughout the territory, in order to market certain products and / or services. Generally, the enterprise (the franchisor) obtains from the franchisee an amount of money corresponding to the annual turnover, together with a strict commitment to respect the company quality standards. On the other hand, an assignment agreement is a contract by which the holder transfers the ownership of his/her IP rights to the assignee in exchange for a lump sum or royalties. The IP rights assignment can be made as a separate transaction of intangible assets or may occur as part of larger acquisitions of assets such as sales of business assets, mergers, or stock purchases. To be valid and effective, an assignment of intellectual property rights should comply with requirements that vary depending on the jurisdiction, and will relate to the form of the assignment agreement (written agreement or not), the identification of the parties, and sometimes with the obligation to declare and record the assignment within a specific register.

Article 40 of the TRIPs Agreement recognizes that some licensing practices or conditions pertaining to intellectual property rights which restrain competition may have adverse effects on trade and may impede the transfer and dissemination of technology. Member countries may adopt appropriate measures to prevent or control practices in the licensing of intellectual property rights which are abusive and anti-competitive. Also the United Nations Convention on Contracts for the International Sale of Goods (CISG) sets forth principles which may apply to IP agreements between businesses of the signatory countries, such as many specific IP international laws, often indirectly or through national implementation, such as the Paris Convention and the EU Regulations and Directives.

8   The New Technological Challenges of IP Rights in International Trade

The increasing importance of the Internet, and the advent of more disruptive technologies such as Artificial Intelligence (AI), Big Data, Blockchain, 5G and the Internet of Things (IoT), are continuously transforming the world at an unprecedented speed, radically changing societies and economies and running a concrete transformation in the way we produce, distribute and access products and creative content. As stated by the 2014 working group of Member States' experts within the European Commission, the Open Method of Coordination, national and local authorities, policy makers and businesses are becoming more aware of the important role and potential fulfilled by the creative industries in driving innovation and growth in the economy.

In this context, the European Commission (EC) in 2015 decided to embrace the digital revolution through the creation of a Digital Single Market (DSM), where the *"free movement of goods, persons, services and capital is ensured and where individuals and businesses can seamlessly access and exercise online activities under conditions of fair competition, and a high level of consumer and personal data protection, irrespective of their nationality or place of residence"*. The DSM Strategy recognised the need to exploit innovations such as Cloud computing, Big Data tools or the Internet of Things, broadband deployment and spectrum management, media policy, competition issues posed by online platforms, and consumer privacy and security (Marcus et al. 2019).

Furthermore, in 2019 the EC proposed the Digital Europe Programme, a programme focused on building the strategic digital capacities of the EU and on facilitating the wide deployment of digital technologies, such as Artificial Intelligence, High Performance Computing and Cybersecurity, to be used by Europe's citizens and businesses.

Making the market fit for the digital age has underlined the need for stronger regulation for the protection of IPRs, allowing for the complete embracement of digitalization. As technologies and regulation have a close relation—technology shapes legal developments and vice versa (Finck and Moscon 2019) the latest digital technologies usually entail radical impacts on the existing legislative landscape.

Indeed, in this fast-changing digital world, the main actors in the market are facing a new challenge: their position is built on a traditional business model, but the ideas and tools they could use to expand and modernize their businesses are changing and becoming more and more complex. Indeed, old businesses need to adapt their models to newer trends: digital reality technologies, cognitive technologies and blockchain are becoming essential for an enterprise to achieve good profits. As an example, digital real technologies are capable of bringing emotional connections among customers and employees

(Deloitte 2020, p. 11), thus improving their well-being and, as a result, their productivity. The same practical results come from learning machines technologies, which may reduce long processes automatically performed by robots and machines, simplifying the whole work production, and increasing profits. The latter represents one of the greatest advantages for the newer businesses. The advantage is reached through automatic machines simulating human cognitive processes: this is known as Artificial Intelligence (AI.

The functioning and examples of these processes will be explored more in detail in the following paragraph.

8.1　The Challenges of the Internet and AI

The advent of the digital age and the development of new technologies have posed several new challenges regarding the protection of the IPRs.

Where copyright is concerned, several creative works (e.g. books, software, music, and films) can be transposed in digital format and thus transferred, modified, and easily disseminated via the internet. Therefore, at international level and EU level, new treaties and legal instruments have been adopted in order to tackle the difficulties arising from the digital era, such as the mentioned WIPO Copyright Treaty, the E-Commerce Directive (2000/31/EC) and the EU Digital Single Market (DSM) Directive, which aims at the modernization of certain aspects of the Union copyright framework to take account of technological developments and new channels of distribution of protected content in the internal market. In particular, the DSM Directive has as its main objectives: the adaptation of certain key exceptions to copyright to the digital and the cross-border environment, the improvement of licensing practices and the assurance of wider access to content, and the achievement of a well-functioning marketplace for copyright. The DSM Directive became effective on June 6th, 2019 and must be transposed into national law in all Member States by June 7th, 2021.

This gradual shift to the digital realm has also changed the medias and platforms where trademarks are used, determining different perspectives and factors to consider when evaluating, *inter alia*, their concrete use, distinctiveness and reputation. In particular, the growth of e-commerce and different forms of social platforms where right holders are promoting and using their trademarks, have determined the need to establish common practices for assessing infringements and acquiring online evidence, i.e. evidence extracted from the internet by different means. Indeed, proceedings before EUIPO's Boards of Appeal and other IP offices, as well as before national EU Courts, often imply the submission of proofs retrieved throughout the internet, sometimes also involving the use of new technologies.

Challenges are also raised by the increasing use of Artificial Intelligence (AI) in the creative industry. In 2019 the President of the European Commission Ursula von der Leyen in her Political Guidelines (Von Der Leyen 2019) stated the prioritization of the investments in Artificial Intelligence and the putting forward of the legislation for a coordinated European approach. The usage of emergent technologies, AI and robots among creative sectors has caused several legislative debates concerning, *inter alia*, protection of IP rights of the data taken as input by the technology, as well as the ownership of AI-generated outputs and AI-assisted outputs. The application of AI technologies within creative sectors is deeply rooted: RACTER is an AI computer programme that generates English language prose at random dates to 1983, even though it still needed a human input (Chamberlain 1984). Currently, there are algorithms capable of writing poems, novels, composing music, editing photographs, and even creating music videos in a completely autonomous way. A technological revolution is unfolding and the interaction between computers, creative processes, and the rights related thereto need to be reviewed.

Some countries have already implemented legal provisions dealing with machine created content,[2] admitting the protection of intellectual works created by AI and thus allowing companies to continue investing in the process of creative technology and development. Indeed, one of the main issues concerns the regulation of AI-generated outputs and AI-assisted outputs (Goodman 2016). Moreover, in many situations drawing the line between AI-generated or AI-assisted creative output is not straightforward. This entails an ethical problem of AI transparency on how humans are informed when they are accessing AI-produced and not human-created works. The digital society will be increasingly characterized by the interaction of human actors and non-human technological actors or virtual agents. In order to boost technological and industrial capacity as well as AI uptake, a crucial challenge will be to foster discussion on the evolution of EU policy to ensure an appropriate ethical and legal framework.

8.2   Enforcement Issues

The assessment of the probative value and reliability of digital evidence is often problematic, due to the nature of the internet itself, which makes it difficult to establish the actual content available online as well as the date or period of time when such content was in fact made available to the public. Moreover, from the rights holders' perspective, it might be burdensome to establish the effective use of their trademarks on the internet. Hence, the Trademark Directive (EU) No. 2015/2436 which aims to further approximate

---

[2]For example, Section 9 of the UK Copyright, Designs and Patents Act 1988 (CDPA) states that: "In the case of a literary, dramatic, musical or artistic work which is computer-generated, the author shall be taken to be the person by whom the arrangements necessary for the creation of the work are undertaken", while Section 178 of the CDPA further defines a computer-generated work as one that "is generated by computer in circumstances such that there is no human author of the work".

the laws of the Member States relating to trademarks, has established a stronger legal basis for cooperation in procedural rules regarding trademarks.

WIPO has recently introduced a tool to ascertain internet related evidence: WIPO-Proof. WIPO Proof is a new digital business service that provides a date- and time-stamped digital fingerprint of any file, proving its existence at a specific point in time. It is specifically designed for granting proofs of ownership that could be successfully used in infringement proceedings.

Another underlying aspect, especially for small companies, regards the reduction of the costs related to IP protection, which might be achieved by providing legal certainty and common standards in the ways to provide evidence for the enforcement of owners' rights, and thus improve the efficiency of trademarks' use throughout their life cycle. As outlined in EUIPO's strategic plan 2020–2025, the development of a close partnership with Member States IP offices play a crucial role for improving IPRs' use by SMEs, due to the geographical, cultural and linguistic closeness of such national offices. Fostering accessible services and the development of technological extended skill sets for dispute resolution is fundamental for ensure an effective enforcement of IPRs.

Also, the newer trend consisting of AI technologies applied in business is bringing new challenges for the enforcement procedures. There is the issue of liability of robots/software agents, which could be legally treated as mere machines, instruments in the hands of their human creators who would remain responsible for their activities (Spindler 2019).

Furthermore, the growing autonomy of AI is generating unknown risks. Hence, new rules are needed to provide sufficient safeguards for the efficient allocation of liability, also concerning IP infringement cases.

9   Conclusion

Intellectual property rights play a fundamental role in the competitiveness of businesses in a globalized market. They became fundamental for the development and internalization of big undertakings, but also of SMEs and start-ups. Intellectual property, if properly verified, protected, certified, monitored and defended, is a crucial element for the success of a product on the market and for the success of a company over its competitors.

Furthermore, for companies interested in marketing their products in their own or other countries, it is essential to ensure that their competitive advantage on these markets remains safeguarded. The possibility of counting on a strong brand, or on an innovative design, represents a marketing tool of extraordinary importance as well as the ability to exploit these intangible assets through a network of license or franchise agreements.

Adequate protection of intellectual property rights can form the basis for the development of portfolios of securities capable of functioning, both as an element of attraction towards venture capital, and as an advantage over other competing companies for eligibility and access to public funds (national and EU) and private financing. The novelties posed by the new technologies represent both challenges and opportunities for undertakings. When properly used, new technological means will bring opportunities for stronger and more effective strategies in international trade. The interaction of new technologies and intellectual property will require a detailed review in order to uphold rights of organizations and persons inventing new products. It will further need to be clarified how IPRs generated by algorithms are to be treated in future.

Finally, suitable management and exploitation policy of intellectual property rights can generate positive repercussions on the entire economic system: large companies, small and medium-sized enterprises, already established or newly established, as well as public research bodies and public institutions.

Exercise 3-A

A company based in Pakistan has invented a new technology within the telecommunication sphere. The company wants to use this invention and protect it in Pakistan and other countries. What would you advise this company to do first?

Exercise 3-B

A company, a well know supplier in the sailing industry, is based in Italy and has been using a distinctive logo (trademark) registered in several jurisdictions on the Internet and worldwide for a long time. As the company expands into the international market, it is discovered that in some states within the pacific region similar products with very similar logos are sold by competitors. The Italian company wants to take legal steps against the use of their logo. What would you advise them to do?

References

Bently, L., & Sherman, B. (2009). *Intellectual property law* (3rd Ed.). Oxford University Press.

Bertelli, G. (2020). The influence of digital innovation and patent management on SMEs: A systematic review. *Ius in Itinere*, Part 1/2, February 2020.

Chamberlain, B. (1984). *The Policeman's beard is half constructed (introduction)*. Grand Central Pub.

Deloitte Insights, Tech Trends. (2020). https://www2.deloitte.com/us/en/insights/focus/tech-trends.html [20 November 2020].

European Commission (DG Grow). (2019). Communication on intellectual property action. Bruxelles: European Commission.

European Intellectual Property Office. (2019a). IP contribution study. Alicante: European Intellectual Property Office.

European Intellectual Property Office. (2019b). High-growth firms and intellectual property rights. Alicante: European Intellectual Property Office.

Ezell, S., & Cory, N. (2019). *The way forward for intellectual property internationally.* Information Technology & Innovation Foundation, April 2019. https://itif.org/sites/default/files/2019-way-forward-ip.pdf [20 November 2020].

Finck, M., & Moscon, V. (2019). Copyright law on blockchains: Between new forms of rights administration and digital rights management. *International Review of Intellectual Property and Competition Law, 50,* 77–108.

Goodman, J. 2016. *Robots in law: How artificial intelligence is transforming legal services.* Ark Group.

Gurry, F. (2013). *Re-thinking the role of intellectual property.* MLS News: University of Melbourne.

Khachigian, L. M. (2020). Pharmaceutical patents: Reconciling the human right to health with the incentive to invent. *Science Direct, 25*(7), 1135–1141.

Kur, A., Dreier, T., & Luginbuehl, S. (2019). *European intellectual property law.* Cheltenham: Edward Elgar.

Organisation for Economic Co-operation and Development. (2014). *Uncovering Trade Secrets - An Empirical Assessment of Economic Implications of Protection for Undisclosed Data.* Paris: Organisation for Economic Co-operation and Development.

Raffoul, N. (2019). Utility models and industrial designs – IP rights worth considering. *IAM Yearbook: Building IP value in the 21st century 2020.* October 2019.

Marcus, J. S., Petropoulos, G., & Yeung, T. (2019). *Contribution to growth: The European digital single market.* European Union.

Spindler, G. (2019). Copyright law and artificial intelligence. *International Review of Intellectual Property and Competition Law, 50,* 1049–1051.

Stigler, R. (2014). Ooey GUI: The Messy protection of graphical user interfaces. *North-western Journal of Technology and Intellectual Property, 12*(3), 215–250.

Volkov, D., & Garanina, T. (2007). Intangible assets: importance in knowledge-based economy and the role in value creation of a company. *Electronic Journal of Knowledge Management, 5*(4), 539–550.

Von der Leyen, U. 2019. Political guidelines for the next European Commission 2019–2024. https://ec.europa.eu/commission/sites/beta-political/files/political-guidelines-next-commission_en.pdf [20 November 2020].

Ecosystem Evaluations in Business Development

Henning Hinderer and Ludwig Martin

1   Connections and Interdependencies in Business

If companies want to succeed in any kind of market they need to interact with numerous players in their business environment. Without interaction customers would neither know about nor ever buy the companies' products. Suppliers would not know what product or service is expected to be delivered. Governments set the contexts through rules and regulations and would not appreciate companies contravening such rules and laws. Interaction takes place through the exchange of information and artefacts such as products, parts, raw material, data and documents, even services or money. In any case the purpose of action is always the demand and thus the requirements of a customer are supposed to be fulfilled. At the end of the chain of value creation there will always be the satisfaction of a human need (see Fig. 1). It can be stated that the driving forces behind economic activity are human needs expressed by the consumer.

Doubtless it has to be noted that numerous authors hold the view that value creation or the idea of a *supply chain* has to be criticized because it ignores the fact that products have to be disposed of if they cannot be re-used or recycled and thus cannot be considered as a sustainable model (Fournier et al. 2013). In this case this restricted view is supposed to only depict and to help to understand why companies interact at all and how they interact.

H. Hinderer · L. Martin (✉)
Pforzheim University, Pforzheim, Germany
e-mail: ludwig.martin@hs-pforzheim.de

H. Hinderer
e-mail: henning.hinderer@hs-pforzheim.de

© The Author(s), under exclusive license to Springer Fachmedien Wiesbaden GmbH,   57
part of Springer Nature 2021
L. Martin (ed.), *International Business Development*,
https://doi.org/10.1007/978-3-658-33221-1_4

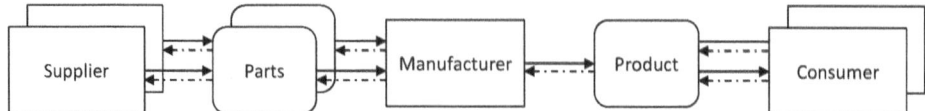

Fig. 1 Schema of interaction in a chain of value creation

Interaction in the value creation process is usually bi-directional. The specification of a required part can be sent by a digital document after having communicated about prices and conditions person-to-person. The shipping of a tangible artefact is the core activity of interaction along such a supply chain. The efforts necessary to produce and to ship a part or product will be compensated by the exchange of money. This value chain and bi-directional characteristic is depicted in Fig. 1. Furthermore, such a value chain may be multi-layered. In order to produce a product, various suppliers will be engaged in supplying artefacts, or parts needed to create a product for consumers. Supply chain management literature describes the distance to the manufacturer as tiers. A supplier directly engaged with a manufacturer is regarded as a 1st tier supplier; suppliers rending services or parts to the 1st tier supplier are regarded as a 2nd tier supplier from the point of view of the initial manufacturer (see also Chapter "Sourcing Strategies and Trends: Global Versus Local").

2   Human Need as Driver for Businesses

A commercial business has to add value for its customers. If not, the company would not be able to find customers for its offerings, it will not be able to make money and thus, at least in the long run, would lose its reason for existence. On the other side, if a company manages to find its niche in the market it can prosper and grow and contribute with its business model to the value creation for all its stakeholders (Osterwalder and Pigneur 2010).

If a product can be offered to a market successfully it obviously addresses a need of its customers. Customers are found in Business to Business (B-to-B) as well as in Business to Consumer (B-to-C) settings. Furthermore, markets can be differentiated by location: domestic vs. international markets. If the products are offered to other companies they are either meant to be production or non-production material. In case of production material, the products will be part of the customer's products and will later be sold again and leave the customer's company (Zenz and Thompson 1994). If the products are non-production material or services they are dedicated to help the customer to do his job. A machine can be used to produce other products, a computer can help the employees to achieve their targets and a service might be necessary to improve working conditions. In any of these cases the products are destined for the customer and will remain at the customer's company (Crumley 2008, p. 50). However, the ultimate endeavour is always, and must be, to help the customer with his own challenges and tasks to satisfy the customer's own market. Hence a business customer will only buy a product if it will assist in improving or doing this customer's job to fulfil a need of its customer. At the end of this chain of companies interacting might again be businesses, aiming to satisfy the needs of their customers.

The value proposition is a characteristic of the product offered and it is the result of all efforts of a company. The value proposition has to be recognized and appreciated by the targeted customers. If the customers are not at the centre of all considerations and the prospective user does not value the proposed product or service he or she will not be willing to pay for the product (Osterwalder et al. 2014). All players who participate in these efforts share a common reason for existence. The fulfilment of end-user needs can assure the survival and growth of all players involved by means of the interchange of their artefacts. Hence, it is essential to have customers willing to pay for the product or service (March 1991).

It can be stated that at the 'end' of such a chain of value creation, however, there will be a human need to be fulfilled, a need of an end consumer. With regard to the required sustainability within such a value chain it would be better to see such a chain as a part of a circular economy. Products should be designed in a way that they can be re-cycled completely as soon as they cannot be used for the purpose they were originally developed for. It can, however, be argued that firstly, for now with societies not embracing circular economies in full the aim is still to satisfy an end consumer need; secondly in circular economies product cycles only develop due to this end consumer need in the first place. The recycling (or even upcycling) of products is a step back into the chain of value creation, providing one part or ingredient to such a supply chain, which aims at satisfying a need again. Examples for human needs are such basic ones as nutrition, safety or health benefits as well as profane needs such as entertainment, excitement or even mobility. Maslow's hierarchy of needs can serve as a first guidance here (Maslow 1958).

3   Ecosystem Theory

In order to use the term ecosystem in a business environment, it is just to briefly look at some of the base concepts which have led to the current overflow of apparent ecosystems in the business environment. Tansley (1935) is regarded to be the first to introduce the term ecosystem. At this stage it was closely linked and embedded in discussion in the field of biology. These systems, described as ecosystems, are regarded as complex systems. Many interdependencies exist within these systems, and it is postulated that the anticipated order is an equilibrium, characterized by stability. Various factors rely on others and circular links can be observed. Three key determinants for (biological) ecosystems are commonly found:

- Scalability : Size and scale are not limited, hence the view of an ecosystem is a matter of zoom (Levin 1992), perspective and time.
- Interaction : The system is full of causal relationships; various factors influencing each other. Biotic and abiotic matter interact and cannot be separated as the ecosystem is to become unstable; but biotic-biotic relations also exist and add to the ecosystem.
- Dynamic: The ecosystem is dynamic, ever changing (O'Neill 2001), and the factors involved are intertwined and develop in complex congruent patterns.

The apparent stability of ecosystems, including the investigations on how these stable conditions can be disrupted are the focus of many studies in the field of biology with regards to ecosystems. Disruptions are encountered, often induced from an ecosystem on a scale above, and ecosystems self-regulate their own recovery. The outcome, however, is open, yet finding a stable equilibrium appears to be the ultimate aim of biological ecosystems. What is common in biology is hence research into the flow of energy, and equilibria, within such systems (Picket and Cdenasso 2002).

3.1   Business Ecosystems

Using the thinking out of the context of biology and applying this elsewhere is an obvious progression. The term ecosystem found its first appearances in the field of management in the late 1980s. Frosch and Gallopoulos (1989) coined the term industrial ecosystem. Similar to biological ecosystems the idea here is the flow of material and energy. In the industrial context this is less sunlight but has more to do with goods and materials as well as the exchange of money. While the metaphor of an ecosystem was already used in the field of (material) management, Moore (1993) established a more prominent use of it. Moore's take on business ecosystems is that particular companies are (lead) actors in ecosystems. These companies feed, enhance and live within this system of businesses together with other companies also representing actors of such an ecosystem; expressed in biological terms, this is a type of symbiosis. This approach focuses on the description of companies within these ecosystems, different actors or players who fulfil roles, and each of them filling a certain function to help the ecosystem to survive and prevail within a certain industry sector. Intensified competition inside an industry requires closer cooperation of the players resulting in the postulation of a co-evolution of partners engaged in complementary contributions to the system. Later work extends the view on competition and competitive networks (Moore 1996). However, Moore's concern was strategic management and how to use this understanding of ecosystems and the interdependencies herein. The players within the ecosystem are linked and interdependent. It is, however, postulated that a business ecosystem is built around a core business. In the inner layer of the model, the core business, value creation is provided directly by manufacturers and their suppliers and distribution channels. The view is extended by including the supply chain referring to the suppliers' suppliers as well as customers and the customers' customers. The idea of co-evolution and co-existence is further extended. Players such as investors, labour unions and even other stakeholders who all are identified to be affected by and contributing to the business ecosystem are added. The roles of governments or other regulatory organizations are acknowledged too. They define the rules and boundaries for the co-existence within the ecosystem. Hence these parties take on a regulatory role. Here a reverse dependence exists too and governments reap benefits from well-functioning business ecosystems. Tax revenues as well as the provision of work opportunities for members of communities are just some of these benefits. On the other hand, infrastructure provided by governments and local authorities are prerequisites for prospering businesses and for the ecosystems they are a part of. Figure 2 shows Moore's multi-level approach.

Authors, such as Winter (2014) or Iansiti and Levien (2014) refer to these basic thoughts of Moore and extend the approach. The common thread in these approaches is the player-orientation within these business ecosystems. The term players here is meant to include all stakeholders co-operating and mutually dependent on the existence and performance of the other players in order to be able to prosper or even just survive. The characteristics of the contribution of these stakeholders within an ecosystem are viewed to be complementary rather than competing. This includes the insight that even competitors can benefit from each other by the continuous challenge to improve, by creating new advancements in technology or by improving the attractiveness of an industry, which might help to improve skills and attract talent.

The contribution by stakeholders to the ecosystem may be a direct one, such as the creation of value for the core product or service. More indirect contributions are possible too. An example could be providing frameworks such as legislation or machine standards to assist and support the process of creating an actual product or service. It is important to note that these indirect contributions are key for the success of ecosystems as well. Without these the inner players would not be able to fulfil their roles.

Fig. 2 Business ecosystem
(Moore 1996)

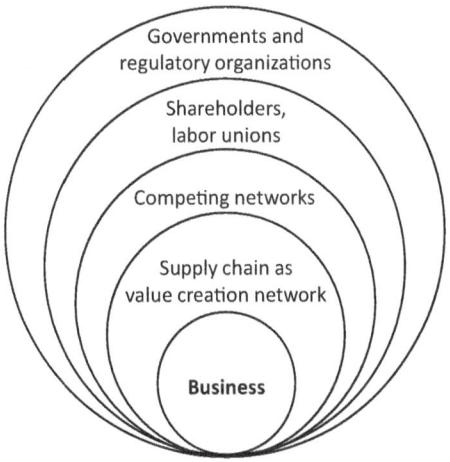

3.2   Product Ecosystem

A further variant of the ecosystem analogy is the ecosystem of products. The term product ecosystem describes the relationship and interdependence of various products and components. These artefacts in their entirety offer solutions to the requirements put forward by customers; they function as interdependent and joint sets of products and hence are seen as an ecosystem (Pickett and Cdenasso 2002; Blanke 2014, p. 61; Kehle and Hinderer 2016). Examples for product ecosystems can be found in entertainment (e.g. smartphones and their access to applications or content) or in business management software (e.g. enterprise resource planning which comprise various modules and open or restricted interfaces to the solutions of third-party providers) (Backhaus and Voeth 2014). These systems may feature artefacts, designed in such a manner that connecting into such a system with an "alien" design or interface may result in failure. A good example for such a restrictive or closed product ecosystem is the products by Apple Inc. Contrarily, open systems, such as open source software systems, are characterized by freely accessible interface specifications; there is no barrier to such a system. Their aim is an easy extension with new contributions. The advantage of such an open system is obvious: broad acceptance by customers is envisaged. This is not the primary aim of creators of closed product ecosystems. The aim of the creators of such restrictive product ecosystems is to capture a market segment and making it difficult for customers to change their systems to a competitor's offering.

Product ecosystems can be depicted in a similar fashion to business ecosystems. Core products are embedded in complementary products, related parts, components, (supporting) services or infrastructure in a concentric way (see Fig. 3). The level of integration, e.g. expressed through proprietary or openly defined interfaces, determines the level to which a product is embedded in and dependent on an ecosystem.

Fig. 3 Shell model of a
product ecosystem

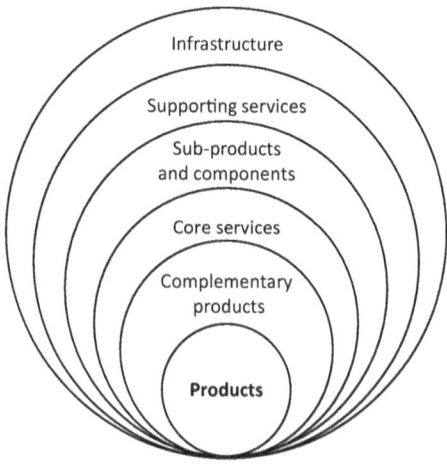

Using the allegory of the biological ecosystem, it is the product which is the biotic component within such a system. Artefacts develop along technological advances, lines of customer needs, competitive forces, or face distinction due to disruptive innovations (Bower and Christensen 1995). The product itself is often the result of a mirroring design of the manufacturing company's own organizational design. Some authors argue that companies and products develop jointly; thus, including company infrastructure and supporting services, as well as the understanding of the product as being core to the company (Ethirj and Posen 2014).

The product and its components as well as the services supporting the product's functionality can only unfold their effects together and only within a given environment. Such an environment is characterized by the artefacts which build the infrastructure and conditions within which the products work. In case the products need energy for a certain functionality, the networks to share and provide this energy, the laws that regulate the generation and billing of it or the rules that define the tolerated amount of emitted green houses gases, are examples of such artefacts of the infrastructure.

3.3   Ecosystems in Other Contexts

The term 'ecosystem' is also used in many other contexts too. Some of these uses of the term ecosystem are closely linked to either the above business (player) or product focused use of the term. Yet some deviations and perspectives are interesting to note.

The metaphor of ecosystems can be found in the field of information and communication technology too. The digital ecosystem (Chang and West 2006) is important to mention here. Interested readers should be referred to the work of Skilton (2016). Similar interchangeable terms are used elsewhere, such as in the field of mobile services (Winter 2014).

A review on innovation ecosystems is offered by Durst and Poutanen (2013). The concept of innovation ecosystems has found some traction recently. Researchers on innovation use this concept frequently. It allows for taking different contexts into consideration and seeing innovation embedded in a network or system of players. Nonaka and Konno (1998) referred to the "Basho" in their work on knowledge creation; the larger place or network in which knowledge is created. The concept of innovation ecosystem has a high degree of congruence to the above discussed industrial ecology, or business ecosystem. However, innovation deals with developing new ideas and hence changing the status quo. Critics of the use of the ecosystem metaphor in this context exist too. Cross-pollination between players and culture (Wallner and Menrad 2011) exist and impact on innovation. And critics maintain that the ecosystem metaphor only offers limited parallelism to this; an open system approach is favoured by Wallner and Menrad (2011).

3.4   Comparison of the Approaches

The leading idea in a business ecosystem metaphor is that it is players who interact and require each other for co-existence. Each player has his role and lives from the results others produce and provide as well as him contributing to the existence of others. This may also include competitors as long as they altogether provide useful contributions to the system. It can hence be deducted that the results or contributions of the different players, such as the products or services provided, are taken as an asset of these ecosystems but are not literally displayed.

On the other hand, there is the product ecosystem metaphor, using products and services as the unit of analysis; it can be stated that solely these products and services and their interdependencies express the leading idea in this metaphor. Technologies are developed for and applied in the products and their components to fulfil a customer need. Innovation within the solution and its constituents can be allocated. Missing features or functions for an even more advanced and more appropriate solution may be identified. However, the view will be object-focused, not showing the actors providing the particular solutions.

The other approaches follow similar ideas. While reducing the view to one dimension they help to understand distinct aspects of the described (sub-) ecosystem by the explanation of the co-existence of its various building blocks such as software components or the aspects of innovations.

Many attempts exist to describe ecosystems. These attempts aim to describe a certain purpose of the respective ecosystems. All these attempts are somehow self-centred. However, it is just that a more combined, polycentric interpretation seems to be beneficial for a better understanding of the inherent multi-dimensional interdependencies. The perspectives following the product view as well as the business-oriented role-player view should be incorporated allowing for a solid basis for argumentation across disciplines and requirements. Such a model, aiming to offer a construct fulfilling this, is shown here.

4   Need-Driven Ecosystems

Combining the actors with the products leads to further insights into intersections of interests, product dependencies as well as potential counter-intuitive contexts for businesses. Only a view combining businesses interacting and products coexisting and supporting each other allows for a full understanding of interconnections and hence an overview (Hinderer and Martin 2017). Figure 4 depicts the general need-driven ecosystem (NDE) model. The novelty of portraying an ecosystem in such a manner is threefold:

- It combines the perspective of the product and the business view
- It maintains the end consumer needs at the centre of all thinking
- Using various needs at the centre, the coexisting business and product environments can be grasped swiftly.

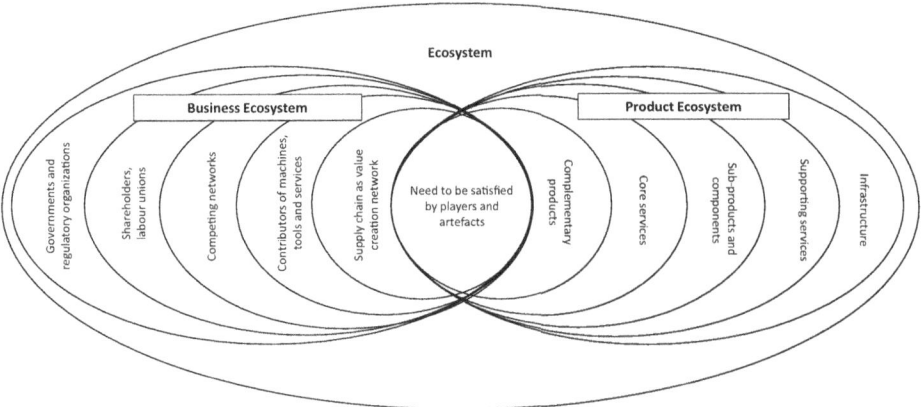

Fig. 4 Twofold shell-model for need-driven ecosystems (Hinderer and Martin 2017)

A further extension to this NDE model is the understanding of the end consumer, who has got at least one of the human needs. One of these needs stands as the epicentre of each single NDE. This two-dimensional NDE model seems to be sufficient for the purpose of evaluating business development opportunities abroad. The use of this model in an international context cannot be underestimated. In particular, at an early stage of business decision making, the clarity on markets with its products and players offered by the application of the NDE model is unchallenged.

5   Analyzing International NDEs

In the context of the internationalization of companies, their constant search for new markets and assessment of opportunities the NDE approach offers unique insights. The complexities of markets abroad and their own position in such markets in terms of the business itself but also the product or services offered can be depicted. An inside-out analysis of existing ecosystems allows for an assessment of the potential impact of a company with its product. But an outside-in analysis of the ecosystem can also be conducted; such an approach gives insights into the overall framework of a market and its impact on the possible operations there.

The NDE approach further offers post market entry a tool to keep abreast with developments in the ecosystem abroad for companies which have their head offices elsewhere. The constant change in the ecosystems through new entries of actors but also product innovation makes the NDE approach a useful tool to keep track of change and reconsider one's own position. In order to do so a constant update and research on the relevant topic is necessary. The NDE approach can be used on various levels using different strata of timeframes too, which can help to define the level of detail for the required research and analysis.

Using a three-level approach in analogy to well accepted decision-making models in management of organizations (e.g. Dillerup and Stoi 2016), the NDE model can be applied on three levels in international management:

- Strategic
- Tactical
- Operational

5.1   Strategic Level

The NDE can be applied in the context of evaluating markets and opportunities abroad. In order to do so, the purpose of such an evaluation needs to be clearly defined from the onset. Typically, in a first step in business development abroad a strategic level or view is taken on the target market. A two-prone approach is appropriate for such a use of the NDE.

Firstly, the centre of all concern is the central need. Hence a first assessment of a market abroad needs to be concerned with an evaluation of the size or quantity of this need. This will entail collecting data on populations of countries or regions relating to the need identified and linked to one's own business endeavour. Of particular importance is the knowledge on the proportion of need covered or satisfied already. For instance, a need may be mobility. Using population data, including age distribution, country information (urban vs. rural characteristics) as well as data on vehicle penetration and availability on public transport services, a first grasp of the need as well as uncaptured quantity thereof can be gathered. Sometimes this first assessment of an uncaptured need may be of such a nature that already at this stage any further strategizing may not be warranted. In such a case the clear consideration of the central need may have saved valuable resources for planning and managing an investment abroad upfront. However, if the uncaptured need is deemed to be worth the effort, the application of an NDE thinking can play out its full strength and the second phase in developing a clear picture of the ecosystem can be attempted.

Following the quantification of the central need, the outer rings of the NDE need to be understood. Overall available infrastructure (product side) as well as governmental or supra-national institutions need to be mapped out. This information is of particular interest since the strengths and abilities of such institutions directly impact on companies seeking to engage in work abroad. Their role in enabling businesses to invest in a country cannot be underestimated. Furthermore, a good grasp of these players may assist in engaging players from a company's home country on this level too. The assessment of potential political support can only be done, when the players abroad are clearly defined and identified.

Further information has to be collected coming from the outer rings in order to develop a full understanding of the NDE. The approach to narrow down on the previously identified central need coming from the outer rings is the preferred method when entering unknown territory. The outer frameworks shape the inner circles. When trying in a first step to find information on markets abroad, NDE offers the required guidance and structure. Furthermore, the understanding of the macro environments of products and players first allows for swift interventions. While it may be possible, for instance, to develop suppliers and their parts delivered over an appropriate time period, the players and products sitting in the outer rings are more often difficult to sway. For instance, legislation on labour unions and their enactment of their rights may be a strong red flag for some foreign investors in their considerations to develop their business abroad. However, negotiating with a supplier on the quality of their product certainly is in the realm of an investor. The approach to populate the NDE starting from the outer rings hence gives opportunity to precisely understand one's own position and set strategies at an early stage, but also to highlight potential hard stumbling blocks.

When gathering information to populate the NDE model on a strategic level, macroeconomic assessments of the target market are useful to lift the required information. Information gathered through approaches such as PEST or PESTEL assessments may be useful. NDE offers a concise framework to use the gathered information and to focus all efforts on the ultimate need. The full grasp of the ecosystem allows management to decide and shape a strategic approach to a particular market abroad.

As the strategic planning does, however, not end with the market entry of a company abroad, the use of NDE can also be seen in ongoing strategy formation. Companies can use the developed picture of a particular NDE for scenario planning and managing future steps. For instance, known upcoming changes to regulations, such as the creation of free trade zones, need to be constantly mirrored back onto the NDE allowing one's company to understand possible impacts at an early stage and to get into an advantageous position. Future developments with regards to actors but also artefacts in the NDE need to be monitored. Constant forecasts on the shape and features of future NDEs can be made and monitored accordingly through the application of an NDE thinking.

5.2   Tactical Level

The tactical level of management encompasses enacting the strategies set at an earlier stage. In the context of international business development this may be at first the stage following the decision to enter a market abroad. A strategy is formulated through the application of the NDE model and gathering the required information for a strategic decision, based on the evaluation of players and products in a particular ecosystem. However, the strategic level is by definition set at a level higher and with a longer time horizon. The application of the NDE model at the strategic level will also not have the same depth of detail as required when engaging in tactical management tasks.

However, the first grasp of the NDE will suffice in many areas, since not all products and players in the NDE will directly impact on a company's endeavour to enter a market.

The NDE may, for the purpose of a tactical management only, be refined in certain areas of particular interest. The company's own position as a player, as well as the position of the product offered needs to be considered. The tactical level will be engaging in supply chain development efforts, lobbying for regulatory changes, or formation of industry standards which work in the company's favour. Hence the zoom of the company may be taken off the entire ecosystem, but rather focus on areas (players and products) impacting on the mid-term establishment, operations and survival of the company. Adjacent rings within the NDE model become the playground of tactical management. And tactical decisions need to be framed in this context, with the awareness that any change in the ecosystem may bring some overall unbalance to the very same ecosystem—with risks and opportunities opening up. It is hence of importance for management to develop more of an understanding of the NDE, and in particular of the areas concerned with by the company. This additional information is often gathered by unstructured information gathering in an international expansion project. Existing and future supply chains (its players and parts) become clearer to managers through engagements with other players. Underlying networks, linkages and interdependencies may surface too. This information needs to be captured in the NDE, allowing these to be mapped.

Tactical management may be concerned with developing links to other players in the same ring of the NDE model, strengthening their common position. Or it may collaborate on the development of a new part or product, changing technical standards for doing business. The scope of tactical management, being mid-term and there to roll-out previously decided strategy, makes it necessary to focus on some areas of the developed NDE, yet not changing the entire ecosystem. Tactical management and its understanding of the linkages within the NDE assist in shaping the structure and approach to be taken on a day to day basis—operational management. At this level isomorphism (Di Maggio and Powell 1983) may be experienced—companies start to react and partially adapt to environmental conditions.

5.3 Operational Level

Operational management is concerned with day to day operations of a company's activities. The management decisions are often rather of a short-term nature. They are concerned with the operations, i.e. the manufacturing of parts or products using the optimal level of resources, time and achieving the necessary quality or the acquisition of new customers. The knowledge of the previously assessed and depicted NDE can be further used here. While on an operational level the concern is often raw materials input and producing parts or products and selling this output, the NDE view allows operational management to frame any changes occurring in the market environment or rather the ecosystem better. This assists in the planning of daily activities.

The operational interlinkages with other players and products can be mapped out. As in operational realities where influences from beyond direct business partners are experienced, operational managers can, following their own linkages, understand the circumstances of suppliers as well as of customers or even of competitors better. Changes in their own environments may make suppliers or customers change their own tactics including purchasing behaviours. The impact of changes stemming from customers are obvious, the understanding of the reason behind these changes however often require a wider view—into the customer's adjacent ring of the NDE.

Changes in the supply chains are often more difficult to grasp. Changes are often detected through a change in quality of materials or parts received. While improved quality typically is less of a concern (if the price remains the same), a deterioration of quality will trigger alarms. Here NDE can assist in understanding the contexts which the players of the supply chain have to work in, and how this may also impact the materials and parts delivered. In particular in international settings, with different cultures collaborating, such understanding of the contexts of others can prove to be important for further negotiations.

5.4 Issues When Applying the NDE Approach

However, the application of the NDE does not have to follow any of the described sequences above. The strength of the NDE model is that the final state of the model will depict the required information to make appropriate decisions at a glance. The final depiction of the NDE is the ultimate aim.

A drawback when applying the NDE approach to international contexts may be the uncertainty and availability of information. In order to portray the full ecosystem abroad in its required width and depth a good understanding of the environment there is required. However, this is not a problem of the application of the NDE per se. The uncertainty of situations in unknown markets is common to any approach to be taken. In contrast, the NDE offers a clear template for the required information. This information needs to be populated through available intelligence accordingly. The required effort in populating the NDE is highly dependent on the use of the NDE approach itself. The level of detail necessary for the analysis of an NDE, and hence market, is determined by the purpose of the analysis.

5.5 Assessing One's Own Situation

Notwithstanding the application of NDE thinking on a strategic, tactical or operational level, some communalities need to be pointed out in any of the applications. NDE offers a tool for an outbound but also inbound view of a company's own situation and setting on all levels. Clarity on external forces but also internal abilities may become enhanced through the development of an NDE for a particular need and a company's own product and business environment.

The understanding of external forces is pivotal for companies entering and engaging in markets, and hence ecosystems abroad. As described by di Maggio and Powell (1983) *"competition, state, or the professions"* shape organization and make organization akin. The uniqueness of companies with their Unique Selling Proposition (USP) turned into a competitive advantage is, however, often the key to success. Hence understanding underpinning forces from the onset and monitoring these through an outbound view may assist in retaining such a USP and advantage. The assistance of governments or para-governmental bodies flanking the efforts of companies entering markets abroad (see Chapter "Project Management Standards") need to be assessed and its value weighted before fully relying on these.

Similarly, it is important for companies broadening their footprint through endeavours abroad to understand their internal abilities. A resource-based view on companies (Sharma and Erramilli 2004) is in order here. A company's own abilities in acting, surviving, and prospering in a market abroad, read ecosystem, need to be assessed and considered too. This pertains to physical resources / assets available to a company, monetary resources, as well as knowledge and capabilities. The boundaries in deploying such internal resources need to be considered too in an international context. Cross-border financial streams, the free movement of employees, as well as international patent laws (see Chapter "Legal Aspects of Launching Products Internationally") are themselves regulated and bound to given (legal) frameworks. Given that the interrelations between certain playersrequiring communication, analogue as well as digital communication channels are used (see Chapter "Digital Communication in B-To-B Sales"). The deployment of resources may hence not be as swift and simple as required. Careful consideration is thus needed to grasp the full complexity of ecosystems and on how to enter, shape, and possibly succeed in these.

Case study: The mobility ecosystem

Mobility can be considered to be one of the vital needs of human beings. Ever since they tried to move from one location to another, not only by walking but also at first using animals such as horses, donkeys or camels and later by using machines, this has led to a globally spread industry that provides vehicles such as cars, bicycles, buses, trains or planes as well as mobility services.

A huge number of international players is involved in this business, starting from manufacturers of such vehicles that can be sold or provided to the people who want to move themselves. Due to the technological complexity the manufacturers need suppliers who take care of parts like engines, braking systems or wheels but also who can provide software solutions for driver assistant systems or even autonomous driving. Since the industry sector is so huge and globally present in literally every single country of the world many competing networks can be identified. To provide reliable rules and boundaries on what is allowed in mobility and to provide the required infrastructure such as laws, standards and restrictions or even streets and energy supply is a challenge for administrative authorities and governments worldwide.

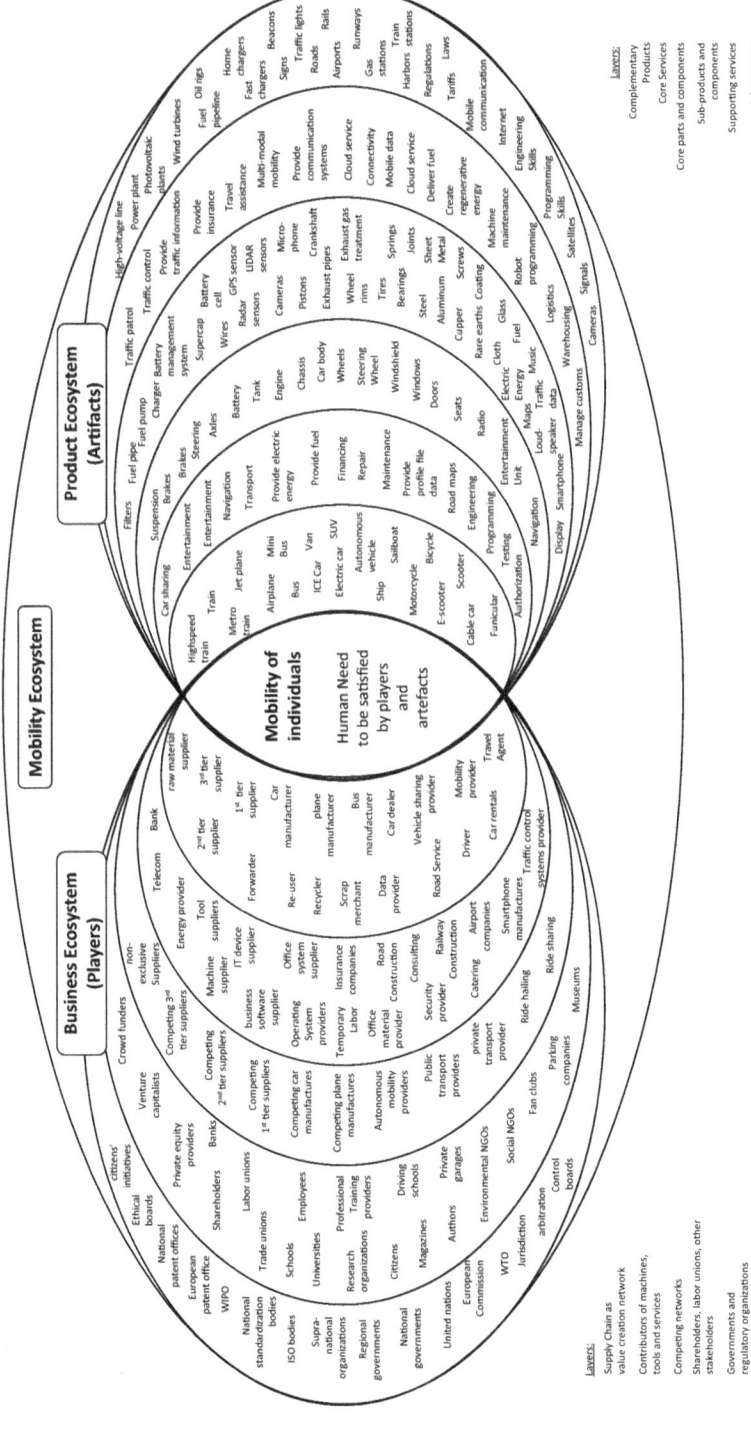

Fig. 5 Extract of the mobility ecosystem for international market analysis (Hinderer and Martin 2020, extended)

These and many more players and artefacts build the NDE for mobility. Figure 5 shows an overview of the ecosystem, which is still showing only a very superficial abstraction of the real situation. At the same time the situation in mobility is changing constantly and rapidly due to several effects such as climate change and the aim to reduce greenhouse gas emissions and thus the consumption of crude oil or the necessity to relieve metropolitan areas from excessive traffic congestion. New vehicles with new propulsion technologies based on renewable energies as well as new mobility solutions which focus more on the core need mobility than on owning and parking cars will put pressure on the ecosystem and accelerate change even more.

However, due to that rapid change in the NDE such a depiction can always and only show a snapshot on the existing situation with a certain bias. Having that in mind, the NDE of mobility as shown here allows an understanding of the complexity of the ecosystem itself and helps businesses to find the position of the artefacts they provide to the system as well as their own position as players now and in the future as well as in their home and in their future international markets. ◀

Case study: BEC GmbH in their NDEs

BEC GmbH is a medium sized company located in Reutlingen, Germany providing innovative robotic solutions in four main different business areas. BEC develops and applies advanced solutions in industry, entertainment, simulation and medical wherever a high level of automation is required. BEC comes into play with its ability to build and apply safe but at the same time highly interactive robot applications, especially as soon as a close interaction between robot and human being is needed.

These different business interests indicate that BEC is active in different NDEs. They mainly act as provider for solutions with Automatic Guided Vehicles (AGV) in the industry sector. Such AGVs are applied in industrial production whenever parts have to be moved and high precision is required in reproducible settings, maybe even in hostile environments. The strength AGV solutions have is the flexibility to handle changes in the setup. Conventional automation systems convince in situations with fixed robots and conveyor belts, which are favourable for high volumes and repetition rates. However, any kind of adjustments to the setup end up in high costs and an interruption of the process. In contrast, AGV can react ad-hoc to new challenges such as variable part sizes and weights or obstacles in their predefined route through a plant.

Automation of production is always dedicated to a certain supply chain that provides products or services for a specific human need. As described above, in the automotive industry, where automation is applied in ample variations, the need to be satisfied in the end is mobility. This leads to the finding that BEC is playing the role of a supplier that provides indirect goods within the NDE. Even though BEC does not consider themselves to be part of the automotive industry BEC is still affected by changes in the global economic situation of this industry due to new trends or influences in the NDE. As a player in this NDE it is of interest to understand these changes and recognize new challenges at an early stage in order to be prepared for new business opportunities rising on the horizon of innovation in any of the international markets relevant to BEC.

In the entertainment industry, however, BEC develops solutions for amusement parks or game shows. The companies that have such offerings to the public are very much driven by the preferences of the local population in international markets. In this context the human need of entertainment is in the epicentre of activities. The role of BEC is substantially different in this NDE. In this context they appear as the player that has the skills to build and provide the robotic solution to the company operating the amusement park or producing the game show. Thus, BEC is not allocated in the outer rings of the business view of the NDE but can be considered a 1st tier supplier and their solutions are directly in touch with the entertainment park customers being entertained. This changes the perception of their own role significantly. Here BEC is not the supplier's supplier but is directly in the position to communicate with final operators of the devices and thus has a much more direct access to market requirements, but is also subject to changes in an immediate and direct way here.

A similar assessment of the business position and allocation of the solutions can be found in the medical industry. Here the human need that directs all activities is health. BEC provides solutions e.g. for the positioning of patients in radiotherapy or for a very individual and reactive training and rehabilitation of injured athletes. Thus, the company is to be considered a 1st or 2nd tier supplier in the health NDE depending on line-up and arrangements of the projects, which might be managed by a general contractor or by the hospital operators themselves.

What can be seen in all three examples is that even a medium sized company has to act in several ecosystems at the same time. The concept of the NDE can help to understand their own position and interdependencies that can appear in each of the contexts more easily. Having a good overview of these situations enables management to take appropriate strategic, tactical as well as operational decisions affecting all international markets the company is active in. ◄

---

6   Conclusion

Businesses in the process of broadening their market engagements to market abroad need to carefully investigate these markets to fully understand them. Only a comprehensive overview of the markets abroad will allow businesses to position themselves in an advantageous position and manage possible challenges and risks from an early stage onwards. The application of an NDE thinking in evaluating market environments can assist in this endeavour. Broadening the understanding of the term ecosystems as often used in a business environment and setting the end consumers' needs at the centre of such thinking is pivotal to the NDE approach. The powerful approach of centring all thinking on the needs of an end-consumer uses the vectors of market forces to shape a business's overall outlook. Additionally, NDE combines the product as well as the business ecosystem thinking.

Businesses entering markets are well advised to carefully consider their position. Production value chains and the interdependencies and interconnections of players and products become visible through NDE thinking. NDE thinking can be used with a different zoom or level of resolution of the ecosystem under investigation. This strength of NDE thinking can hence be used on various levels of management. Strategic management is concerned with long-term higher-level issues. Therefore, NDE is used in this context as grasping the big picture. Players, such as governments, regulatory bodies, competitors and also suppliers on the one side, but also products, such as legislation, tariffs, general infrastructure, available materials (raw and production), as well as existing services in the field and complementary products, can be mapped out on a high level. The exercise of mapping the existing NDE allows strategic management to assess their own potential position and contribution to the ecosystem in future.

NDE thinking can, however, also be applied on tactical and operational management levels. A closer look at the more immediate setting as a business but also of its own product can be used on a tactical level, concerned with rolling out strategy and being a mid-term horizon task. Observing and mapping competitors as well as suppliers and customers in the NDE assists in actively creating the desirable market environment, or at least maintaining it. Changes in product supply chains, but also central consumer needs can better be understood using an NDE view, and thus can be appropriately managed.

NDE offers clear guidance to managers on an operational level. Linkages of the business and its products are depicted allowing managers in their daily activities to manage these. Upcoming changes can better be framed and not only the interdependencies within supply chains, but also the businesses own market can be managed.

The main obstacle in applying NDE thinking in general, but in an international context in particular, is the reliability of information gathered. Uncertainty is the norm when entering markets abroad. However, using a structured approach based on an NDE can assist in overcoming this obstacle.

The application of NDE can be manifold. The end-consumers' needs are at the core of the NDEs. These needs can be mobility, nutrition, health or any human need comprising the final market.

Exercise 4-A

Discuss the advantages of mapping an environment of a business from the end-consumer's perspective depicting a business and a product side to this environment, compared to traditional ecosystem approaches in business management.

Exercise 4-B

Core to the thinking of the NDE approach are the end-consumers' needs. As a global supplier of carbon-reinforced masts to the mobile phone infrastructure industry your company is envisaging entering the UK market. Map the relevant businesses as well as products which may impact on your product offering there.

Exercise 4-C

Considering the drive to 5G networks and the apparent use of this technology in the Internet-of-Things market. How would an NDE for the above company change?

References

Backhaus, K., & Voeth, M. (2014). *Industriegütermarketing* (10th ed.). Munich: Vahlen.

Blanke, T. (2014). *Digital asset ecosystems. Rethinking crowds and cloud.* Kidlington: Chandos.

Bower, J. L., & Christensen, C. M. (1995). Disruptive technologies: Catching the wave. *Harvard Business Review, 1,* 43–53.

Chang, E., & West, M. (2006). Digital ecosystems the next generation of the collaborative environment. The Eighth International Conference on Information Integration and Web-based Applications Services, 4–6 December, Yogyakarta, Indonesia, pp. 3–24.

Crumley, R. (2008). *Selling the moment. Values, needs and relationships; turning ordinary sales into a lifetime of success.* Amherst: HRD Press.

Di Maggio, P. J., & Powell, W. W. (1983). The iron cage revisited: Institutional isomorphism and collective rationality in organizational fields. *American Sociological Review, 48,* 147–160.

Dillerup, R., & Stoi, R. (2016). *Unternehmensführung. Management & Leadership: Strategien – Werkzeuge – Praxis* (5th ed.). Munich: Verlag Franz Vahlen.

Durst, S., & Poutanen, P. (2013). Success factors of innovation ecosystems – Initial insights form a literature review. In R. Smeds & O. Irrmann (eds.), *CO-CREATE 2013: The Boundary-Crossing Conference on Co-Design in Innovation,* Espoo, Finland, 16–19 June 2013, 15, pp. 27–38.

Ethirj, S. K., & Posen, H. E. (2014). Do product architectures affect innovation productivity in complex product ecosystems? Collaboration and competition in business ecosystems. *Advances in Strategic Management, 30,* 127–166.

Fournier, G., Hinderer, H., Schmid, D., Seign, R., & Baumann, M. (2013). The new mobility paradigm: Transformation of value chain and business models. *Enterprise and Work Innovation Studies, 8,* 9–40.

Frosch, R. A., & Gallopoulos, N. (1989). Strategies for manufacturing. *Scientific American, 261*(3), 144–152.

Hinderer, H., & Martin, L. (2017). The concept of a Need-driven ecosystem and its application to mobility. In *Proceedings of the International Conference on Engineering, Technology and Innovation (ICE /ITMC)),* Funchal, 27–29 June 2017, The Institute of Electrical and Electronics Engineers (IEEE), pp. 747–754.

Hinderer, H., & Martin, L. (2020). Towards understanding the impact of innovation – An application of the need-driven ecosystem theory. *International Journal of Innovation, Management and Technology, 11*(6), 159–164.

Iansiti, M., & Levien, R. (2014). *The keystone advantage: What the new dynamics of business ecosystems mean for strategy, innovation, and sustainability.* Boston: Harvard Business School Press.

Kehle, F., & Hinderer, H. (2016). Szenarien für die Neuordnung der Mobilitätsbranche. In H. Hinderer, T. Pflugfelder, & F. Kehle (Eds.), *Elektromobilität – Chancen für Zulieferer und Hersteller* (pp. 23–62). Springer Fachmedien: Munich.

Levin, S. (1992). The problem of pattern and scale in ecology. *Ecology, 73*(6), 1943–1967.

March, J. G. (1991). Exploration and exploitation in organizational learning. *Organization Science, 2*(1), 71–87.

Maslow, A. H. (1958). A dynamic theory of human motivation. In C. L. Stacey & M. DeMartino (Eds.), *Understanding human motivation* (pp. 26–47). Cleveland: Howard Allen.

Moore, J. F. (1993). Predators and prey: A new ecology of competition. *Harvard Business Review, 71*(3), 75–86.

Moore, J. F. (1996). *The death of competition – Leadership and strategy in the age of business ecosystems.* New York: HarperCollins.

Nonaka, I., & Konno, N. (1998). The concept of 'Ba': Building a foundation for knowledge creation. *California Management Review, 40*(3), 40–54.

O'Neill, R. V. (2001). Is it time to bury the ecosystem concept? *Ecology, 82*(12), 3275–3284.

Osterwalder, A., & Pigneur, Y. (2010). *Business model generation A handbook for visionaries, game changers, and challengers.* New York: Wiley.

Osterwalder, A., Pigneur, Y., Bernarda, G., Smith, A., & Papadakos, P. (2014). *Value proposition design. How to create products and services customers.* Hoboken: Wiley.

Pickett, S. T. A., & Cdenasso, M. L. (2002). The ecosystem as a multidimensional concept: Meaning, model, and methaphor. *Ecosystems, 5*(1), 1–10.

Sharma, V. M., & Erramilli, M. K. (2004). Resource-based explanation of entry mode choice. *Journal of Marketing Theory and Practice, 12*(1), 1–18.

Skilton, M. (2016). *Building digital ecosystem architectures.* Houndmilles: Palgrave MacMillan.

Tansley, A. G. (1935). The use and abuse of vegetational concepts and terms. *Ecology, 16*(3), 284–307.

Wallner, T., & Menrad, M. (2011). Extending the innovation ecosystem framework. In *Proceedings of the XXII ISPIM Conference*, 12–15 June, Hamburg, Germany, p. 9.

Winter, J. M. (2014). *Success factors of mobile business ecosystems – From hardware-centric to content and advertising based business models.* Aalto University.

Zenz, G. J., & Thompson, G. H. (1994). *Purchasing and the management of materials* (7th ed.). New York: Wiley.

Assessing International Markets

Ludwig Martin

1 Reasons for Market Assessments: A Two-Pronged Approach

Companies grow due to their participation in economic activities. And as shown in Chapter "Ecosystem Evaluations in Business Development" companies are set in an environment to do so. This is true for their actual business activity as well as for their product offerings. The growth of companies is mostly driven by their ability to supply a demand stemming from customers. Hence, such growth is enabled through the product side of the activities of companies. The trigger for the initial invention of a product may well be earlier in time. But also, at that stage companies already experience their first small growth due to their offering. This is especially true for start-ups.

However, with the growth of companies also comes the ability to expand further. If the business is managed well and growing locally, financial resources become available to look for more places where demand for the product offering might be present. Other countries may hold the promise to be the next destination for selling products. The external market demand (extrinsic) and the internal ability to satisfy such demands (intrinsic) need to be balanced out. The rationale for the step of developing business abroad needs to be understood within a company in order to position itself (Lem et al. 2013). Ample advice for companies is available from consultants and academics. They typically offer some advice on how companies can position themselves following internal considerations on how a company might view its own setting. The step towards understanding a

L. Martin (✉)
Pforzheim University, Pforzheim, Germany
e-mail: ludwig.martin@hs-pforzheim.de

© The Author(s), under exclusive license to Springer Fachmedien Wiesbaden GmbH,   77
part of Springer Nature 2021
L. Martin (ed.), *International Business Development*,
https://doi.org/10.1007/978-3-658-33221-1_5

company's position is, however, difficult to outline. The accompanying uncertainty adversely affects any intention of developing business activities abroad.

Overall in international management the application of the (international) product life cycle (Vernon 1966) is an often-used way to explain internationalization of businesses. The main thrust in this explanation is product-centred. In the initial model postulated by Vernon (1966) products undergo three stages of product development: new product, maturing product, standardized product. Later a fourth stage: decline, was added. Variations of this initial product life cycle model exist, see also Chapter "International Business Development in Context—History, Trends and Realities". Linked to the product are consideration of location (markets) as well as the production sites of the product. The product life cycle model links the considerations companies might have with regards to markets for their products explicitly to considerations of production location. In many cases internationalization is seen as a result of a mix of available capacity and opportunity to capture markets shares elsewhere, resulting in profits. Companies seek markets abroad in order to gain from economies of scales in production. In early phases of the product life cycle this is often achieved through exports of produced goods. As the markets mature and competition sets in, a strategy of reduction of costs though production of goods in less costly locations is often followed. Production sites are shifted abroad, typically these production locations are set in the regions of the new markets for the product.

The international product life cycle depicts many cases in businesses and the development path of their products well. However, internationalization may also occur without the actual product. Internationalization can also be a pull towards the supply chain. Considerations of companies to use particular advantages of other markets to their benefit in terms of relocating production facilities or other departments without an intent to serve the market there exist too. An extreme example here would be companies prospecting for minerals or fossil fuels all over the world. Companies within the commodities market often enter countries due to the opportunities to secure supplies. But also, for companies in the manufacturing sector, this is an often overlooked second drive for internationalization of companies: offshoring. Frequently cited advantages for relocating some departments into other countries are access to skilled labour as well as cost of production / labour; all part of the input rather than the output of an economic activity of a company. More efficient and globally coordinated performance is at the core of reasons for offshoring (Pisani and Ricart 2016).

In the context of this chapter, however, the more traditional view on international business development, the product-based approach in explaining the routes companies may take in the quest to cover other countries, is taken. Yet it is important to note that internationalization may occur as a supply pull as opposed to a product push too.

Similar considerations prevail in terms of basics for an assessment of market places abroad. Such assessments are important steps in companies' decision making and strategy development. And this is true for both important aspects of such assessments of opportunities to go abroad: the external environment and internal abilities.

2   External View

The aaim of a market assessment is to derive a solid base for a decision on entering a market or not. Before deciding on expanding a company's presence into another country, it is prudent to first assess the potential and risks of the target market. Such an assessment can take many different forms. It varies as much as the product offering of a company differs from one company to the other. The overall product-market strategy, see also "International Business Development in Context—History, Trends and Realities", needs to be considered. However, some standards in the approach to conduct such external assessments can be found.

The target market is often not just the customer. These potential customers are surrounded by their own settings, as also described in Chapter "Ecosystem Evaluations in Business Development" of this book, by the use of the term need-driven ecosystem (NDE). It is important to quantify the perceived potential in a market abroad for a thorough market assessment. The application of NDE thinking and its potential for evaluating business context can assist in this effort. As depicted in the NDE, the product is placed in the context of other products. This is particularly true for Business to Business (B-to-B) activities. But more importantly, the company deciding to engage in a market abroad is placing itself in this ecosystem too. Market assessments need to grasp the contextual factors of the target market on various levels (Douglas and Craig 2011). It proved to be a good approach for the assessment of markets to differentiate this target market on two main levels, namely:

- macro level and
- meso level.

The macro level is concerned with data on country or geographical area level. An assessment on this level will result in an overall broad overview of the target market, its potential and possible uncertainties. The meso level is concerned with more industry specific information in the target market. Establishing a presence abroad and becoming part of an ecosystem there will require this closer and less broad look too. Additionally, a micro level can be added to a market assessment. This level of assessment will yield contextual information pertaining consumers, and is hence important for companies in the business to consumer (B-to-C) market. Focusing on B-to-B in this chapter it is hence not further discussed here.

2.1   Macro Level Assessment

When conducting market assessments, the probably most common approach to such assessment is outlined by the PEST(EL) analysis. Aguilar (1967) is generally recognized as the founder of this approach—although it was not called PEST(EL) at that stage. PEST was born through a description on how business environments could be scanned and what the important factors to consider are. This approach posits that business environments have four factors to consider: political, economic, social as well as technological. Later the ecological/environmental and the legal factors were added in line with a more modern view on companies as being part of a wider fabric within societies. Essentially this approach to a macro level assessment assists in giving structure in the search for information and knowledge about a potential market. Generally, the information gathered on this (flight) level is very coarse and unspecific with regards to the company's needs of an assessment. This PEST(EL) type of assessment often has a company-independent flavour. The facts considered and investigated on this high level of assessment, the macro level assessment, are of a fixed or given nature. Single companies will usually not be able to change or influence the realities given at a macro level, or at least it will be very difficult for them. Facts considered through a high level PEST(EL) analysis are setting the framework for the activities of companies.

Certainly, cases of change on this macro level due to external influence and government backed companies exist. An example could be the rise of Built-Operate-Transfer infrastructure development deals within Zambia in the last few years: Chinese construction firms are backed by Chinese government loans to Zambia and political influence to change the macroeconomic approach by the Zambian government on how to deliver infrastructure (Burke 2007). Political deals directly impact on economic realities. Markets for (Chinese) companies are created. Such and similar political coverage are also discussed in Chapter "Political Coverage for International Ventures" of this book.

The external environment on a macro level is, however, deemed to be fixed for most companies seeking to develop their business activities abroad. However, the factors making up this macro level, with their very own sub-factors, are to be viewed from a particular company perspective. Every company with its product is embedded in its own ecosystem, of which the macro level is the first important level to understand. The macro level is the wider framework which a particular ecosystem and a company is set in. Each company with its product will need to assess this framework in line with its own needs. The PEST(EL) analysis offers a skeleton for such an assessment, as all major macro level considerations and factors are typically covered under one of the six headings.

Political factors include inter alia information on the governmental system, level of democracy, political stability, and general government policy (including tax, labour, and trade). Good sources of information on these are manifold. Publications by the respective governments and also policy reviews done by well-known think tanks may be available to create this wider understanding of how the political realm of the target market can be viewed.

Economic factors are often easier to pin down. Sub-factors in this group include data on economic growth, currency exchange rates, inflation rates, unemployment rates (incl. youth unemployment), and income levels. Data on this can often be found in government publications, publications by the various offices of the United Nations, Central Bank publications, national or international statistics bureaus as well as in many other sources.

Social sub-factors aim at depicting the situation of a society in the country abroad. In order to form this picture data on demographics (e.g. birth rates, age distribution), income, health and lifestyle and many more can be used. Typical sources for such data are similar to the sources for data underpinning the economic factor.

Technical factors include inter alia drive of innovation (e.g. patents registered as a marker), research and development efforts, existing infrastructure (ports, roads network etc.). The technical factor is of particular importance for companies entering a market with an established product. The technical context of a target market translates directly to technical necessities of products. Sources of information on this can be publications of professional bodies, institutions for standardization, data from patent offices, and general reviews by tech consultants (e.g. Gartner reports).

Ecological/Environmental sub-factors include all aspects relating to the real natural world. Information on climate, weather, flora and fauna may be important to some companies. Further the impact of climate change and country efforts to counteract such change and brace for the change could be interesting to consider. Existing environmental laws (e.g. regarding emissions), particularly important for companies seeking new production locations, may be part of a first assessment in this rubric too; this could, however, also be covered in the legal factors. Sources for such information on ecological/environmental sub-factors are manifold. Reports of the World Wildlife Fund (WWF) or the UN Intergovernmental Panel on Climate Change and also local resource centres hold information aplenty.

Legal sub-factors are often covered in one of the other rubrics already since the laws of a country are influenced by political, economic and societal considerations. The importance of the legal aspects of doing business abroad, however, warrants its own rubric. Environmental laws (see ecological sub-factors), antitrust laws, employment regulations, such as labour relations as well as patent and trademark laws (see also Chapter "Legal Aspects of Launching Products Internationally") are important sub-factors to consider. Export/import duties and existing rules on tariffs need to be assessed. Consideration should also be given to potential foreseeable changes in existing rules and regulations impacting the business activities in future. Government publishers as well as reviews by legal consultants are good resources to consult on information on the legal sub-factors.

With PEST(EL) providing a skeleton for information on a potential market or host country, it is up to the company to discover all the relevant information on this macro level. Since information on any of these six rubrics is generally aplenty, the task of defining relevance for a company's own setting is not trivial. Novices to this task tend to go too far with capturing relevant information. While the picture drawn will become bigger and possibly more colourful, the actual focus and aim of such an assessment might be missed. The work of macro market assessments by external consultants is similar. Without a good understanding of the actual perspective of the company on the macro environment, such macro level assessments often fail to address the needs of companies on such assessments.

An assessment on this (flight) level is not to be confounded with a market assessment. The information gained through a PEST(EL) like exercise generally lacks the required detail for a market assessment. However, some of the data collated may well be used as a proxy or marker for particular market features which are to be expected. This is, however, highly dependent on the market segment and product which a company aims to operate in. While, for instance, a supplier to the baby food industry might find birth-rates of countries to be a key factor for considerations for an engagement in that market, a supplier in the automation industry might not find data through a macro environment analysis which is directly linked to the potential business opportunities in a foreign country. The market assessment will require a closer view in order to create the required solid base for any decision making on a market entry.

2.2   Meso Level (Market) Assessment

The meso level of a company shall be defined as the closer environment of a company. An assessment of this meso level will need to look at an industry level assessment of a host country and the target market. Suppliers, customers as well as competitors need to be considered.

In his seminal article Porter (1979) describes the forces within an industry driving competition. What is interesting to note in this work is that not only the direct competition (another company producing the same or similar product) is considered. The approach of Porter is multi-pronged, distinguishing between five forces. The strength of these five forces determines, according to Porter, the profit potential of an industry. The five forces considered are (Porter 1979):

Jockeying for position: The actual competition within an industry needs to be considered. The likely actions and reactions of market-players in a market with regards to pricing, production volumes, efforts of standardization, level of fixed cost and embeddedness in industries of competitors all influence their behaviour. When entering a market an adaptation and development of a company's own value proposition may be required in order to gain traction in a market. This is typically set in a competitive environment and responses of existing competitors can be expected.

Bargaining power of customers: Customers themselves might be powerful too. This is of particular truth if product offerings are very industry or customer specific, e.g. large-scale paint shop conveyor systems and the automotive industry. Further, large volume customers bear particular importance to companies, adding bargaining power to the buyer. But also, the characteristics of the product and the lack of value proposition offered may deter customers.

Bargaining power of suppliers: Suppliers to an industry may use their own power to gain higher profits. Depending on the market structure and dominance of few suppliers in an industry, supply chains have great effect on companies and their leverage to push back high prices offered by individual suppliers.

Threat of entry: New companies might emerge in the market. The strength of this force depends on various factors such as barriers to entries and the existing competition. The threat of entry is of particular interest for companies evaluating opportunities in other countries and their markets. These threats also exist for the new-entrant itself. According to Porter (1979) the barriers of entry are: Economies of scale, product differentiation, capital requirement, cost disadvantages independent of size, access to distribution channels and government policy. Further the responses from existing rivals need to be considered (price war, increase in production and flooding of market, overall downturn to detriment of all).

Threat of substitution: This force relates to the product offered itself. Products, once a standard, might see substitution by more competitive products with a change of technology and modern production, offering to customers a better return on investment. Disruptive technologies or the likeliness for such a disruption in a market place need to be considered.

It can be argued that this model of Porter is dated and new technologies, globalization etc. have changed market environments. This is certainly true. However, the model of the five forces provides a good base-line of aspects to consider when evaluating markets abroad. Further, through the accelerated internationalization of businesses in the past two decades an assessment of target countries on a meso level needs to consider networks too. In an update of their well-known Uppsala model (this is introduced in Chapter "Establishing Local Business Units" of this book) Johanson and Vahlne (2009) point out that internationalization cannot only be viewed in a neoliberal way, viewing markets as places of supply and demand. They argue, using Johanson and Mattsson (1988) as a base, that relationships and networks become more prevalent in the business environment. This is possibly also due to the ease of travelling to and communicating with business partners, suppliers as well as customers due to a growing aviation industry and the rise of digital communication (see also Chapter "Digital Communication in B-To-B Sales" on this topic).

Social capital, a concept which found its base in sociology through Coleman (1988), explains the importance of networks in communities. This concept was broadened and applied in business contexts too (Burt 2000) and remains a focus of many scholars in business science as well as international management in particular (e.g. Menzies et al. 2020). Social capital has an economic value for individuals or companies. Social capital can be understood on a structural level and its affiliated networks are characterized by clusters and structural holes. Simplified, social capital is a measure of how well an individual or company is tied in within a network (through alliances, joint ventures, previous business contacts etc.). The ability of networks and the actors within these, to recognize structural holes (read: gap in the market) can become a key advantage of companies. Social capital and the affiliated network are to be considered to be crucial aspects of doing business and for decision making when entering foreign markets. This goes beyond the five forces of Porter, at times negating some of these too. Networks can become driving forces for development of business, this is particularly true for ventures with a perceived high risk. Networks can lower the risk for the individuals within networks. This is an important aspect when looking at international business development decisions.

However, it is not an easy task to evaluate a full network and to bring this information to paper and into a formal decision-making process for entering a new market or country. Personal relationships, undocumented connections, informal agreements etc. may shape such networks. And the strength of a company network, often based on the social capital of managers, can only be judged by the very managers themselves.

Case study: IMS Gear—network pull

IMS Gear SE & Co. KGaA is specialized in gear and transmission technology. Its headquarters are in the South of Germany. IMS Gear is a supplier in the globalized automotive industry with physical presence in the form of production sites and/or sales offices in Germany, Mexico, USA, Japan, South Korea as well as China. The total headcount of employees is approximately 3100. The history of IMS Gear dates back to 1863, founded as Johann Morat and Söhne. Beginning of this century, partially due to the globalization, the name of the company was changed to IMS Gear. Starting in the early 1990s the company increased its international presence with a strong focus on the automotive market (IMS Gear, n.d.). Automotive companies such as Daimler, BMW and VW as well as first-tier suppliers such as Bosch, Conti or ZF started to build their production facilities in the early 1990s in the USA. IMS Gear, by then already a supplier to the first-tier companies in Germany, opted for increasing their production capacity in close proximity to these major customers. A similar approach was followed in China.

In such international business development scenarios not only the market opportunity, presented through an increase in production capacity of customers, but also established networks and business contacts are part of the market assessment. The final decision to follow customers—a case of coat-tailing—is hence based on market considerations as well as on a network (business partner) approach to do business. ◄

2.3   Market Realities

When considering doing business abroad and a product is taken abroad, the question of market size is an important question to answer. Information on the environment has been gathered through tapping into multiple sources. Macro and meso level information has to be compiled and a solid picture of the NDE needs to be sketched.

A market assessment can be differentiated into three strata of markets a company plays a role in:

- suppliers,
- competitors, and
- customers.

As indicated in Fig. 1 a company will itself take on three positions compared to other players in the wider market and will conversely have three strata of markets to consider. Companies will have suppliers and possibly a choice of suppliers to choose from. Second-tier suppliers (indicated far left in Fig. 1) are at times to be considered too. Companies will have direct competitors; this competition may also be in two directions: competition for customers as well as competition for suppliers (resources). Further, companies will have to assesses the actual customer market. In many cases companies in the wider marketplace can be clearly categorized into one of the three markets. However, as also indicated in Fig. 1 companies may also cross markets and extend their reach upstream or downstream. When conducting a market assessment, it is (mostly) good practice to differentiate between the three mentioned strata of the markets. The boundaries of such strata might prove to be blurred. As good practice, the company's own boundaries (start and end of value adding in the wider value chain) can be used to differentiate the externalities. This allows for a defined assessment and lowers the risk of not searching for and finding relevant information in particular directions.

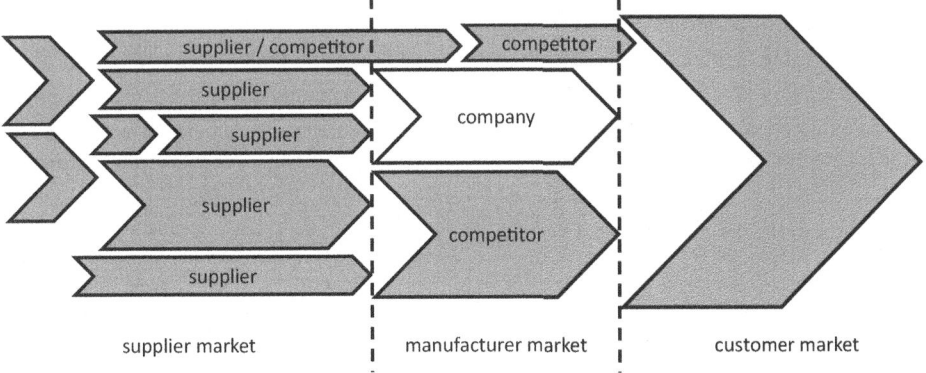

Fig. 1 Three strata of market assessment

2.4   Supplier Market Assessment

Moving a company, or parts thereof, to another country or launching a product internationally, results in companies finding themselves in new ecosystems. Depending on the business structure and proposition, companies are often reliant on a well-functioning support system: their suppliers.

An assessment of the supplier market strata has the following two parts to consider:

- quantitative evaluation of existing suppliers in target market and
- assessment of quality of suppliers.

The importance of such an assessment stems from typical mid- and long-term views on how companies can do business abroad. The term supplies includes a vast array of possibly required products or services when entering a foreign market. The obvious suppliers are suppliers who deliver (raw) products or semi-engineered parts to the new venture abroad. But there are more suppliers to be considered too. Depending on the nature of the business this might include an assessment of: locally registered lawyers, IT support companies, security contractors, facility management firms, etc. An assessment of the markets will yield information on availability of such suppliers including their capacity and first insights on cost structures attached. First-tier suppliers are the focus. However, depending on the structure of the industry at times second-tier suppliers are to be considered too. Companies entering a new country enter an existing network of companies. When assessing the supplier market, it is hence just to gain information of the suppliers' commitments elsewhere. A supplier might officially have sufficient capacity to produce and deliver supplies. However, commitments to competitors or elsewhere may well lead to a situation where such a supplier might not be able to supply at all. This can also be due to exclusivity clauses by potential suppliers with existing customers. The bargaining power of suppliers is assessed here. Publicly available information on potential suppliers such as turnover and balance sheets (if listed) reveal great first insights. Further scouting for potential suppliers and direct contact with potential suppliers, including visits to production sites will add to an overall understanding of the available supplier market.

The importance of supplier market assessments may not be underestimated. A thorough understanding of the upstream part of the business or venture aboard, prior to committing to a new market will reduce risks of failure. The quality of suppliers in terms of reliability, level of work, timely delivery etc. will have a great impact on the future venture. The development of the supply side of a venture abroad is also discussed in Chapter "Sourcing Strategies and Trends: Global Versus Local" of this book.

2.5   Manufacturer Market Assessment: Competitors and Products

The existing competition needs to be gauged on a second strata level. Information on companies active in the same market segment in the target country as well as products available is crucial for any decision. A first qualitative picture of the market can be drawn through the application of the NDE approach (see Chapter "Ecosystem Evaluations in Business Development"). A quantification of this market is required prior to making decisions involving investments, as is the case with any decision to enter a new market and develop business abroad. Referring to Porter's Five Forces, the "jockeying for position", it is the assessment of the existing market forces and their potential response to a new entry that need to be evaluated here.

When assessing the closer market and in particular the competition within the market, some first insights for a possible future positioning of a product or the company itself need to be gained. Competitors have to be identified and assessed. The identification of competitors in markets abroad may at first seem an easy task in a globalized world—using the internet and its various information portals. However, in particular in a B-to-B environment the identification of competitors is often cumbersome. Competitors will at times not reveal their customers; and potential customers may be reluctant to reveal their suppliers. This information gap can, for instance, be closed through interactions within the wider industry network. Trade fairs, professional associations, local trade and industry chambers may prove good sources of information.

The dimension of timing must be considered. Depending on the timing of a market entry, the assessment of the market will be different, or at least will have different nuances. Market situations change over time due to the occupancy by competitors in the market. The advantages of a first mover (Lieberman and Montgomery 1988) when entering a new market can be considered as one extreme. However, if markets already exist and a company enters as a new entry, the assessment ought to be different in nature.

In the cases of companies entering a new market as a first-mover, by definition no direct competition within the target market exists. Companies can choose their "location" (Prescott and Visscher 1977) or position within the market. It is then, however, good practice to look further: What further competitors might enter the same market soon, possibly imitating products or offerings and using their home-based resources to capture market share. Decision in such scenarios will hence require foresight of potential moves of competitors and an evaluation of possible active measures to retain the advantage of first-mover for a prolonged time. Such active measures may include binding suppliers in exclusivity clauses (see Sect. 2.4).

In cases where markets already exist, the assessment will primarily look at the target market itself. Based on information on competitors regarding market share, total sales, registered patents, level of human resources (quality and quantity), cash reserves etc., a company developing their footprint abroad is able to better paint an overall picture of the target market. In addition to competitor specific information, product information is crucial too. When entering a market abroad with a product, a replacement of existing products in that market may be part of the strategy. Knowing characteristics and features of products (and affiliated services) of competitors will allow a company to derive a better judgement of the response of the actual customer market to a new offering. The position and the marketing strategies of competitors, their branding as well as their communication / sales channels are important to note. This information will guide own development of the brand and the routes to customers to be taken.

2.6   Customer Market Assessment

The customer market is the place where revenue is generated. It is hence the possibly most important market to assess within the three strata of the market: No customer, no market. In order to measure the market demand of a product three dimensions are to be considered (Kotler et al. 2017, p. 100):

- time,
- product, and
- space.

According to Kotler et al. (2017) each of these three base dimensions has their own ranges. The task at hand is to determine a suitable level and horizon to measure potential market demand for a product. While in an effort to develop a company's international footprint in a particular host county, the unit of analysis for the dimension "space" is the target country, the time horizon (short-term, mid-term, long-term) for such demand needs to be decided upon. Further, company policy and strategy will determine the level for the assessment in terms of the product level. The level for such an assessment ranges from an assessment of the turnover of the actual product to the overall turnover in the industry. Depending on the industry and the actual product on offer, the most suitable unit of analysis to determine the actual demand in the target country needs to be selected. In order to do so the market segment targeted by the company needs to be defined.

Knowledge on pricing in the market is of particular importance. If pricing structures in the market are far below forecasted costs, it will be difficult for companies to become commercially successful in the target market. Information on pricing is hence of utmost importance to judge on the attractiveness of a target market. It must, however, be noted that the final pricing of a company's own product is not set at this stage of assessment yet. The gathering of information on the pricing levels of products by competitors is cumbersome. This is particularly true for B-to-B deals, where no publicly available information is available. Further data informing a company of possible switching costs (Lieberman and Montgomery 1988) to customers may be of interest at this stage of assessment. Switching costs are costs which customers may incur additional to purchase costs due to changing their set-up to a new set-up. A typical example in the consumer market is the cost of changing from Android based mobile telecommunication products to iPhone or vice versa. In a B-to-B environment switching costs are often related to setting up new logistics channels, transforming production units or IT system changes. Switching costs, therefore, are good markers for actual realistic chances to attract and secure future customers.

The initial pricing is, however, not the only criteria which is used by customers to decide upon a product. In the B-to-B environment the total cost of ownership is an important measure of investing in new equipment or other assets. Total cost of ownership takes a long-term view on investment. Costs affiliated to this are purchase costs, running costs as well as indirect costs. Further the divisor 'time of use' is important. The 'time of use' is often linked to the quality of a product or its longevity. Understanding the value proposition offered by competitors in this regard can be existential for companies entering new international markets.

Due to differing political and legal circumstances the peculiarities of markets abroad may shape the demand as well as business models and offerings of market players. The full understanding of business approaches taken by competitors in target markets will assist in shaping one's own view on a company's position. A close look at a company's business model circulating around the product and resources available is of importance for further decision making. As a new entrant into a market it is up to the company to master the hurdles as described by Porter's model of the five forces.

Case study: moulding equipment—own position in the market

A manufacturer of moulding equipment is active worldwide (Company ABC—anonymized name). Their effort in capturing market share is based on a close cooperation with the users of their equipment and consulting these customers on the best suited moulding machine. The moulding machines are sold all over the globe, partially through partners and partially through own sales and service centres abroad.

Moulding machines are used for forming plastic parts. Plastic parts can be found in our daily life, such as packaging, electronics, medical etc. To assess the global market the consumption of plastic may serve as a proxy. However, not all industries have the same use of plastics in their various forms. And data on moulding machines in use is essentially non-existent. There are ample equipment manufacturers in this market, supplying producers of plastic parts with moulding machines and equipment. Assessing Company ABC's market share may prove to be difficult.

When the above manufacturer had to evaluate its own strategy on the best suited presence in a particular world region, a market assessment of this region needed to be conducted. Having already operated in the regions for many years allowed a good overview of existing customers as well as potential customers. Further, through information gained by its sales representatives in the region, some data on other manufacturers selling and servicing their own moulding equipment in the region was available. The data on the market was hence collated from various sources of information. An overall high-level market study based on available data (secondary sources) was conducted. Further, a desktop type of study of the existing customers and respective outlooks for future needs of moulding equipment—estimating growth rates in their respective industries—was done; this was combined with insights of sales representatives present in the region. The insights of the sales representatives were weighted high, since they were close to the primary source (the potential customers) of data on demand.

The final step was the strategic decision and take on Company ABC's own position within the market. While the market showed a steady upward trend, the company needed to estimate its own (future) market share. The uncertainty on the current market share, due to a lack of well-established information, added an unavoidable uncertainty to this task. The subsequent management decision on how to structure the company's presence in the region took this into consideration too. ◄

3   Internal Reality

Parahalad and Hamel (1990) is an often-cited source advocating a resource-based view on companies. The topic of core competence is at the centre of their argument on what makes companies successful. Core products of companies are, for Parahalad and Hamel, the *"embodiment of core competencies"*. They argue that core competences must fulfil three sets of criteria: They provide access to wide range of markets, they add to (perceived) customer benefit and they are difficult to imitate.

Using these three tests, internal realities on the path to grow internationally can be checked. This check is, however, not as simple; it involves a critical assessment of abilities too. Self-overestimation, or underestimation can skew such an assessment. What is crucial to any company, however, is to clearly establish for themselves as to what the core competencies are they possess. Capabilities are important to grasp.

However, it is not capability alone that will determine success when developing its business footprint abroad. Prior to the decision to go abroad, and linked to the market assessment, a company's capacity to make such a step needs to be considered too. Capacity is understood as a measure of depth—how much is available? Companies targeting markets abroad will have to determine their level of country expertise, financial capacity, human resource capacity, production capacity, capacity to innovate and capacity to scale up among others. Existing physical infrastructure, such as IT servers, need to be checked for its free resources and availability for an expansion in business. Competencies with regards to (international) management, technology use or strategy development need to be grasped. In particular, what is interesting in situations in which companies are seeking to broaden their footprint abroad are assessments of the capacity and capability of the sales department. The development of sales channels generating leads and prospects (see also Chapter "B-To-B Sales Approaches" of this book) through agents or own staff becomes crucial in endeavours of selling products abroad. Differing cultural factors as well as business culture abroad and the ability of a company to accommodate these need to be considered. In many cases only a small number of staff will be taken abroad when establishing a local business unit, see also Chapter "Establishing Local Business Units" of this book. Prior to the decision to enter a market, a firm strategy needs to be devised on how such a market entry can be conducted with the resources at hand. Social capital and existing networks need to be added to the equation.

The deployment of any resource with its accompanying risk of failure needs to be considered. Risks of failure will be higher if internal capabilities and capacities are not well judged beforehand. A realistic view on internal abilities and hence possible responses to looming crises in the future need to be developed. Stemming from a market assessment first tasks and risks will be known already. In the second step, the assessment of internal abilities will gather evidence on how a company is positioned to deal with any of these tasks and potential risks.

Following the NDE model, the product view is of importance too. The product is the link to customers and is embedded in its own ecosystem. The product's features and (particular in the B-to-B environment) the technical fit will be of importance. Further the factor cost is not to be underestimated. Shifting a product or even its production to a new country will require a good knowledge of costing of product offerings. The cost position relative to competitors will become important. An assessment of cost structures within the company will yield insights on flexibility to respond to the market. Here the accounting department has to set a realistic view on costs and margins expected for the products on offer.

Various formal internal capacity assessment approaches exist. McKinsey spearheaded the Organizational Capacity Assessment Tool (OCAT). OCAT is particular useful for companies looking at growth perspectives. The VRIO analysis (Barney 1991) is an approach for looking at company resources and their relation to competitive advantage. The acronym stands for valuable-rare-inimitable-organized. The VRIO analysis looks at the competitive edge stemming from the resources—similar to the argument of Parahalad and Hamel's (1990) on the importance of core competencies.

4   Matching External and Internal: Decision Making

Having gathered information on the external and the internal realities given, companies need to decide upon their approach on a new market. In the first step a wealth of information is gathered; the analysis of the implications on a business endeavour is the second step to be taken. At this analysis stage a broader corporate view of markets, their meaning, their potential and the trajectory of a company needs to be taken. Prior strategic management decisions and their implications for the overall final analysis and resultant decision making need to be considered. And here some of the realities of business may appear: the opportunity to enter a market may well counter any previous strategic decision. At times opportunities knock on doors and companies are well advised to reap the benefits of such opportunities. Matching the strategic outlook of companies on internationalization with such opportunities may however be difficult, as resources may have to be diverted from the originally decided strategic path. Other times opportunities have to be created first, these are typically based on a strategic path taken initially and will require proactive shaping of products and markets.

The final decision to enter a new market will hinge on many different factors to consider. Further, the information gathered embodying these factors will be accompanied with uncertainty: Uncertainty regarding correctness and accurateness of the data gathered as well as uncertainty about future developments. It is the task of the manager to comprehend all factors, accumulate the wealth of information gathered, process it and decide upon the most suitable way ahead. Some standard approaches have been established to fulfil this task, making the wealth of information gathered at times more comprehensive and thus allowing for a decision-making process with a clear track of a decision-making path.

4.1   Portfolios—CAGE Distance Framework

The General Electric / McKinsey portfolio analysis is one such tool to condense important information. It is of particular use when various opportunities need to be assessed against each other. This is the case when companies seek opportunities in various countries and available resources are limited. Decisions on prioritizations may need to be made. It is the task for management to decide upon which opportunity to tackle (first). A portfolio of various markets can be depicted in a single graph, see Fig. 2 (left).

In order to derive such graphs, the results stemming from market assessments are condensed to an overall market attractiveness. The combination of information on suppliers, competitors and customer, all set in a macro setting (PESTEL), will determine this market attractiveness. The market attractiveness is hence a measure of attractiveness derived through external indicators.

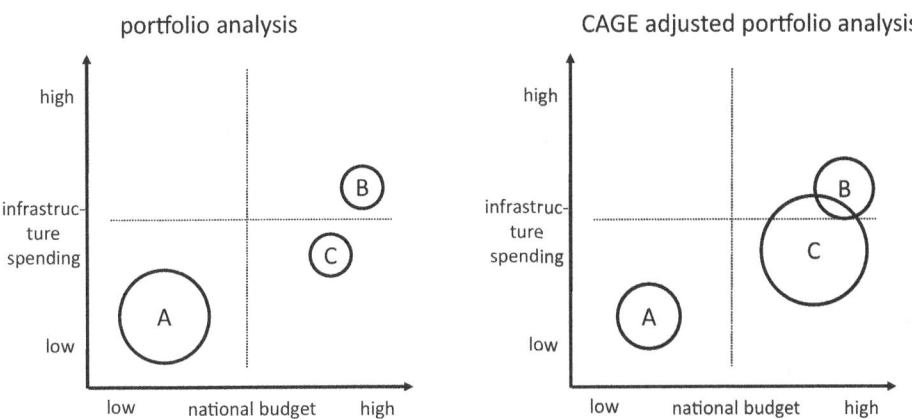

Fig. 2 Country portfolio analysis and adjustment for CAGE distance (after: Ghemawat 2001)

The example in Fig. 2 is based on the construction industry and a particular service offered. A normal portfolio analysis will depict various countries as bubbles (Countries A, B, C). The position of the bubbles in the matrix represents the overall market. The size of the bubble represents the potential revenue (implicitly the company's ability to generate revenue). Market position and potential revenue in combination are a measure of market attractiveness.

The results of a PEST(EL) and a market analysis do not give many insights on the relative place of a target market and a company's own position. These analyses yield some insights on market size and attractiveness. Further, some indicators of otherness of markets abroad can be detected during the gathering of data for these assessments. This otherness or "distance" is the focus of the work of Ghemawat (2001). A measurement of distance to own reality and to the base of a company (launching its efforts in international business development) might be of assistance in checking the feasibility and realistic gains of going abroad. A thorough assessment of the market at a meso level will bring insights into this otherness of a market. It allows for a measure of distance and can hence be included in an analysis. Ghemawat (2001) postulates that this distance, in terms of business endeavours, has four dimensions: Cultural, administrative, geographic, and economic (CAGE). The strength of this CAGE framework is the clear definition of attributes of the four dimensions and the impact these attributes might have on product offerings abroad. An assessment of distance, using the CAGE framework, will change the perception of market attractiveness. If this distance has not been considered before, portfolios can thus be adjusted to reflect this reality. Following Ghemawat (2001) Fig. 2 depicts such an adjustment. Considering the CAGE distance, a different estimate on potential revenue in the markets may be the result. This is depicted by the change of size of the bubbles, shown in Fig. 2 (right). In the example of Fig. 2 such adjustment results in the realization that Country A may not be as attractive as initially considered. However, after adjusting the portfolio matrix Country B appears more attractive to the company. Country C, initially deemed to be the least attractive market (smallest bubble in the portfolio analysis), appears after adjustment more attractive due to some closeness of the market-to-company CAGE dimensions. A comparison of overall market attractiveness might, therefore, come to another conclusion when adding the four CAGE dimensions to market assessments.

4.2   Portfolios—Attractiveness Analysis

Flowing from such a realization that not all markets are equally attractive when considering CAGE distance, a company-based view is another option to judge market opportunities. Finding the perfect match between company and market is the aim. A measure of business attractiveness is hence introduced. Business attractiveness is determined by internal indicators. Capacity, capability and abilities in terms of products as well as value adding processes are to be considered here.

The use of a variation of the portfolio matrix is a powerful tool to graphically represent the various opportunities a company might have. Various countries (or market segments) can be judged using two dimensions: market attractiveness and business attractiveness (Kotler et al. 2019, p. 357). This gives a basic structure of a 2×2 matrix (Fig. 3). Two important deciding factors are hence combined for decision making in such market-business attractiveness diagrams: External realties and internal abilities. Where opportunities presented in a host market are deemed to be high (high attractiveness) and the internal strengths (business attractiveness) are high, the most attractive overall opportunities are situated. Unattractive markets or ill-fitting product offerings to markets are the least overall attractive opportunities, compare Fig. 3.

In an extension to the simple two-dimensional marking of attractiveness, other information can be added to the graph. The size of the market (e.g. number of customers or

Fig. 3 Market-Business attractiveness base diagram

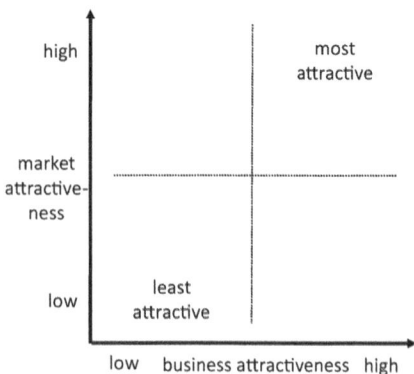

Fig. 4 Market-Business attractiveness diagram with market size/share

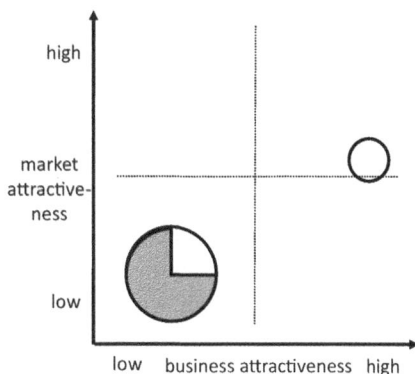

expected sales volume) can be represented in this base matrix by the use of bubbles. The larger the bubble the larger the size of the market. Should companies already be present in a market or forecasts on future market share are available, this information on market share can be added too. This can easily be represented as a segment of a bubble, see Fig. 4 as an example. The portfolio analysis, with its output in a portfolio matrix diagram, is swiftly understandable and comprehensive, and thus a good base for a decision-making process with clear decision paths.

4.3   SWOT

The SWOT analysis (strength-weakness-opportunities-threat) is an often-used tool to assess the internal and external realities and the potential match of companies to enter a new market. Puyt et al. (2020) traced the beginnings of SWOT analysis back to the early 1950s. In its early form it was used as an intra-firm, bottom-up approach to inform managers on coupling strategic plans with operational plans. Since then the use of SWOT analysis has developed and it is an important strategic management tool.

Strength and weakness are by definition related to internal abilities. Opportunities and threats are external realities. The combination of the internal and the external realities make a SWOT analysis a simple, comprehensible tool to draw the full picture in a very abbreviated manner. Its simplicity is its beauty.

The information required for the SWOT analysis, showing fit and discrepancies between internal abilities and external realities, is produced through the market assessments as well as the internal review. Information on the external realities are often fairly objective and are existing through the market assessments. The internal realities, strengths and weaknesses, are often less objective to measure. Thus, companies run the risk to see themselves in an unrealistic way. Some weaknesses detected through exercising a SWOT analysis often have their cause on a business unit or even individual staff member level. Due to conducting a SWOT analysis internal company politics may surface. Conducting a SWOT analysis will hence not only result in an overview of company-market match. It will assist companies to detect and confront own weaknesses and improve upon these.

SWOT is the standard for many businesses and decision makers. However, its beauty is also its stumbling stone. The simplification of realities and interconnective nature (Strength—Opportunity; Weakness—Threat) of a SWOT analysis can lead to skewed decisions. Tacit knowledge, embedded in companies and/or the managers' realm, are typically overlooked in any of these analyses. Knowledge about future paths of companies and strategic directions wished for by shareholders, may guide the final decision more than any in-depth analysis of Strengths or Threats.

4.4   Market-Company Matching

The need driven ecosystem (NDE, see Chapter "Ecosystem Evaluations in Business Development") argues for an understanding of business activity as set within two spheres of an ecosystem: company and product. Within this wider ecosystem the product as well as the company need to find their niche and contribution towards satisfying the needs of the consumer. This consumer need is deemed at the centre of the NDE. The NDE combines a resource-based view as well as a product-based view on a market-company interaction.

In order for a company to analyse a potential fit to a new international market, both product and available resources need to be checked against the market. Some of the theoretical foundation of this approach can be found in Ansoff (1957). Figure 5 depicts the links (arrows) between company and market which need to be analysed for their level of matching and need to be tested for their respective strengths.

The analysis takes the view of matching the product as well as resources available against the target market. This analysis rests on two pillars: it is product-based as well as resource-based. The importance of the individual links differs from company to company. The analysis will give an indication of the match and strength of the various possible link. The strengths of the link reflect a measure of existing convergence between market and company.

For instance, for some products the macroeconomic level and the results out of the respective macro level assessment, may in fact be irrelevant. A low level of match

Fig. 5 Market-company links for matching analysis

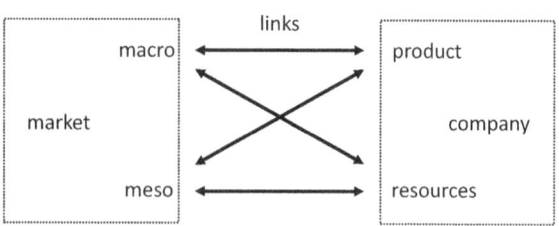

between macro level and product attributes may be acceptable; albeit the strength of the link could be found to be high. In this case however the link of the product to the market meso level would have to show some degree of matching and strength in order to deem a company's venture abroad worth considering. Through such an analysis the need of product development (Ansoff 1957) can be detected too.

Similarly, the analysis of matching the company's resources and the opportunities presented in the target market on a macro as well as meso level need to be conducted. Such analysis may reveal a seamless match or it may reveal available potential to improve the use of resources (e.g. capacity, capability). The understanding of a company as existing of product and resources, and using this in an exercise of market-company matching and measuring the strengths of links will deliver information for managers. This information assists in decisions about the internationalization route to be taken by a company. In many cases it will further flag information on areas within the company (product or use of resources) which would need improvement prior market entry.

5 Summary

Many companies seek opportunities to develop their business further. A typical route of such business development is to enter international markets. Here companies may enter with products or simply set-up production facilities. The product life cycle model by Vernon (1966) is a well-known model to explain the paths of products and companies to foreign markets. However, such decisions to enter markets abroad, with a product or a production facility, are to be carefully considered and analysed.

Market assessments are a standard way to gather the required information and insights into the target markets. Such assessments are important for any decision for companies hoping to enter international markets. These target markets need to be checked and measured. Market assessments need to distinguish various levels: macro and meso level. Information and realities found on a macro level are often fixed, given to be accepted by any new entrant. However, it is the meso level where companies find themselves engaging in the market. In many cases it is good practice to gather data relevant to the particular company and its product offering on this level of assessment. Differentiating the meso level on three strata: supplier, competitor, customer, enables an orderly and organized way to paint the full picture of a target market. Quantitative data relevant to the company and its offering will be gathered at this stage of assessment.

However, the pure presence of attractive markets may not be enough. Companies will have to check their own abilities to actually make this step into an international market. Internal capability and capacity will have to match the challenge ahead. The real potential of a company needs to be weighed up against the opportunity presented through an internal analysis and check for realities. Additionally, companies are part of wider environments and contacts within the industry network (social capital) will induce decisions. Any of the opportunities earmarked will have to be checked for risks too. Through assessments of these international markets data is gathered allowing management to weight up opportunity and risk.

Matching the external factors of the target market with the internal factors of the company is the final task for managers before deciding on any future venture abroad. In particular, some form of portfolio analysis of market attractiveness and also an adjusted attractiveness matching to the company's own abilities is good practice for companies with an array of opportunities or alternative choices. Taking further strength and weaknesses but also opportunities and threats (SWOT) into account, managers are tasked to decide which path the international business development of a company will take. Through an analysis of existing matching between company and target market, managers are informed of areas of improvement in their own product offering or use of resources in order to make a market entry successful.

The knowledge gained through the external assessment needs to be matched with internal realities. And despite all the theoretic underpinnings for such task, managers often take further factors into consideration too. Their tacit understanding of opportunities and abilities, their gut-feeling based on experience will often direct future developments of companies.

Exercise 5-A

A German-based company produces hydraulic actuators. These actuators are commonly used as jacks for heavy duty trucks as well as in hydraulic lifting gear.

A major client of this company is opening a new assembly plant for their trucks in India. You are tasked with drawing up a mid-term plan to secure future purchases from this client and its plant in India and evaluate the overall attractiveness of the Indian market for the hydraulic actuator producing company. How will you proceed?

Exercise 5-B

List various factors that could be used as proxies to indicate "market attractiveness" for the above example.

References

Aguilar, F. J. (1967). *Scanning the business environment*. New York: Macmillan.
Ansoff, H. I. (1957). Strategies for diversification. *Harvard Business Review., 35*(5), 113–124.
Barney, J. (1991). Firm resources and sustained competitive advantage. *Journal of Management, 17*(1), 99–120.

Burke, C. (2007). China's entry into construction industries in Africa: Tanzania and Zambia as case studies. *China Report, 43*(3), 323–336.

Burt, R. S. (2000). The network structure of social capital. *Research in Organizational Behavior, 22,* 345–423.

Coleman, J. S. (1988). Social capital in the creation of human capital. *American Journal of Sociology, 94,* S95–S120.

Douglas, S. P., & Craig, C. S. (2011). The role of context in assessing international marketing opportunities. *International Marketing Review, 28*(2), 150–162.

Ghemawat, P. (2001). Distance still matters – The hard reality of global expansion. *Harvard Business Review, 79*(8), 137–162.

IMS Gear, n.d. www.imsgear.com [25 November 2020]

Johanson, J., & Mattsson, L.-G. (1988). Internationalisation in industrial systems: A network approach. In N. Hood & J.-E. Vahlne (Eds.), *Strategies in global competition* (pp. 468–486). London: Croom Helm.

Johanson, J., & Vahlne, J.-E. (2009). The Uppsala internationalization process model revisited: From liability of foreignness to liability of outsidership. *Journal of International Business Studies, 40*(9), 1411–1431.

Kotler, P., Armstrong, G., Harris, L. C., & Piercy, N. (2019). *Grundlagen des Marketing* (7th ed.). Hallerbergmoos: Pearson.

Kotler, P., Keller, K. L., & Opresnik, M. O. (2017). *Marketing-Management: Konzepte – Instrumente – Unternehmensfallstudien* (15th ed.). Hallerbergmoos: Pearson.

Lem, M., van Tulder, R., & Geleynse, K. (2013). *Doing business in Africa: A strategic guide for entrepreneurs.* Utrecht: Berenschot International B.V.

Lieberman, M. B., & Montgomery, D. B. (1988). First-mover advantages. *Strategic Management Journal, 9,* 41–58.

Menzies, J., Orr, S., & Paul, J. (2020). SME internationalisation: The relationship between social capital and entry mode. *Management International Review, 60,* 623–650.

Pisani, N., & Ricart, J. E. (2016). Offshoring of services: A review of the literature and organizing framework. *Management International Review, 56,* 385–424.

Porter, M. E. (1979). How competitive forces shape strategy. *Harvard Business Review, 57*(2), 137–145.

Prahalad, C., & Hamel, G. (1990). The core competence of the corporation. *Harvard Business Review, 68*(3), 79–91.

Prescott, E. C., & Visscher, M. (1977). Sequential location among firms with foresight. *The Bell Journal of Economics, 8*(2), 378–393.

Puyt, R. W., Lie, F. B., de Graaf, F. J., & Wilderom, C. P. M. (2020). Origins of SWOT analysis. *Academy of Management Proceedings, 1,* July.

Vernon, R. (1966). International investment and international trade in the product cycle. *Quarterly Journal of Economics, 80*(2), 190–207.

Political Coverage for International Ventures

Jorge Del Castillo

1   Introduction

Governments know that local products, traded or not by private firms, can have an important impact at international level and some of them will be exploited by third parties without benefiting local communities, if not appropriately protected. Widely recognized international brands, businesses and products take advantage of the lack of regulation on where they get resources from and have no positive impact in local communities that took care of such resources for a long time. Additionally, there are other initiatives that can fast forward the process of international participation of local enterprises and there are different tools to strengthen such inclusion. It is then in the interest of governments to protect these products, promote these policies and constitute what can be called diplomatic or political coverage of them.

Among 193 countries, only 18 are considered biodiversity hotspots, home to approximately 80% of the world´s plants and animal species, according to the Convention on Biological Diversity. Those countries are: Australia, Brazil, China, Colombia, the Democratic Republic of the Congo, Ecuador, India, Indonesia, Iran, Madagascar, Malaysia, Mexico, Papua New Guinea, Peru, the Philippines, South Africa, the United States and Venezuela.

Peru is a good example of a country trying to preserve, promote and protect its products and cultural heritage although, in attempting to do this, it finds obstacles coming from different corners, starting with scarce resource allocation by its own government in order to follow up on Intellectual Property Rights (IPR) processes and gathering enough

J. Del Castillo (✉)
ESAN Graduate School of Business, Lima, Peru
e-mail: jdelcastillor@esan.edu.pe

© The Author(s), under exclusive license to Springer Fachmedien Wiesbaden GmbH,
part of Springer Nature 2021
L. Martin (ed.), *International Business Development*,
https://doi.org/10.1007/978-3-658-33221-1_6

information to protect genetic resources belonging not only to the state but mostly to ancient and indigenous communities.

On a related subject, Peru is in the process of consolidating its country brand and uses it to back its products abroad. This goes in line with the protection of products through denomination of origin and genetic resources, and traditional knowledge.

The following lines will present the way in which Peru develops political protection of its interests, more precisely through denominations of origin, biopiracy protection, development of a country brand and, as additional political coverage (used for instance by Argentina and Brazil in the region), the use of export credit agencies.

2   Denomination of origin and government assistance

The first way to address political coverage of products by states is denominations of origin. A denomination of origin is one that uses the name of a region or geographical area in order to designate, distinguish and protect a product based on its special characteristics derived, specifically, from the geographical environment in which it is made, paying attention to its natural, climatic and human factors. It is one way to differentiate products on the market. The entity upholding rights for denominations of origin is national states, however the denomination of origin can be used by producers legally credited in the exploitation of such a product and carefully observing the established requirements.

A denomination of origin indicates to the consumer not only the geographical origin of a product, but also indicates that it has certain qualities that make it special, thus it will be appreciated by its uniqueness or typicality. By differentiating a product by a denomination of origin, producers are accrediting its origin and quality. Products achieving such recognition will be more appreciated by the consumer and acquire higher value in national and international markets. It also prevents people from outside the production area from unduly benefiting from the good reputation of the protected products. The Lisbon Agreement for the Protection of Appellations of Origin and their International Registration of 1958 is the international agreement in charge of protecting geographical denominations.

It is important to address the difference between denominations of origin and geographical indications as both refer to the importance of where certain products come from. Certainly, the difference between them is very narrow and it is not always clear. Both are industrial property rights with the aim of protecting consumers from unauthorized use of misleading information or practices in general towards the fabrication of a product. The denomination of origin is a type of geographical indication. In simple terms, the denomination of origin refers to a product obtained from its initial steps until its final touches in a specific area. The geographical indication refers to, at least, one or more stages of production taking place in a specific area. Overall, both refer to the natural conditions that can affect that product. The peculiarity of the geographical characteristics (climate or soil) where products are fabricated or even grown have an impact on the result. According to European Union parameters, those are certifications to provide peace of mind in regards to ensuring that the system in place ensures food safety and that there is a monitored quality in product standards. It also allows sustainable farming showing respect for the environment while traditional farming is well kept and, of course, ensuring all production comes from one specific place (World Intellectual Property Organization 2016).

Peru´s emblem product in terms of diplomatic protection is what is considered its national drink: PISCO. According to the Peruvian National Institute for Defence of Free Competition and Protection of Intellectual Property (INDECOPI) and following World Trade Organization (WTO) principles, its product PISCO is protected given its special characteristics and distinction since it comes from a specific geographical location where it takes its name from. A denomination of origin is a good example of diplomatic defence of national products since they can be negotiated using trade agreements that can be bilateral or multilateral. It is a two-way tool: If you recognize my denominations of origin, I will recognize yours.

Indeed, the denomination of origin looks after protecting a product based on its special geographical characteristics but also taking into consideration natural or human factors. Also, it is important that it uses the name of the country, location or determined geographical region of origin and thus it differentiates products coming from specific regions providing customers with a better idea of specific processes when it is being produced and what makes it achieve specific characteristics.[1] Evidently, if customers can differentiate their qualities or categories, value increases in markets looking for it. In this way, local producers are going to receive the benefits of the increasing fame of such products.

Among the benefits that the denomination of origin Pisco creates (just like other denominations of origin) are: the strengthening of a national identity[2] and the possibility of promoting community/local development through productive and economic activities. These activities entail the generation of labour opportunities for local residents. The likelihood of engaging in such activities can be scaled up and with help from other investors and the government, add value for such products in international markets and then improve the possibility of competing internationally. Other factors to pay attention to are linked to sustaining a permanent quality in the different phases of production while

---

[1]According to the Peruvian National Association of Pisco (CONAPISCO), there are 5 pisco regions where the drink can be produced: Lima, Ica, Arequipa, Moquegua and Tacna. Most of them crops different types of pisco grapes: Quebranta, Negra Criolla, Mollar, Italia, Moscatel, Albilla and Torontel. A different type of grape: Uvina is only cultivated and produced in the districts of Lunahuana, Pacaran and Zuñiga, within the province of Cañete, in Lima.

[2]Other good examples of denomination of origin supporting national identities can be found in the experiences of Colombian coffee, Argentinian wines, Dominican and Guatemalan rum.

keeping up with traditions, recognizing the product´s exclusiveness in some specific regions and promoting decentralization. It is also important to protect those producers from counterfeiting, which seems to be ready to mimic products with no consideration whatsoever for producers' rights and consumers.

Similarly, the case of Tequila in Mexico replicates what Pisco is to Peru. Tequila can only be produced in Mexico as a result of mixing up agave fermented liquids. Historically, this process was conducted in the surroundings of the town of Tequila, state of Jalisco, in the western part of Mexico and its denomination of origin protects its production within the state of Jalisco and a few municipalities in Nayarit, Guanajuato, Michoacan and Tamaulipas. According to Mexican law[3] tequila is defined as follows: (…) alcoholic beverage obtained by distillation and rectification of musts, prepared directly and originally from the extracted material, within the factory facilities, derived from the grinding of the mature heads of agave, previously or later hydrolysed or cooked, and subjected to fermentation with yeasts, cultivated or not. It can also be enriched by other sugars up to a proportion not greater than 49%, on the understanding that cold mixes are not allowed. Tequila is a liquid that, according to its type, is colourless or yellowish when it is matured in oak or oak wood containers or when it is poured without maturing.

2.1   Scenarios for protecting the denomination of origin Pisco

It is known that Chile, which neighbours Peru, also produces an alcoholic drink that Chileans like to call Pisco. However, the Chilean strategy for its protection has a different approach in comparison to the Peruvians. Chile´s strategy is that of homonymy, where Peruvian and Chilean Pisco coexist in as many different markets they compete in. Peru which boasts its authentic way of processing Pisco only accepts its own drink and protects it worldwide.

The Peruvian government foresees three different scenarios about the protection of the denomination of origin Pisco:

1. Protection in countries that only recognize Peru as the sole producer of Pisco. As in the case shown before the Intellectual Property Appellate Board of India (IPAB) that ruled the geographical indication tag for alcoholic beverage Pisco was eligible for registration. The Geographical Indication application had been requested by Peru in 2005, but opposed by Chile. IPAB made clear that the word Pisco is without doubt a denomination of origin exclusively from Peru.[4]

---

[3]Norma oficial mexicana NOM-006-SCFI-2012, Bebidas alcohólicas-Tequila-Especificaciones.
[4]Indian Intellectual Property Appellate Board. Case OA/1/2010/GI/CHN Embassy of Peru vs Mohan Devan.

2. Protection in countries recognizing homonymy between Pisco and other countries producing an alcoholic drink with the same denomination. As an example, back in 2017 an Australian winemaker started distilling a blended drink out of local Australian grapes varieties. He started calling it Pisco, even though he was producing it in his cellar located in Cowaramup, Australia.
3. Protection in countries recognizing only Chile as a sole producer of Pisco. As it is the case only in Zimbabwe and Chile.

Case study: Spirits selection

The Concours Mondial de Bruxelles of Spirits takes place every year in different locations worldwide. In 2017 it took place in La Serena, Chile. According to Chilean law, they reserve the denomination of Pisco to a liquor produced and bottled in the Chilean regions of Atacama and Coquimbo. In order to comply with Chilean law, Peruvian Pisco samples taking part in the contest had to enter Chile under the denomination of Peruvian brandy and not under its real name: Pisco. The Peruvian Ministry of Foreign Affairs talked to the Belgian organizers exposing the following reasons: According to article 4.2 of the Concours, the registration of each product had to be made according to the exact denomination of the product in line with the regulations of the country of origin. Also, the European Commission Regulation 1065/2013 had registered Pisco as a geographical indication from Peru. Despite the fact that Peruvian producers tried to participate, no concessions were given and all Peruvian producers preferred not to participate in the Spirits Selection of 2017. ◄

---

3   Genetic resources and traditional knowledge

Besides the protection given to products that have a geographical identification, there is a protection oriented to the misappropriation of genetic resources and traditional knowledge by corporations and foreign research organizations. Peru and countries such as Brazil and India that have a huge biological and cultural diversity have been developing a different strategy in favour of genetic resources and collective knowledge of indigenous origin. Their aim is not only to prevent cases of biopiracy but also to share possible benefits of genetic resource exploitation. Such resources and knowledge are so varied that not many of them are registered although these products have been used for centuries by local communities. These countries have pushed what is called defensive disclosure which is: "information or documentation intentionally made available to the public as prior art in order to render any subsequent claims of invention or discovery ineligible for a patent" (Hansen and VanFleet 2003).

Previous efforts came along after the 1992 Rio Convention on Biodiversity, which officially took the first steps in the fight against biopiracy. More precisely, the Nagoya

Protocol pushed for the incorporation into national laws of provisions for the creation of a system for prior registration or authorization of genetic resources, also ensuring that those resources were shared with indigenous populations.

The above-mentioned countries' approaches towards biopiracy are based on the Bonn Guidelines on Access to Genetic Resources and the Fair and Equitable Sharing of Benefits Arising Out of Their Utilization of 2002 (Secretariat of the Convention on Biological Diversity 2002) which were created to assist parties and governments in facilitating steps for genetic resources and benefit sharing legislation and policies.

According to the World Intellectual Property Organization (WIPO), both genetic resources and traditional knowledge and folklore are protected. Genetic and other biological resources must be understood as microorganisms, plants, animal breeds, genetic sequences, nucleotide and amino acid sequence information. Traditional knowledge is all the information origin in indigenous communities that have subsisted since ancient times. Such information can be about natural products that have been appropriately documented. Problems appear when different entities use that traditional knowledge or the genetic resources without previous consent from the communities of origin or not even sharing profits at all.

It must be said that investigations of possible and innovative uses of genetic resources and traditional knowledge must be encouraged and countries should grant access to them. It is not only about protecting them but promoting the responsible use and sharing of genetic resources and traditional knowledge. These countries try to prevent the patent registration of genetic resources and traditional knowledge since patents require originality upon their creation and precisely that is what they lack since local communities used them and knew about them beforehand. There is not a unique approach to such protection and agreeing a method is still in the making. However, there are creative ways of protecting them.

All three countries mentioned above, protect their genetic resources and traditional knowledge in an uncontentious manner although they have different approaches.

India, passed the National Biodiversity Act in 2002 which tries to protect indigenous communities' knowledge by preventing the large-scale exploitation of traditional knowledge with the clear aim of protecting biodiversity. This effort came jointly with what was called the Traditional Knowledge Digital Library (TKDL), a project pushed by the government of India that created a database containing a list of local traditional knowledge that can be reviewed by patent entities worldwide. The publication of such an immense database has proven successful in the registration of more than 200 patents of traditional Indian knowledge. (India 2017). It is interesting to know that the registration of such a big amount of traditional knowledge was possible in India. This traditional language was coded in written language and had to be translated some others from Tamil or Urdu into English. Such writings have been systematized and fed into its TKDL.

The case of turmeric is a good example here. Tumeric is a plant of the ginger family and had been used in India for centuries. The case study shows how the traditional knowledge of communities is protected by governments.

Case study: Indian Tumeric

In 1995 two expatriate Indians at the University of Mississippi Medical Centre (Suman K. Das and Hari Har P. Cohly) were granted a US patent (no.5, 401,504) on use of turmeric in wound healing. The Council of Scientific & Industrial Research (CSIR), India, New Delhi filed a re-examination case with the US PTO challenging the patent on the grounds of being known before. CSIR argued that turmeric has been used for thousands of years for healing wounds and rashes and therefore its medicinal use was not a novel invention. Their claim was supported by documentary evidence of traditional knowledge, including ancient Sanskrit text and a paper published in 1953 in the Journal of the Indian Medical Association. Despite an appeal by the patent holders, the US PTO upheld the CSIR objections and cancelled the patent. The turmeric case was a landmark judgment case as it was the first time that a patent based on the traditional knowledge of a developing country was successfully challenged. The US Patent Office revoked this patent in 1997, after ascertaining that there was no novelty; the findings by innovators having been known in India for centuries.

(Source: India 2020). ◄

Brazil´s approach to genetic resources and traditional knowledge exploitation is only given to Brazilian entities according to Medida Provisoria 2186-16/2001 (M.P. 2186). If foreign institutions want to recollect samples for possible future exploitation, they must do so associated with a Brazilian institution and obtaining what is called a prior informed consent (PIC) by the owner, which according to Brazilian legislation is: indigenous communities, the competent body if access occurs in a protected area or the maritime authority. This approach is complemented by a similar database as India´s TKDL gathering.

While the procedures for obtaining a prior informed consent (PIC) seem reasonable since Brazil is trying to empower indigenous communities by deferring to traditional social organizations, there is a practical problem of which entity can officially give PIC. This problem was experienced by the Kraho Indians, as the case study shows.

Case study: Kraho Indians of Tocantins state

In 1999 Brazilian pharmacologists from the Federal University of São Paulo (Unifesp) sought and received the consent of three Kraho villages to engage in bioprospecting for commercial ends. The contract established that the Kraho would have royalty rights to whatever drug was developed from their traditional knowledge. Unifesp did not seek permission from the Indian National Foundation (FUNAI) because it already received what it believed to be the consent of Wyty-Cati, the legal entity representing three villages in the reserve. In 2000, the Unifesp researchers learned of Kapey, another indigenous association that said it represented all seventeen villages of the Kraho nation. When the fourteen villages learned of the agreement from which they were excluded, they protested. Unifesp said that it held another meeting involving representatives from all seventeen Kraho villages. In the meeting, the representatives agreed that three villages, two represented by Wyty-Cati and one represented by Kapey, would participate in the Unifesp study and that any benefits derived from the use of Kraho traditional knowledge would be shared by all seventeen Kraho villages. Apparently this did not satisfy all parties involved because some Kraho complained to FUNAI and the Ministério Público and demanded twenty-five million reais (approximately $11.4 million), twenty million reais for an access charge, and five million reais for pain and suffering. Unifesp refused to pay because it maintains that it had a valid contract entered into with the PIC of the Kraho nation.

(Source: Tustin 2006). ◄

Peru has created the National Commission for the Protection of Access to Peruvian Biological Diversity and to the Collective Knowledge of the Indigenous Peoples (hereinafter The National Commission), which, since 2004, has been searching for patent applications filed or granted worldwide and that have included a Peruvian biological resource or traditional knowledge historically managed by any of their national indigenous groups. Once cases of interest are found, a task force is oriented to inform the country where such a product is trying to be registered not to grant patents, protecting Peruvian interests and those of its indigenous communities. The construction in Peru of a database following up on the defensive disclosure approach has been complicated since the ancient Incas lacked a written language; hence in some cases there are no tangible registries. However, there is an oral tradition that has been registered by researchers.

As a pioneer in pushing for the protection of genetic resources and traditional knowledge protection, The National Commission, works on a technical report proving the lack of novelty in the possible products likely to receive a patent. It is an important effort of constant monitoring plus drafting of reports and additional coordination with the Peruvian Ministry of Foreign Affairs, which makes sure that such reports are received by the patent office in the countries of destination.

Case study: Peruvian Sangre de Grado

In 2018, the species known as Sangre de Grado, whose scientific name is Croton lechleri was trying to be patented in Mexico, Australia, Canada, China, Korea, Colombia, Costa Rica, Argentina, the United States, Uruguay, among others, by Jaguar Health Inc. The National Commission against Biopiracy became aware of such processes.

The National Commission determined that such patent applications were improper. They did not meet the patentability requirements (regarding inventive level) required by the patent laws of the different intellectual property offices. Also, they were not eligible to be protected since some laws ban the patentability of therapeutic methods, so the Commission proceeded with the preparation of observation documents for detected applications. Moreover, the submission of such documents through Peruvian embassies was coordinated with the Ministry of Foreign Affairs, except for patent applications that were filed to the Intellectual Property Office of China (SIPO), in which the filing of a Mandarin Chinese language document was required. Also, the high fees and legal procurement demanded by the United States Patent and Trademark Office (USPTO) made the attempt difficult to achieve.

In May of the same year, the Commission, through the Ministry of Foreign Affairs, sent a letter addressed to Jaguar Health Inc. This letter stated that all known patent applications had been made known to different intellectual property offices that were related to a derivative of Croton lechleri, a native species of the Amazon rainforest and known as Sangre de Grado. In addition, it was stated that these requests involved access to a genetic resource of Peruvian origin and traditional knowledge of native communities, so they made a request for the document proving legal access to that resource. Shortly after, in July 2018, Jaguar Health sent a letter to the National Commission saying that they have changed the strategic approach of their businesses. Therefore, they were going to abandon the requests observed by the National Commission against Biopiracy.

Once again, the mission of The National Commission is blocking the granting of patents unduly requested based on traditional knowledge. The other type of protection is avoiding the access to genetic resources. During 2019, more than 24 cases came to be known by the National Commission and are related to products such as Maca, Ungurahui, Maiz Morado, Sangre de Grado and Yacon. All of them have been observed before the patent offices where they were presented addressing letters to the companies intending to do such registrations. (Valladolid 2020). ◄

In the end, the protection exercised by the countries mentioned does not work to its best because it is a vast world to cover. Many resources or traditional knowledge is used or incorporated in so various products around the globe, often infringing on the rights of others. Benefits and profits obtained from the incorporation of those resources into modern products are to be shared with the collective groups owning such knowledge. More regulations and creative ways to implement cooperative efforts are to be developed in order to create a better system.

4   Government backed foreign direct investment initiatives

There are numerous ways in which national economies provide governmental support to local companies to progress with foreign direct investment initiatives. Governments are helpful when opening the door of their businesses overseas. These are initiatives that boost the internationalization of even small or medium size enterprises. Among the ones

Fig. 1 Marca Peru logo

that are offered by Peru and appreciated by Peruvian exporters are: the country brand and financing of internationalization plans. The Peruvian government provides good examples for both initiatives.

The Peruvian Ministry of Trade and Tourism has created two different brands. A general country-brand named MARCA PERU and a second more focused brand named SUPERFOODS (Promperu 2011).

Marca Peru is an official sign of the Peruvian State and it is used as a promotion tool for the country´s tourism industry, exports and investments (see Fig. 1). It is not an exclusive brand since it can be used for free to favour the promotion of important tourist destinations, promote competitiveness of Peruvian exports, increase the flow of tourists to Peru, attract investments and improve the image of the country as a whole. The general idea is to use the country brand in institutional participations, on its products or events in which any company from any sector thinks it is worth accompanying their ventures with. Among the different sectors prioritized by the Peruvian government to use MARCA PERU are agricultural businesses, garments and decorations, fishing, gastronomy and tourism industries.

The second country brand promoted by the Peruvian government is SUPERFOODS. Natural and healthy products that are considered part of a balanced diet: cereals such as quinoa, maca, purple corn, cocoa, golden berries, lucuma, grapes and other produce cultivated in the country. If companies dare to export any of those products they can benefit from the promotion that the country does for them and add that brand onto their product packaging.

Lastly, the program denominated Program for Internationalization Support (PAI per its acronym in Spanish) has as an objective the promotion of internationalization through the financing of research studies and activities to improve capacities and management skills in the process of exporting and selling Peruvian goods and services in destination markets. Once that company receives the state support, it is committed to participating in any promotion activities suggested by the Peruvian State (Peru 2016).

Alongside these supporting initiatives, there are others which are a bit more precise and of short scope such as the financing for participation in international fairs or match-making services and searching for business contacts mostly done by commercial offices based in destination countries.

5   Role of export credit agencies

A last tool for states to express support for international ventures of local companies is by keeping up with financing an export-driven approach for national products. This is a result of a political decision in order to enhance a country´s possibility to take on world trade. In order to do this, export credit agencies are to be created to provide guarantees and build a financial framework to support the presence of national goods in foreign markets. It is a fact that: "the activities of export credit agencies thus become more significant in the provision of the required financing for trade in times of crisis." (Turguttbopbas 2013).

By definition an export credit agency will be of assistance to private companies when injecting money through government-backed loans, guarantees and insurance. They will be of great support when the business opportunity is too risky for conventional corporate financing (Thenard 2002) and will promote the country's exports and generate foreign investments.

Latin American examples of such agencies are the Brazilian Development Bank (BNDES) and the Argentinian Foreign Trade and Investment Bank (BICE). The former is the main financing agent for development in the country, supporting initiatives related to exports, technological innovation, sustainable socio-environmental development among others. It is BNDES' mission to finance the expansion of Brazilian companies beyond their borders and it does that by financing the production of local companies and facilitating access to export credit.

On the other side of the border, Argentina keeps providing loans to increase the volume of their exports abroad. In fact, BICE finances other banks within the Argentinian system fostering growth of global trade. BICE improves the financial conditions for Argentinian international business in order for them to be competitive when entering trade zones where Argentina does not have negotiated tariffs.

6   Summary

All in all, this chapter succinctly showcases different alternatives that mostly developing economies in Latin America uses to provide coverage for their international ventures, these being protection for the originality of their products or genetic resources and traditional knowledge as well as the promotion of country-brands or credit-export agencies. Similar efforts can be seen elsewhere on the globe too.

Denominations of origin are a more restricted interpretation of a geographical indication. Geographical indications refer to a specific product geographical origin given its qualities and/or reputation. Denominations of Origin is a type of geographical indication and portrays a stronger link with the place of origin since it relates to the production, processing and preparation of such a product. Biopiracy protection is oriented to identifying and following up on patents applications done globally.

The needs of businesses are different and they change depending on the sector, size of companies, experience dealing with internationalization and product commercialized. The role of government backed branding initiatives cannot be underestimated. Further, export credit agencies, lowering the risk exposure of exporters, are an important tool used by many governments in fostering their export economies. Overall these political coverages may vary from country to country but typically governments try to enhance and promote their national interests through the participation of their companies in the international market.

Exercise A

A particular herbal plant is known among an indigenous community for its health benefits. Discuss the possible approaches an internationally active pharmaceutical company might have to make use of such knowledge. Particularly consider the international initiatives to fight and prevent biopiracy.

Exercise B

Discuss the role of government-backed export credit agencies and their impact on fair competition.

Exercise C

Brainstorm and discuss possible additional uncontentious ways to defend genetic resources and traditional knowledge. If you work for an international company that wants to use a product that potentially has been used by indigenous people, what actions can be taken to prevent or to answer a possible protection request.

References

Hansen, S. A., & VanFleet, J. W. (2003). *Traditional knowledge and intellectual property: A handbook on issues and options for traditional knowledge holders in protecting their intellectual property and managing their biodiversity*. Washington (DC): American Association for the Advancement of Science.

India. (2017). *Annual report 2016-2017 office of the controller general of patents, designs & trademarks*. Mumbai: Intellectual Property India.

India. (2020). Bio-piracy of traditional knowledge. https://www.tkdl.res.in/tkdl/langdefault/common/Biopiracy.asp?GL=Eng [1 October 2020].

Peru. (2016). Programa de Apoyo a la Internacionalización Resolución Ministerial # 147-2016-EF/15. Lima: Adex.

Promperu. (2011). Reglamento para el Uso de la Marca País aprobado por Resolución de Secretaría General # 153-2011-PROMPERU/SG. Lima.

Secretariat of the Convention on Biological Diversity. (2002). *Bonn Guidelines on Access to Genetic Resources and Fair and Equitable Sharing of the Benefits Arising out of their Utilization*. Montreal (Quebec).

Thenard, E. (2002). Export credit agencies and sustainable development. CIEL Issue brief for the world summit on sustainable development (WSSD).

Turguttbopbas, N. (2013). Export credit agency activities in developing countries. *The International Trade Journal, 27*(3), 319.

Tustin, J. (2006). traditional knowledge and intellectual property in Brazilian biodiversity law. *Texas Intellectual Property Law Journal, 14,* 131–162.

Valladolid, A. (2020). *Biopirateria: Logros 2019 y avances a futuro*. Lima: Indecopi.

World Intellectual Property Organization. (2016). *Understanding industrial property*. Geneva: WIPO.

Project Management Standards

Ansgar Kühn

1   Project Management in International Business Development

International business development has many faces: bringing innovation to life, launching new products, services or the combinations of both, implementing innovative business processes or whole business models, expanding business operations to new regions and/or products to name only some. All of these activities aim at maintaining the long-term well-being of the company. Hence, they are to be considered an integral part of business strategy.

The key to successful strategic management is the combination of setting the right strategic goals and ensuring their successful execution throughout the organisation. These mostly temporary undertakings reveal their particular nature; specific goals are to be achieved off the beaten track with a high level of novelty and uncertainty, cooperating with numerous different people, disciplines or organizations. They fulfil all characteristics of projects according to ISO Standard 21500:2012 and are to be perceived as a unique group of processes comprising target-oriented coordinated and controlled activities with defined start and completion dates. Despite a lot of similarities among different projects, each of them is considered unique *"primarily [..] by the uniqueness of its conditions in their totality"* (DIN 69901-5: 2009). The nature of projects contrasts widely with the typical set-up of most companies, with permanent structures, installed functions, well-run and repetitive operational processes. Therefore, managing projects

A. Kühn (✉)
Pforzheim University, Pforzheim, Germany
e-mail: ansgar.kuehn@hs-pforzheim.de

© The Author(s), under exclusive license to Springer Fachmedien Wiesbaden GmbH,   115
part of Springer Nature 2021
L. Martin (ed.), *International Business Development*,
https://doi.org/10.1007/978-3-658-33221-1_7

successfully within the organization requires distinct managerial, often technical and other skills and the use of specific project management methods and techniques.

Commonly, project management is considered as the discipline of initiating, (defining), planning, executing/controlling and terminating activities aiming at achieving specific goals (the project goals) under various constraints.

The hour of birth of modern project management, as an academic discipline, is, according to most sources, the US development of nuclear weapons in the 1940s, the so-called Manhattan Engineering District Project or Manhattan Project. Approaches and first techniques developed in this complex and interdisciplinary undertaking have since then been used exclusively in US aerospace programmes in the 1950s and found their way through military dominated projects into industry where they experienced further refinement and extension. During the Cold War in the 1960s, transatlantic cooperation brought this knowledge equally to Europe, first mainly in defence projects and from there spreading to other civil sectors. Over the past five decades project management evolved from its military and aerospace origin to a widely accepted and applied, general academic discipline.

Due to the more dynamic and competitive global environment, development and product life cycles have decreased significantly with an increasing degree of complexity. Project management became an integral part of how companies manage their activities besides their regular organisation. Nowadays, in terms of economic value, the role of project management is considered dominant: research by the Deutsche Gesellschaft für Projektmanagement (GPM) among 500 German companies unveiled that in 2013 more than 34% of the working hours were spent in project-related work totalling to almost 880 bn EUR (GPM 2015). A percentage of approx. 40% project-related work was forecasted for 2019. PMI (Project Management Institute) predicted a 15.7 million increase in project management jobs globally for the period 2010 until 2020 resulting in total to 52.4 million project-related jobs with an economic impact of over 18 bn USD (PMI 2013). More recent research by the same authors (PMI 2017) for 2017 already showed 65.9 million project-related jobs globally clearly exceeding their original prediction for 2020. From first publications in the 1960s it took some time until distinct project management standards und certifications developed. A forum of project managers to exchange experience in international projects started in 1965 under its former name "Internet International Project Management Organisation" (INTERNET); later on, Internet changed its name to IPMA (International Project Management Association) and a first international conference on project management took place in 1967. In 1969, the Project Management Institute (PMI) was founded. In 1985, a first standard the "Body of Knowledge (BOK)" for project management was issued by PMI and became the foundation for the first certification (PMP—Project Management Professional). Besides these two organizations and their methodologies, other organizations and standards have been launched: PRINCE 2 in 1989 and PM^2-Alliance just some years ago. The latter has been launched by the EU Commission, as one project management methodology for Europe. (PM^2-Alliance 2020).

Historically, the project management landscape could be divided into three generally applicable management organisations, PMI, IPMA and PRINCE 2, representing traditional project management. The term traditional stands for a more prescriptive approach with detailed activity planning upfront, usually coming along with a waterfall-model, where project phases are followed and completed (mostly) sequentially. In the context of traditional project management other standards for specific industries might be mentioned, e.g. the German HOAI (Honorarordnung für Architekten und Ingenieure vom 10. Juli 2013/ Official Scale of Fees for Services by Architects and Engineers dated July 10, 2013) which addresses preparation and execution of construction projects along its nine work phases.

In parallel to the classical project management methodologies, alternative project management standards evolved from the late 1980s mainly in the software and IT-environment. Due to the nature of software and system development projects, the environments required an accelerated process with more frequent and earlier testing as well as customer feedback. This is done to already detect deviation contrary to the project goals during development. Therefore, most of the newer methodologies break up the rigid, sequential phase-oriented concept of traditional project management in favour of parallelisation and iterative development: Since the mid-1970s Hermes has been in use for Swiss federal projects and, after major revision, since 1986 the mandatory methodology for all federal IT-projects in Switzerland. Hermes provides scenarios pre-customized for different project types (mainly IT-related) and comes along with a sequential process model of initiation, concept, implementation and deployment. In 1992, the German Army released the methodology "V-Modell" being a specific software development methodology for all German defence projects. Since then, two revisions (Beauftragter der Bundesregierung für Informationstechnik 2020) "V-Modell 97" and "V-Modell XT" have been launched. "XT" stands for "eXtreme Tailoring" underlining flexible adaptation to various project environments. The model comprises 22 predefined process modules which are chosen and arranged into a specific process model. Activities aim at generating products (documents). The latter will pass through four different states: "planned, in progress, provided and accepted". Interdependencies of products and activities are noted. The temporary order of activities is a result of availability of required products in a defined state and not predefined by the model.

Among the newer methodologies, originating from software development, Scrum is by far the most relevant with high impact on today's project management methodologies. It was launched by Schwaber and Sutherland in the early 1990s. Scrum combines elements of lean management with methods of software development. It is based on three pillars:

- Transparency: project progress and obstacles are continuously visualized for all participants.
- Revision: results and functionalities are delivered and evaluated regularly
- Adaptation: requirements for products, plans and procedures are not fixed but continuously adapted in detail.

Scrum does not reduce the complexity of tasks but aims at structuring them into smaller and less complex pieces, the increments. Therefore, Scrum uses a long-term plan, the product backlog, which is continuously refined and in addition the so-called Sprint Backlog, a short-term, detailed planning. The sprint backlog comprises activities for the next sprint, a one to four-week long cycle, which should ensure maximum focus on the essentials.

Among all agile methodologies, Scrum is the most commonly used one—75% of all participants in a 2020 survey by digital.ai claim to use Scrum or a hybrid that includes Scrum (digital.ai 2020).

The agile philosophy underlaying Scrum and other methodologies has been described in the Agile Manifesto by a group of people among others Schwaber and Sutherland et al. (The Agile Manifesto 2001). Some key points are:

- emphasize the importance of individuals and their interactions more than processes and tools;
- value the delivery of a working software more highly than a comprehensive documentation;
- consider real collaboration with the customer more valuable than contract negotiations;
- believe that responding to change is more worthwhile than following a plan.

Traditionally, companies either practise classical project management (PMI, IPMA, PRINCE 2) or pure agile project management. Also, different fractions can be seen among project managers: some being dogmatic, emphasising their approach being the only applicable one. But a rather big and steadily growing group, the pragmatic fraction, has tried to understand the other approach, embraced certain elements and developed all different kinds of combinations between both methodologies, which are commonly referred to as hybrid project management. It has to be further noted that in the meantime all traditional PM-organisations included agile approaches in their methodologies, while agile standards have developed guiding frameworks to provide some structure for bigger projects.

An attempt to facilitate the choice of the right project management approach—prescriptive, hybrid or agile—is often referred to as "Stacey complexity model" in project management, adapted from work on complexity and organisational creativity by Stacey. Figure 1 shows a matrix inspired by Stacey, where the increasing degree of uncertainty about the technology ("how") is shown on the horizontal axis, and the increasing degree about the requirements "what") is shown on the vertical axis.

While the lower left part is considered "simple" and can be solved with classical project management, moving right or up in this chart, will turn the environment into "complicated". Moving further up and/or right will turn the environment from "complicated" to "complex". Finally, the upper right end with its exceedingly high uncertainty is perceived as "chaotic". Some authors argue that complicated environments require hybrid

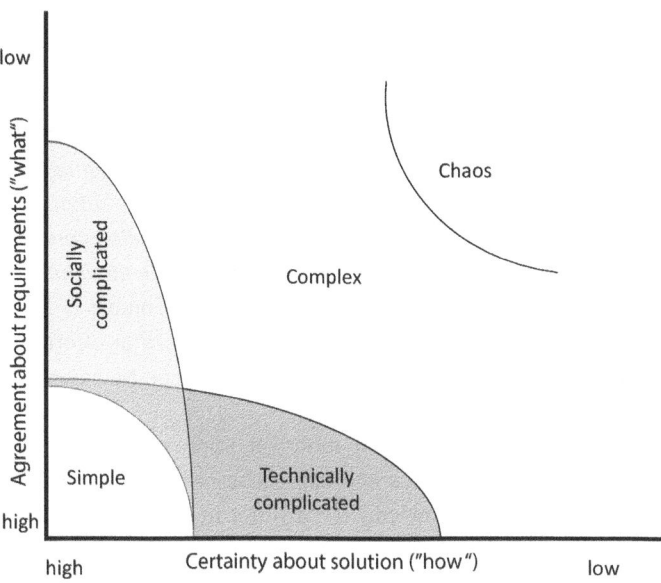

Fig. 1 Uncertainty, complication and complexity in projects inspired by Stacey

project management approaches, whereas others argue that at least technically complicated situations can be managed preferably with traditional project management methodologies. Most authors consider uncertainty in complex environments be best addressed by agile methods.

2   Relevant Standards and Methods

When comparing existing methodologies, some general differences can be noted: Some methodologies are process-oriented and others are competence-based; some emphasize the importance of sound planning and consider soft skills essential in successful cooperation, some focus more on the application of standardized tools and techniques and focus on execution and control. Nevertheless, there are commonalities in the standards. According to Grau (2013) "standard" in project management can be seen in the context of official, de-jure-standards, e.g. the aforementioned relevant ISO or DIN standards. Due to their general acceptance and wide-spread use by many professionals and organizations, these methodologies can be considered as "de-facto"-standards (Grau 2013). This chapter gives an overview about the most commonly used standards in the world, their development, their approach and core elements of the standards. Furthermore, it provides information about their overall importance and regional spread as well as on training and certification available.

2.1   PMI

The Project Management Institute (PMI) was founded in 1969 as a non-profit organisation at the Georgia Institute of Technology. In 1975 PMI depicted their objectives as to *foster recognition of the need for professionalism in project management; provide a forum for the free exchange of project management problems, solutions and applications; coordinate industrial and academic research efforts; develop common terminology and techniques to improve communications; [..] and to provide guidelines for instruction and career development in the field of project management* (Chumas & Hartman 1975).

In the 1970s the organisation participated in standardization efforts in the USA as well as internationally with European International Project Management Association IPMA, then called INTERNET.

In the 1980s and 90 s PMI focussed more on improving and standardizing project management methods, procedures and approaches which led to the first edition of Project Management Body of Knowledge (PMBOK) in 1996. Later editions including the recent sixth edition (2017) have been recognized as the American National Standard by the American National Standards Institute (ANSI). The seventh edition has already been announced for 2021.

Today, PMI, headquartered in Pennsylvania, USA is by far the biggest professional organisation for project management. It counts more than 600,000 members in over 200 countries (PMI 2020). PMI develops various standards to provide guidance and support in all aspects of project management. They can be sorted into three categories:

a) Foundational standards—providing the foundation for project management knowhow in the relevant areas of the profession:
   - PMBOK Guide (6th edition)—focussing on project management and building the base for the PMP-certification
   - The Standard for Program Management (4th edition)—principle-based standard addressing individuals and organisations
   - The Standard for Portfolio Management (4th edition)—providing reference to portfolio managers
   - The Standard for Risk Management in Portfolios, Programs, and Projects—comprising all aspects of risk management
   - The Standard for Earned Value Management—focussing on continuous improvement and maturing practices
   - The Standard for Organizational Project Management—supporting framework to allow better alignment of project management practices with organizational strategy
   - The PMI guide to Business Analysis—focussing on business analysis as critical leadership competency.

b) Practice standards and frameworks—depict the use of tools, techniques and processes laid out in PMBOK or one of the foundational standards, e.g. estimation, scheduling or project configuration management. Further, an Agile Practice Guide, created in cooperation with the Agile Alliance, has been issued in 2017.
c) Practice guides and extensions—provide information and instruction to individuals and organisation in applying PMI standards. Practice guides can become part of a (foundational) standard. Extensions comprise concepts on how to adapt PMBOK in specific industries, e.g. construction or software.

The Project Management Body of Knowledge (PMBOK) is the most relevant guide to understanding the fundamentals of PMI's project management methodology. The current edition, released in 2017, will be replaced by the 7th edition, to be released in 2021.

PMBOK covers topics which are specific to project management such as work breakdown structure or critical path method as well as a broad field of management techniques which are not exclusive to project management, but are essential for managing projects—planning organizing, staffing, financial control and risk management only to mention some of them. PMBOK depicts the most relevant methods and tools applicable to most projects and is therefore to be considered as a guide of good practice for managing individual projects. PMBOK shows a process-oriented approach to project management, comprising 49 processes, organized in five process groups which are (partly) overlapping along the project management lifecycle.

The five process groups are:

1. "Initiating" describes all processes to be performed to defining a new project or a new phase of an existing project as well as to getting authorization to start the project or phase.
2. "Planning" of a project requires processes establishing the scope of the project, refining the objectives and defining the course of action necessary to meet the project objectives.
3. "Executing" contains all processes to be performed to completing the work defined in the project management plan and satisfying the project specifications.
4. "Monitoring and Controlling" features those processes required to track, review, and regulate the progress and performance of the project; furthermore, all processes aiming at identifying any areas where changes to the plan are required and initiating the changes accordingly.
5. "Closing" comprises all processes to be performed to finalizing all activities across all process groups to formally closing the project or phase.

Each process group refers to specific knowledge. This knowledge is laid out in ten so called knowledge areas. The topics within each knowledge area are structured first logically into smaller subchapters, e.g. plan, manage and control, and then around the

ITTOs—Inputs, Tools & Techniques and Outputs—relevant for the specific area. The ten knowledge areas are:

1. Project integration management concerns all processes and activities to identify, define, combine, unify, and coordinate the various processes and project management activities within the project management process groups.
2. Project scope management describes all processes required to ensure that the project includes all the work required, and only the work required, to complete the project successfully, this includes equally the creation of the work breakdown structure (WBS)
3. Project schedule management comprises all processes necessary to successfully manage the timely completion of a project. (Older editions of PMBOK guide refer to this knowledge area as "project time management").
4. Project cost management summarizes all processes from planning and estimating, to budgeting and controlling costs, ensuring the project can be completed within the approved budget.
5. Project quality management states all activities within the organization to determine quality policies, objectives, and responsibilities ensuring that the project will fulfil all requirements.
6. Project resource management groups all knowledge to organize, manage, and lead the project team. (In earlier editions of PMBOK Guide referred to as "project human resource management")
7. Project communications management depicts all processes required to ensure timely and appropriate communication: planning, managing and monitoring communication.
8. Project risk management lays out all processes of conducting risk management from identifying and analysing risk (quantitatively and qualitatively) to planning and implementing risk response and monitoring risk.
9. Project procurement management includes processes necessary to purchase or acquire products, services, or results required from outside the project team grouped in 3 fields of planning, conducting and controlling procurement.
10. Project stakeholder management aims at identifying all people or organizations impacted by the project, analysing their expectations and impact on the project, and planning and managing appropriate strategies to effectively engaging stakeholders in decisions and execution and monitoring the effect on stakeholder relationships.

The 7th edition announced for 2021 promises to address rapid changes in technology and markets and will therefore feature different delivery approaches, from predictive to agile or hybrid. Differently from the current guide, the 7th edition will be structured around project performance domains instead of knowledge areas. Those will include important management practices and explain why the specific domain is important for effective project management but will not be prescriptive (PMI 2020b).

Training and certification for PMI-standards is available. Whereas CAPM (Certified Associate in Project Management) as the entry level, only requires a secondary degree plus 23 h of training before candidates can pass their 150 questions multiple choice exam, the prerequisites for PMP (Project Management Professional) are significantly higher. As PMP is often considered the official proof of qualification for project managers in the USA, candidates have to prove, depending on their educational background, 36 to 60 months experience in leading projects before being admitted to the exam.

Other certifications based on further standards comprise Program Management Professional (PgMP) and Portfolio Management Professional (PfMP) plus further, more specific ones, e.g. Risk Management (PMI-RMP) or Scheduling Professional (PMI-SP).

According to PMI, 1.1 million people globally hold a certificate from PMI (PMI 2020a) The majority of certificates were issued in the USA.

2.2   IPMA

In 1965, a forum for the exchange of experience among international project managers, gathered under the name "Internet International Project Management Organisation" (INTERNET), the predecessor of today's IPMA. It hosted its first international conference in 1967 in Vienna.

After the Project Management Institute (PMI) launched the first edition of "Body of Knowledge (BOK)" for project management in North America in the mid-1980s, INTERNET still enquired among its members whether formal certifications in project management would be beneficial. This led to different professional project management associations in Europe developing their individual bodies of knowledge for competence assessment in project management. Only in 1993, the IPMA Certification Core Team started to coordinate and harmonise the diverse approaches. Finally, in 1997, IPMA Certification Validation Management Board took over the responsibility and in 1998 the IPMA Council approved the universal four level concept and accepted the standard agreement between IPMA and member associations. The Individual Competence Baseline (ICB) version 1.0 was submitted in 1998 and finally published in 1999 as version 2.0, first established in national IPMA-member associations in UK, Germany, Switzerland and France. A major revision to ICB 3.0 was done in 2006 and the current version ICB 4.0 was introduced in 2017.

The ICB does not describe processes or necessary steps in project management and is not considered a textbook to learn from, as does PMBOK. In fact, ICB depicts the inventory of competencies an individual should possess or should develop in order to successfully master work in project, programme or portfolio management. Therefore, ICB 4.0 provides content about the context of projects, programmes and portfolios and points out key competence indicators for the professional competences in the management of these fields.

In total the ICB Version 4.0 comprises 29 competence elements building the "eye of competence". In contrast to other methodologies like PMI, ICB4.0 covers projects, programmes and portfolios in one document and partly simultaneously. Relevance and extent of the competence elements vary according to their application in projects (ICB Chapter "Ecosystem Evaluations in Business Development" "Individuals Working in Project Management"), programme (ICB Chapter" Assessing International Markets" "Individuals Working in Programme Management") or portfolio (Chapter "Political Coverage for International Ventures" "Individuals Working in Portfolio Management"). The "eye of competence" falls into three areas:

1. "Perspective competences" ("perspective")
   "Perspective" deals with the context of projects, programmes and portfolios. Understanding and managing these external drivers and their influence on the project work is essential. Therefore, "perspective" summarizes all methods, tools and techniques by which an individual interacts with his environment. Furthermore, it deals with fundamental thoughts motivating individuals, organizations and societies to start projects, programmes or portfolios. In total "perspective" contains five competences:
   "Strategy" (perspective 1) is formally and explicitly following distinct objectives, projects and programmes mostly contribute to these objectives while portfolios of projects and programmes will be prioritized according to these objectives. "Governance, structures and processes" (perspective 2) build the formal framework for a project, programme or portfolio. Their complexity strongly depends on the amount and interdependency of the project, programme or portfolio interfaces with this context. In particular, it has to be mentioned that inappropriate or obsolete processes or structures, established under other circumstances can slow down and hinder the project, program or portfolio. "Compliance, standards, regulation" (perspective 3) represent relevant perspectives and influence factors, as they comprise laws and standards and tools reflecting priorities and good practices and requirements of the organisation, industry and society. The informal and often implicit "power and interest" (perspective 4) of individuals within an organisation can have strong influence on projects, programmes or portfolios. This perspective also considers that individuals are not only driven by formal and explicit objectives (as stated in "strategy") but equally follow their personal goals. Understanding informal and implicit "culture and values" (perspective 5) of an organisation or a society are often a crucial precondition to success of a project, programme or portfolio.
2. Individual and social competences "people"
   All individual skills and competences which individuals need to successfully collaborate in or lead projects, programmes or portfolios fall under "people". Among the 10 elements, the first two deal with basic attributes of the individual: "self-reflection and self-management" (people1) as well as "personal integrity and reliability" (people 2). The importance of communication is emphasized in "personal communication" (people 3) as well as the ability to build relationships with others in "relationships and engagement" (people 4).

Three elements deal with aspects of leadership, namely "leadership" (people 5), "teamwork" (people 6) and how to handle "conflict and crisis" (people 7).

Different ways of (conceptual and holistic) thinking as well as analytical and creative techniques are featured in "resourcefulness" (people 8). In addition, this competence element focusses strongly on the ability to create a working environment for the team, which is open, creative and allows each one to contribute in an ideal way. Element "people 9" takes into account how "negotiations" can lead to results being favourable for the project, programme or portfolio and at the same time being acceptable for other parties.

Approaches for individuals to motivate and lead the team to reach optimal results are described in "results orientation" (people 10).

3. Technical competences "practice"

"Practice" includes specific methods, tools and techniques, used in projects, programmes or portfolios to successfully carry them out.

"Project design" (practice 1) provides a rough sketch stating the relevant general decisions and priorities for the project, programme or portfolio. These might comprise decision on make-or-buy, linear or iterative approach, financial options and resource considerations. All of these top-level decisions need to filled with life by applying the other technical competence elements:

"goals, requirements and objectives" (practice 2) shows how to manage demands and expectations with respect to objectives and outcomes and how to prioritise them.

The exact boundaries of a project, programme or portfolio are defined in "scope" (practice 3).

The competence element "time" (practice 4) concentrates on the timely order and planning of the delivery. The appropriate organisation of the project, programme or portfolio including the information flow, plus organization of communication and documentation are outlined in "organisation and information" (practice 5). In terms of "quality" (practice 6) ICB distinguishes between process and product quality. The competence element deals with requirements, organization and control of both.

Three elements deal with inputs and their constraints to projects, "finance" (practice 7), human and other "resources" (practice 8) and "procurement" (practice 9). Procurement is often essential for the acquisition of material and resources needed in projects.

All activities need to be integrated and controlled which is described in competence element "plan and control" (practice 10). In addition, the individual has to identify, analyse and minimize "risk and opportunity" (practice 11) as well as to analyse and interact with

"stakeholders" (practice 12). Realizing the benefits is often closely linked with "change and transformation" (practice 13).

Finally, but limited to the management of programmes and portfolios is the competence element "select and balance" (practice 14) seeking to balance programmes and portfolios by selecting appropriate components.

The Individual Competency Baseline (ICB 4.0) represents the general structure of competences for all certification levels. Based on typical activities and responsibilities, the requirements for each of the four certification levels are defined in a taxonomy for assessment. The four-level-certification system (4-L-C) of IPMA comprises level A "Certified Projects Director", able to manage complex portfolios and programmes, level B "Certified Senior Project Manager", able to manage complex projects, level C "Certified Project Manager", able to manage projects of limited complexity or support the manager of a more complex project, level D "Certified Project Management Associate", who "shall have the knowledge in all competence elements and be able to apply it". Exact requirements for these levels might differ slightly among the national IPMA members. Generally, training is available for all levels. In contrast to level D, with no experience being required, the higher levels require proof of experience in project management: For level C three years as responsible project manager in moderately complex projects or responsible leader in complex sub-projects, for level B five years leadership experience in project management, with at least 3 years as project manager in complex projects and for level A, a five year responsible leadership experience in highly complex projects, thereof at least 3 years at strategic level (GPM 2020).

Overall IPMA, counts almost 350,000 certificates (accumulated) in 2019, with the majority being either level D (69.7%) or C (24.7%) (IPMA 2020).

2.3   PRINCE 2

PRINCE 2 is a process-based structured project management methodology emphasizing the division of projects into smaller, less complex and therefore better manageable stages.

PRINCE 2 evolved from an earlier method called PROMPT II (Project Resource Organisation Management Planning Techniques). In 1989 the Central Computer and Telecommunications Agency (CCTA) adopted a version of PROMPT II as a UK Government standard for information systems (IT) project management. The original name 'PRINCE' stood for "PROMPT II IN the CCTA Environment". PRINCE was renamed as an acronym standing for "PRojects IN Controlled Environments" and was released in 1996. PRINCE 2 became popular in many government agencies and departments in UK as well as in the United Nations and can be considered as a standard. Since its launch in 1996 two major revisions of PRINCE 2 have been made in 2009 "PRINCE 2:2009 Refresh" and in 2017 "PRINCE 2 2017 Update".

Since 2013 rights of PRINCE 2 have been transferred from the Cabinet Office, a UK ministerial department, to AXELOS Ltd., a joint venture of the Cabinet Office (49%) and Capita, a UK public listed company, (51%). As of today, PRINCE 2 is applied in many industries and, with more than 2 million certified professionals, is the most widely spread project management certification.

As a project management methodology, PRINCE 2 is based on standardized roles, language and processes aiming at managing time, costs, risks and the scope of projects.

Comparable to the two methodologies mentioned under 7.2.1 und 7.2.2 projects are defined by their project goals. Here, PRINCE 2 refers to six "aspects" or "performance goals": scope, timescale, risk, quality, benefits and costs. In addition to the "magic triangle" of project management focussing on scope, time and costs, PRINCE 2 emphasises the importance of risk, quality and benefits. The aspects are also referred to as "tolerances" quantifying the project and defining the allowed tolerance for each management level. Once the tolerance is exceeded the decision must be escalated to the next higher management level.

The PRINCE 2 methodology is founded on seven principles, seven themes and seven processes. The seven principles lay out the mindset of PRINCE 2. Following these principles provides a framework of best-practice ensuring a project stays in line with the PRINCE 2 methodology.

- The most crucial principle is "continued business justification"—The justification of the project is continuously checked against the business case, which is updated at every stage. In case the justification is no longer given, the project is to be terminated.
- "Learn from experience" requires that each project conducts a lessons log. All projects should continuously refer to their own lessons log as well as to lessons logs from previous and concurrent projects to avoid unnecessary work or repetition of the same mistakes.
- "Define roles and responsibilities": structured in four levels: corporate or programme management, project board, project manager level and project team level. Roles are defined which are separated from individuals, in consequence an individual can take on more than one role or roles can be shared. All primary stakeholders, business, user and supplier, have to be represented in the project management team.
- "Manage by stages": In PRINCE 2 projects are planned and executed in stages. Going to the next stage requires updating the business case, risks, overall plan, and preparation of a detailed next-stage plan reflecting the current situation.
- "Manage by exception" is based on the tolerances ("aspects") defined for each objective. This delegates authority and sets respective limits. In case a management level detects that their respective tolerances will be exceeded, the situation is to be escalated to the next management level for decision-making.
- "Focus on products" underlines the concentration on definition and delivery of products and their quality requirements.
- "Tailor to suit project environment" is the first activity when initiating a new project and equally when entering a new stage ensuring the fit to project environment, size, complexity, importance, time capability and risk.

Closely linked to the seven principles are the seven PRINCE 2 themes. Themes provide the knowledge on how to achieve the principles and are interrelated among each other.

They provide guidance on aspects of project work which should be addressed at various points during the course of the project. The themes also feature specific documents supporting project work (e.g. plans and reports), named "management products". In total 26 "management products" are featured in the manual providing templates for "high level" management of the project. They are grouped into "baselines", "records" and "reports". On the operational level, PRINCE 2 gives some suggestions but in the end, task managers have to decide on and define their own framework managing their tasks.

The seven themes cover:

1. "Business case", relating to the principle of "continued business justification", aims at establishing criteria and mechanisms to continuously evaluate if the project is in line with business requirements and achievable. Management products are "business case" and "benefits management approach".
2. "Organisation", linked to the principle "define roles and responsibilities", describes definition and implementation of project structures with respect to accountability and responsibility. (Management product: "communication management approach")
3. "Quality" is connected to the principles "define roles and responsibilities", "focus on products" and "learn from experience" and focusses on definition and implementation of instruments to verify that products fulfil the desired purpose. Relevant management products are "quality register" and "quality management approach".
4. "Plans" is linked to several principles: "continued business justification", "manage by stages", "manage by exception", "define roles and responsibilities" as well as "learn from experience". PRINCE 2 follows a product-planning approach. Therefore, this theme aims at all means of facilitating communication and control related to delivery of products. Relevant documents comprise "project product description", "product breakdown structure", "product description" and "product flow diagram"
5. "Risk" has links to "continued business justification", "define roles and responsibilities" and "learn from experience" and deals with identifying, evaluating and controlling uncertainty. This aims at improving the project's ability to succeed. Related documents are "risk register" and "risk management approach".
6. "Change" relates to the principles "continued business justification", "define roles and responsibilities" and "learn from experience". It deals with any changes, potential and approved, to the project baselines and provides means for identification, assessment and control of these (management products: "issue register" and "change control approach").
7. "Progress" shows links to the four principles "manage by exception", "manage in stages", "continued business justification" and "learn from experience". It deals with monitoring achievements and comparing the actual ones against those planned. Progress control is based on various plans (project, stage and team), reviews the "registers" and produces reports upon different events (e.g. "checkpoint", "highlight", "end stage" and "end project" reports).

Finally, seven processes describe the activities to be performed during the project. They define who performs the activities, which products are to be created and when. They ensure all critical aspects in project work are covered and treated appropriately. The above-mentioned principles and themes are incorporated within the seven processes.

The seven processes in PRINCE 2 include:

1. "Starting up a project" is about appointing the project team, including an executive and a project manager, and producing a "project brief".
2. "Initiating a project" deals with refining the business case and putting together the so called "project initiation documentation" which is an extension of the project brief.
3. "Directing a project" lays down to the project board the ways in which they control the project
4. "Controlling a stage" dictates how control is exercised in each individual stage, including the way to authorize and distribute work packages.
5. "Managing product delivery" focusses on the connection between the project manager and the team managers. It places formal requirements on how to accept, execute and deliver project work.
6. "Managing stage boundaries" defines the transition from one stage to the next.
7. "Closing a project" covers all formal decommissioning of the project, including actions to follow-on and evaluation of benefits.

In 2018, PRINCE 2 Agile, an extension to PRINCE 2, was launched, which deals with the question on how to adapt PRINCE 2 in order to be deployed with using agile behaviours, frameworks and additional techniques. It considers an agile framework (e.g. Scrum) as a project environment. According to PRINCE 2 this approach turns an agile framework manageable by a project management method as it adds the non-existing decision-making governance and risk management.

As with PMI and IPMA training and certifications are available. PRINCE 2 certifications are awarded by AXELOS after successful completion of the accredited training course and exam. There are two levels of certifications for PRINCE 2 (PRINCE 2 2020). The first level is PRINCE 2® 2017 Foundation certification, confirming sufficient knowledge and understanding of the method and ability to work in a project management team using this method. Here, no proof of experience or mandatory training hours are required to be admitted to the exam. The second level is PRINCE 2® 2017 Practitioner certification. It certifies sufficient understanding of how to apply PRINCE 2 in a scenario situation and ability to start applying the method to a real project with suitable assistance. A prerequisite is the proof of having passed PRINCE 2 foundation exam or any project management exam with e.g. PMI or IPMA. With respect to PRINCE 2 Agile there are equally two certification levels available: PRINCE 2 Agile "Foundation" and "Practitioner".

2.4   Other Standards

Other standards for project management with mainly regional spread or rather new ones can be found. Some selected examples will be briefly depicted:

P2M—Program and Project Management for Enterprise Innovation—is a Japanese standard. Project Management Association of Japan (PMAJ) considers P2M a *body of knowledge combining program management and project management to solve the complicated issues* (PMAJ 2016). These issues result from globalization, global environmental change, advancement of ICT technology (fourth industrial revolution) as well as low birth rate and longevity and lead to individual projects of growing size and complexity. While other project management standards are either objective and/or process oriented with focus *on the process to achieve clearly expected outcome at initiation*, P2M is mission oriented. The methodology considers changes in external environment and opens ways for solving complex challenges, leading to an improvement of business value. The underlying methodology is structured into six parts—comprising three main subjects: (overview and features, program management and project management) as well as three common knowledge platforms (business management, knowledge management and human resources management). The P2M-philosophy is about creating programs which are *directed by organizational mission or strategy. Value creation projects* generate value for the organisation within a program. The program value created exceeds the totality of all values of the projects included, as the business link established by the program ensures an overall optimization in allocating resources according to the top philosophy. In terms of project management, the management areas described have a lot in common with ISO21500—execution of projects comprise the activities check (mission, purpose and goal), define (project scope), organize, prepare (work packages), develop (work flow diagram), implement (schedule control), conduct (cost control) and perform (progress control). Training and certifications ranging from Project Management Coordinator Entry (PMCE) and Project Management Coordinator (PMC) to project management Specialist (PMS) and Program Manager Registered (PMR) are available.

PM^2 is a methodology developed by the European Commission since 2007. Initially it has been created for the needs of European institutions and in use only by them. In recent years the current version 3.0 has been actively promoted by the PM^2-Alliance as *one common free and open project management methodology for Europe* applicable to all kinds of projects and organisations (PM^2 Alliance 2020). The methodology should *enable project managers (PMs) to deliver solutions and benefits to their organisations.* Therefore, PM^2 incorporates *elements from a wide range of globally accepted project management best practices, captured in standards and methodologies* (European Commission 2018). The PM^2-methodology is organized along four project phases—initiating, planning, executing and closing—and additionally "monitor & control" activities are running alongside these phases throughout the entire project life. Phase transitions are marked by three phase gates: Ready for Planning (RfP) marking the end of initiating,

Ready for Executing (RfE) at the end of planning and Ready for Closing (RfC) at the end of executing. The project organization comprises different layers and defined roles and responsibilities. With respect to roles PM^2 points out important competencies, adopted from ICB by IPMA. Among other artefacts, PM^2 postulates the creation of a business case during project initiation, likewise in Prince2. Furthermore, PM^2 stresses ideas of lean management and points out the link to agile methods. Training and certifications are available, but still PM^2 shows a limited spread—per 2018 PM^2 claims a number of roughly 1000 certified individuals (PM^2-Alliance 2020).

2.5   Agile Methods

When it comes to agile project management, two different origins can be identified: lean manufacturing and lean thinking on one hand, iterative and incremental methods for software development on the other.

The first is the lean philosophy which has its origins in industrial production of Toyota, commonly known and referred to as Toyota Production System (TPS). TPS has been developed by Taiichi Ohno. The basic approach of Ohno was to identify and reduce waste within the process. He pointed out seven forms of waste, which are:

1. Delays and waiting times
2. Overproduction
3. Over-processing or running non-value-added activities
4. Transportation
5. Unnecessary movements or motions
6. Inventories
7. Defects in the product

Major elements in this philosophy of eliminating waste comprise a focus on those people adding value in the process, by showing them respect and support in adding (more) value through their own ideas and initiatives. Putting customer satisfaction first, ensures that only non-defective parts are passed on at any time. All activities and processes are subject to continuous improvement. TPS creates stable value streams and establishes a one-piece-flow by continuously reducing and eliminating batch sizes and non-value-adding activities. In the end, a pull-system is created where work is pulled from the downstream, ultimately the customer. It ensures that only what is actually needed is produced. Visualisation in this process unveils differences between the ideal and the current situation at the workplace. Among others techniques, here Kanban is often used to control the production process, reduce the amount of work in progress with limited planning efforts. The ideas of lean manufacturing have widely spread as "lean thinking" (Womack and Jones 2003) to other areas of management.

The second one can be traced back to as early as the late 1950s. In the 1970s, evolutionary project management and adaptive software development emerged. In the 1990s, new methods in software development have been developed to overcome limitation of classical, prescriptive project management which was often considered an overly regulated, over-planned and micro-managed approach. These new methodologies or frameworks comprise, among others, Rapid Application Development (RAD), Unified Process (UP) and Dynamic Systems Development Method (DSDM), and Scrum, all developed in the first half of the decade, later followed by extreme programming (XP) and feature-driven development. All these approaches are now commonly referred to as agile methods of software development as they all reflect the same mindset, which was laid out in the *Agile Manifesto*, by Schwaber, Sutherland et al. (Agile Manifesto 2001) mentioned already in Sect. 7.1 of this chapter. The manifesto describes twelve underlaying principles:

1. Customer satisfaction by delivery of valuable software, early and continuously.
2. Changing requirements welcome, at any time.
3. High frequency in delivery of working software (preferably within weeks rather than months)
4. Close cooperation of business people and developers every day of the project
5. Projects built around motivated individuals, provided with the right environment, support and trust.
6. Face-to-face conversation as the most efficient and effective method of communication in all areas.
7. Progress primarily measured in working software
8. Sustainable development allowing the maintenance of a constant speed for all members throughout the project.
9. Agility enhanced by continuous attention to technical excellence and good design
10. *Simplicity, the art of maximizing the amount of work not done, is essential*
11. *The best architectures, requirements, and designs emerge from self-organizing teams.*
12. Regular reflection within the team on how to become more effective and adjustment of behaviour accordingly

In the following, Scrum will be highlighted more in detail as (1) with respect to its general applicability in projects outside the IT and software industry, and (2) in addition it is the most commonly used agile technique (ref. Sect. 7.2). According to Schwaber and Sutherland, *Scrum is not a process, technique, or definitive method* rather than a *process framework that has been used to manage work on complex products* and within *which various processes and techniques* can be employed (Scrum.org 2015). The term "Scrum" itself goes back to a paper on product development by Takeuchi and Nonaka. It alludes to a Scrum in rugby, where players of each team interlock and attempt to gain hold of the ball at a restart. This metaphor shall illustrate the way of cooperation and intensive team-work within a (Scrum) team.

The Scrum framework is built on three pillars: transparency, inspection and adaptation, representing the basics of empirical process control. Furthermore, the framework comprises Scrum teams, roles, events, artefacts and rules, where each element serves a specific purpose. The rules are the interlinking element of Scrum binding all of them together. The Scrum team shares and lives the values of Scrum, being commitment, courage, focus, openness and respect.

In contrast to other PM-standards, Scrum only knows three different roles, which are:

- product owner, who is representing the customer's voice and responsible for maximizing the value of the product under development. The role is not to be separated among more than one person. The product owner is managing the product backlog, which includes:
  expressing product backlog items clearly and ensuring they fulfil goals and missions;
  optimizing value of the work performed by the development team;
  ensuring visibility and transparency of the product backlog and all items are correct understood (to the degree necessary) by the development team;
  full accountability for the above work, regardless whether done by the product owner or delegated to the team.
- development team, which ideally consists of three to nine professionals to perform the work of delivering an increment at the end of a sprint. Lower numbers will lead to weak interaction and limited productivity gains, as well as such teams suffering from constraints in skills. Managing higher numbers will add too much complexity. The development team is cross-functionally staffed to ensure it possesses all skills required, self-organizing and therefore not told how to transform items into working increments. Regardless of the work performed or the domain covered, there are no subgroups or titles within the team. Despite different specialities in skills or domains, the development team is accountable as a whole.
- Scrum master—supports all members to understand theory, practices, rules, and values of Scrum. Further, the Scrum master interacts with individuals outside the team, checks which interactions with the team are helpful or not and ensures interactions are changes to achieve maximum value generated by the team. The Scrum master further promotes, supports and improves the use of Scrum within the organisation.

The core piece of Scrum is a sprint, which is a time-box of one week to one month, during which a useable product increment, a "done", is created. A concluded sprint is immediately followed by the next sprint. During the whole development, sprints always have the same length. Within a sprint, no changes affecting the sprint goal are made, nevertheless scope might be clarified and re-negotiated based on product owner's and development team's learning. Prior to the sprint, sprint planning is done to define what can be delivered to the increment and how the work needed will be accomplished. Further on, the sprint goal is defined, which will be met by implementing the product backlog. Sprint planning is usually time-boxed for a maximum of 8 h. During the sprint, every day, a 15-min time-boxed event, the daily Scrum, is held. During this meeting the team discusses what each member contributed the previous day, what they will contribute the same day and whether impediments exist preventing the individual or the whole team from reaching their sprint goal. After completion of the sprint, a sprint review is held in order to inspect the result, the increment, and to adapt the product backlog if necessary. Usually such an event takes four hours and aims at demonstrating which backlog items have been "done" and which have remained not "done". Depending on the outcome, likely targets or delivery dates as well as potential changes can be discussed. All information gathered during the review will be used for the next sprint planning. Additionally, the Scrum team will make a usually 3 h long "sprint retrospective" allowing the team to inspect how the last sprint went, with respect to tools and processes, as well as people and relationships. This allows the team to identify potentials to be adapted and implemented.

Another agile technique to mention in this context is Kanban, originating from lean manufacturing, although there is no elaborate concept around Kanban in terms of an overall methodology for project management. Therefore, others consider Kanban as a technique to be combined with Scrum, sometimes referred to as Scrumban, or equally with traditional methodologies. The core piece is the use of a Kanban board, separating work in "to do", "doing" and "done". While Scrum is time-boxed, the main focus of Kanban is to visualize the workflow, establish a pull-system leading to a limited number of work packages to be worked at simultaneously. This leads to a better flow of work and productivity.

Training and certification are available on Scrum. Mainly two organisations, the Scrum Alliance, a non-profit organisation, and Scrum.org, a private company, offer Scrum certificates.

Scrum Alliance requires formal training before applicants can pass a multiple choice online-test; recertification is required every two years. Certificates by Scrum Alliance comprise among others: Certified ScrumMaster (CSM) with no prerequisites followed by Advanced Certified ScrumMaster (A-CSM), prerequisite CSM-Certificate plus one and more years of experience ending with the Certified Scrum Professional ScrumMaster. Analogue certification scheme available for product owner; The developer track starts with Certified Scrum Developer (CSD) with no prerequisites, followed directly by the Certified Scrum Professional available for active CSD-certificate holders.

For Scrum.org formal training is not mandatory, but equally offered. Applicants equally pass a multiple-choice online test once; a recertification is not required. Among others certificates Scrum.org offers certificates according to the Scrum roles: Professional Scrum Master (PSM), comprising three levels, Professional Scrum Product Owner (PSPO), equally comprising three levels plus a one-level certificate for Professional Scrum Developer (PSD).

With respect to Kanban, both organisations equally offer certificates on Kanban. Official numbers are not available about the overall number of Scrum certificate holders with Scrum Alliance but estimates range around one million certificates globally. The chapter for Germany, Austria and Switzerland, names roughly 50,000 certificates (Scrum DACH 2020). For Scrum.org, official numbers are available showing 467,000 certificate holders globally (Scrum.org 2020).

2.6   Review and Criticism

In the preceding chapters details about the specifics of the most relevant methodologies, traditional and agile have been given. Potential advantages and disadvantages of all methodologies exist and will be discussed in the following.

PMI's methodology and the PMP-certificate are popular and widespread especially in the United States and American countries. Its process-oriented approach is often considered too scientific or theoretic. It focusses very much on execution and control of projects as well as on the application of tools and techniques, less on planning, people and their interactions nor required (social) competencies of project managers.

While IPMA's methodology is less wide-spread in terms of certificates, its competence-based approach does not focus on processes and tools, but highlights individual competences of professionals in project management. Criticism can be made with respect to showing only weak links between the standard and the organization's business strategy. The methodology remains quite general which allows a wide field of application, but it does not sufficiently reflect the needs of business development nor does it have special focus on the creation of product. Project managers need to fill these shortcomings by implementing appropriate tools and techniques.

Mandatory creation of a business case and the continuous business justification in PRINCE 2 emphasize the business orientation and can be seen as a big advantage. As can be seen by the number of certificates, the methodology is widely spread and in particular popular in the UK, Australia and partly in Europe. Due to its background, PRINCE 2 appears more suitable for bigger projects within hierarchical structures: While the definition of tolerances and the rigid approach of escalation (management by exception) is a clear advantage in those environments, it might turn out as a disadvantage in smaller projects, less hierarchical environments or wherever requirements are changing dynamically. In those cases, this may lead to excessive work on documents and focus on deliverables for their own sake. With respect to PRINCE 2 and PMP it might be worthwhile to mention, that both acknowledge each other's existence and they might be used alongside of each other.

The approach of PM²-Alliance is worth mentioning, as it combines strengths of different methodologies. The methodology is still quite young and, so far only seldomly applied in practice or discussed in literature. Hence, time will tell whether it becomes more popular and widely used in the future.

The term agile has become more and more popular. Nevertheless, some seem to misinterpret agile as a charter for working without having a clear idea about the desired outcome of the undertaking (lack of objectives) nor rules or guidance within the process. Even when objectives for a project are explicitly defined, a general weakness might be the absence of integration of the methodology within the overall business strategy. As Scrum, in particular has its roots in the development of (IT and software) products, it is undisputedly very suitable for the development of products. Here, the focus on frequent completion and delivery of valuable increments to the customer is a clear advantage. Scrum is most suitable for smaller teams, the methodology encounters limitations with increasing team size. One success factor is the close cooperation and ongoing interaction by personal face-to-face communication. Whenever members are not working in the same place nor on the same time schemes this might become an issue, which can partly be solved by the use of communication technology. A more general critique to agile product development can be made with respect to legal matters, e.g. with regards to defining binding requirements, expected work content and payment in contracts.

3   PM in International Business Development

First of all, international business development implies initiating and executing projects which ensure the successful deployment of a business strategy within own and associated organisations. This ensures the long-term well-being of the organisation. Generally speaking, the use of some kind of project management standard(s) is indisputably a reasonable approach. However, project management is a complex discipline and cannot be reduced to the question of which methodology is the best in general. It is more about understanding the overall project environment and its specific needs. Further, a standard with its existing tools and techniques can be chosen or, if required, it will be enhanced and blended with additional methodologies. Some criteria are quite obvious for the choice of a suitable standard, e.g. availability of and experience with project management standards within the organization. Organizations professionally using project management usually have implemented one or more standards and train their staff accordingly. This facilitates a common understanding on methods and tools to be used, raises transparency and ensures smooth communication among all people involved. Often the implemented project management standard(s) unveil a lot about the organisational culture: importance of predictability, reliability and control for management, transparency and tolerance for mistakes, level of autonomy of and trust in employees. This is closely linked to the self-perception of companies (see also Chapter "Establishing Local Business Units" of this book).

When different organisations participate in a project, it is advisable to decide upon one specific methodology for all parties. In those cases, geographical preferences, practices specific to an industry segment or legal reasons/policies play a role, sometimes the use of a specific standard is simply required by a customer. In international projects, geographically distributed teams, often with different languages and cultures working on different time zones, add another degree of complication. Here, a common standardized project management "language" is a must to simplify communication and coordination. It avoids different perceptions and expectations on objectives, priorities and outcomes within the project. It sets clear rules for the collaboration and helps to manage such project even beyond national borders.

The size of a project and or its criticality for the organisation is a further relevant indicator. While smaller projects with less impact on the organization might be run easily with a limited set of methods, bigger projects showing a higher criticality for the organisation require more framework and management.

Projects in international business development require further considerations: As outlined in Fig. 1, projects become complicated or even complex when social and/or technical uncertainty grows. However, the boundaries between the different fields which cannot be defined precisely and strongly depend on individual perception of the project manager. Therefore, project manager and management should be aware of their general attitude towards uncertainty. This helps to manage expectations and creates the right awareness for risks. In consequence, appropriate tools to analyse, manage and control risks during the entire project lifetime can be chosen and implemented. Regardless of the applied project management methodology (traditional, hybrid or agile) higher volatility and uncertainty require more frequent or even continuous control and revision of risks.

Additionally, developing new businesses means to take entrepreneurial risk. Hence, project manager and management have to understand the link between business strategy and project objective, preferably with the help of a business case for the project. The more volatile and dynamic the project environment is, the more important the continuous business justification of the project becomes as part of risk management. Terminating a project, because of the absence of business justification is a success of project management, preventing bigger harm for the organisation.

Interactions with the customer or final users about the expected outcome and functionalities of products or services often lead to complex environments in business development. Some expectations and goals remain vague and only solidify during the course of the project. These aspects solely might be addressed best with agile approaches. On the other hand, project size, criticality for the organisation and geographical setup or accepted standards among the people involved could call for more structures and stable processes as given by traditional project management approaches. Therefore, reviewing the needs in different stages of the project and the subsequent adaptation of the methodology. This often leads to some kind of hybrid, which will be the most suitable approach to tackle all aspects of project endeavours in the best way.

Although all standards provide clearly defined frameworks and methodologies to manage projects, solely the use of a methodology is no guarantee to successfully complete a project. On the other hand, the more professional the project is managed, with the right attitude, understanding about what is important, the openness for change and a sound methodology ensuring good cooperation among all people involved, the more likely projects in business development will succeed.

Exercise A

Discuss the fundamental differences between Prince 2 and the PMI's project management methodology.

Exercise B

A company produces machines for the food beverage industry. The machines are mostly bottling and labelling units for breweries as well as soft-drink producers.

Each machine is a unique type, custom-made for the client. Machines are manufactured in Germany and Hungary. The installation of the machines at the customers' sites around the world are run as projects, with typical durations between 6 and 10 weeks.

What project management standard would you recommend for such a company to use? And why?

Exercise C

A European pharmaceutical company intends to launch a newly developed cardio-vascular medicine in the US market. In terms of business development point out crucial aspects to be considered. How does that affect your project management standard? Which tools and elements of project management play an important role?

Exercise D

Discuss the benefits for a company to certify their project managers according to a general standard vs. a company specific solution.

References

Beauftragter der Bundesregierung für Informationstechnik. (2020). https://www.cio.bund.de/Web/DE/Architekturen-und-Standards/V-Modell-XT/vmodell_xt_node.html [23 November 2020].

Chumas, S., & Hartman, J. (1975). Directory of United States standardization activities. *NBS Special Publication, 417,* 141.

Digital.ai. (2020). The 14th State of Agile Report.

European Commission, Center of Excellence in Project Management (CoEPM²). (2018). PM² Project Management Methodology, Guide 3.0. Brussels/Luxemberg.

GPM, (2015). Makroökonomische Vermessung der Projekttätigkeit in Deutschland. Deutsche Gesellschaft für Projektmanagement e.V., Nürnberg.

GPM (2020). https://www.gpm-ipma.de/zertifizierung.html [23 November 2020].

Grau, N. (2013). Standards and excellence in project management—In who do we trust? *Procedia—Social and Behavioral Sciences, 74,* 10–20.

IPMA. (2020). Certification and Validation Management Board. IPMA Certification Yearbook 2019. International Project Management Association.

PMAJ. (2016). *P2M Bibelot—Overview of P2M* (3rd ed.). Tokyo: Project Management Association of Japan.

PMI. (2013). *Project management talent gap report*. Newton Square: Project Management Institute.

PMI. (2017). *Project management job growth and talent gap 2017–2027*. Newton Square: Project Management Institute.

PMI. (2020a). PMI Today July/August 2020. Project Management Institute. https://www.pmitoday-digital.com/pmitoday/july_august_2020?pg=4#pg4 [26 September 2020].

PMI. (2020b). A first look under the hood of the PMBOK guide seventh edition. https://community.pmi.org/t5/the-official-pmi-blog/a-first-look-under-the-hood-of-the-pmbok-guide-seventh-edition/ba-p/46#_=_ [23 November 2020].

PM²-Alliance. (2020). https://www.pm2alliance.eu/our-mission/ [23 November 2020].

PRINCE 2. (2020). https://www.prince2.com/uk/prince2-qualifications-explained [23 November 2020]

The agile manifesto. (2001). https://agilemanifesto.org/ [23 November 2020].

Scrum.org. (2015). The scrum guide. https://www.scrumguides.org/docs/scrumguide/v1/Scrum-Guide-DE.pdf [23 November 2020]

Scrum DACH. (2020). https://scrumdach.org/ [23 November 2020].

Scrum.org. (2020). https://www.scrum.org/professional-scrum-certifications/count [5 November 2020].

Womack, J., & Jones, D. 2003. *Lean Thinking – Banish Waste and Create Wealth in Your Cooperation*. 2nd Ed. London: Simon & Schuster.

Sourcing Strategies and Trends: Global Versus Local

Moritz Peter and Philipp Rathgeber

1 Introduction to Sourcing

1.1 Supply Management

Supply chains make the world go around and are therefore crucial to international business development. Hence, supply chain management optimization has gained substantial attention from both practitioners and academics in recent years. Constant attention is given, for instance, to global supply chain issues such as supply chain vulnerability (Wagner and Bode 2006), supply chain social responsibility (Fine 2013) and supply chain performance (Hendricks and Singhal 2005).

Most scholars presume that proficient supply management skills have great potential to enhance the competitiveness of a firm (Christopher 1992; Hendricks and Singhal 2003). Quality, costs and lead time have been identified as important factors in this context (Mason-Jones et al. 2000). In addition to those market qualifiers, supply flexibility is increasingly gaining in importance to achieve a competitive edge (Christopher and Towill 2001). In order to accomplish these competitive goals, the concept of customer-centric supply chains was developed by putting customer value at the centre of attention (Melnyk and Stanton 2017). Monczka et al. (2009) emphasize the strategic nature and long-term perspective of supply management, as they describe supply management as an

M. Peter (✉)
Pforzheim University, Pforzheim, Germany
e-mail: moritz.peter@hs-pforzheim.de

P. Rathgeber
International School of Management (ISM), München, Germany
e-mail: philipp.rathgeber@ism.de

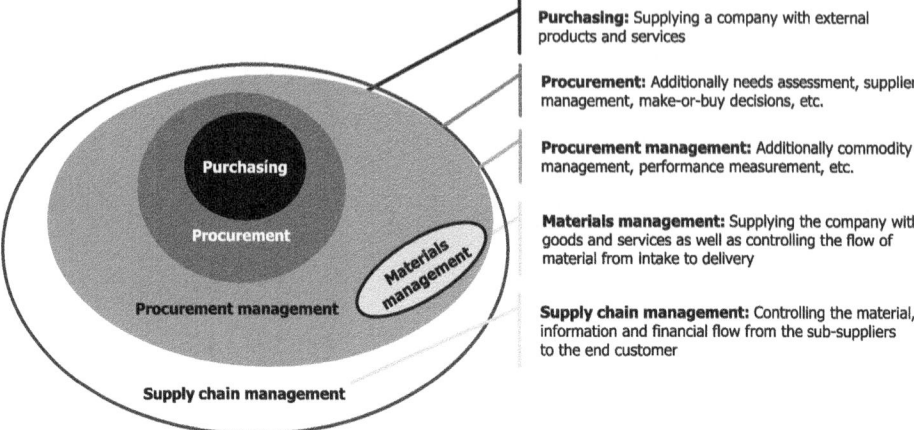

Fig. 1 Supply management related terms, based on BME (2020, p. 5)

inclusive concept, which refers to a strategic approach to cater to the current and future needs of an organization through active supply base management.

While there is little doubt about the competitive potential of modern supply management, there is, unfortunately, still confusion about the scope and relation of supply management terms. Since inconsistent wording is likely to cause misunderstandings, an overview of terms related to supply management is given in Fig. 1.

Among the terms mentioned above, especially procurement and purchasing are used as equivalents in most of the publications and everyday language. However, in line with Van Weele (2014), procurement can be understood as a broader term than purchasing, serving as an interface or a bridge between the internal customers and the external suppliers. Thereby the scope of procurement activities ranges from planning demands in terms of volume and specifications, selecting and evaluating suppliers, negotiating contracts with suppliers, placing and monitoring orders with selected suppliers, following-up, and finally evaluating supplier performance. Hence, procurement can be understood as an end-to-end concept, which requires total cost of ownership thinking (Van Weele 2014) as shown in Fig. 2.

In the past, procurement and supply management in general was mostly considered to be an operational and clerical function (Aljian 1984; Giunipero et al. 2006; Monczka et al. 2009), that was responsible for obtaining materials, equipment, supplies and services according to the "five rights": right quality, right quantity, right place, right time and right price (Aljian 1984; Monczka et al. 2009). Towards the end of the twentieth century, new management concepts, e.g. lean management, and new supply issues, e.g. risk management, corporate sustainability and product safety requirements, increased the importance of service orientation, cultural and language diversity of a global supply base, legal and compliance issues, as well as rapid IT and technology advancements

Fig. 2 Sourcing activities based on Van Weele (2014, p. 8)

Table 1 Overview of major risks inherent to global supply chains

Peripheral risks	• Catastrophic risks, e.g. earthquake
	• Geopolitical risks, e.g. political unrest
Market-specific risks	• Market risks, e.g. exchange rates
	• Strategic risks, e.g. monopolistic suppliers
Supplier-specific risks	• Financial risks, e.g. financial supplier distress
	• Operational risks, e.g. quality problems

transforming the role of procurement departments into a strategic one (Johnson et al. 1998; Radovilsky and Hegde 2012). Nowadays supply management and procurement in particular are seen as strategic levers for operational performance and profitability, since optimizations can often quickly be realized and have a direct impact on profitability.

Moreover, the attention top managers and researchers are paying to supply management issues is remarkably triggered by the frequency and intensity of disasters and crises (Wagner and Bode 2006). Catastrophic events such as the terrorist attacks on the World Trade Center (2001), the SARS epidemic (2003), Hurricane Katrina (2005), the Fukushima tsunami (2011) or the outbreak of the COVID-19 pandemic (2020) reveal the vulnerability of global supply chains due to inherent risks. These so-called supply chain risks can range from supplier-specific risks to market-specific risks in addition to peripheral risks of global supply chains, as shown in Table 1.

The risks shown in Table 1 are inherent to global supply chains and have therefore to be taken into consideration when developing sourcing strategies, as the occurrence of these risks can lead to severe operational and financial damages.

1.2 Sourcing Strategies

Sourcing strategies consist of a series of strategic procurement decisions that shape the long-term success of supply operations. As mentioned in Table 1, international sourcing activities are accompanied by specific risks. Therefore, the benefits and risks of global supply operations have to be analysed and carefully balanced. Monczka et al. (2009)

Table 2 Pros and cons of global sourcing based on Monczka et al. (2009)

Motivation for global sourcing	• Cost benefits • Access to superior technology • Availability if domestic capacities are exhausted
Barriers to global sourcing	• Increased supply risk • Longer lead times • Lack of skills and resistance to change

identify a number of benefits from global sourcing activities such as cost benefits, access to superior technology, availability if domestic capacities are exhausted and the opportunity to put domestic suppliers under competitive pressure. On the other hand, Monczka et al. (2009) also mention typical barriers to global sourcing, such as an increased supply risk, longer lead times, lack of skills, resistance to change and cultural differences. The pros and cons of global sourcing mentioned in Table 2, make each international contract award an individual case by case decision.

Typically, companies need individual sourcing strategies that are tailor-made for each of their main product groups. Obviously, product group-specific sourcing strategies are necessary due to different supply market conditions. In general, it can be said, that sourcing strategies need to take the trade-off between supply efficiency and supply security into account. Supply chain practices that incorporate redundancy, such as using multiple sources of supply, reduce the immediate impact of a supply chain disruption by buying time (Zsidisin and Wagner 2010). However, these security-oriented tactics lead to additional costs that can be seen as an insurance fee (Sheffi and Rice 2005).

In order to set up a sourcing strategy, companies have to take two basic decisions at the very beginning. The following two basic decisions have a direct impact on the internationalization of the entire sourcing strategy as shown in Fig. 3:

- Make-or-buy decision: In-house production versus outsourced supply
- Internationalization decision: Domestic location versus offshore placement

Practitioners and researchers alike have recognized that a high degree of efficiency can be achieved through outsourcing. Therefore, the need for productivity improvement (Razzaque and Sheng 1998) and the desire to focus on core competencies (Arnold 2000; Quinn and Hilmer 1994) induced the outsourcing trend. However, the widespread practice of outsourcing is based on the reliance on external sources for value adding activities (Lei and Hitt 1995). Therefore, the outsourcing-induced efficiency gain comes at the expense of increasing dependence on the supply base (Kannan and Tan 2002; Zsidisin 2003).

As part of the strategic make-or-buy decision, a suitable supplier has to be identified either domestically or globally. The importance of location has been noticed by research (Porter 1994) and depends on various factors as shown in Fig. 4.

	Domestic	**Offshore**
In-house	*Domestic in-house production* Company produces its products domestically without any outside contracts	*Offshore in-house sourcing* Company uses services supplied by its own foreign-based affiliation (subsidiary)
Outsourced	*Domestic outsourcing* Company uses services supplied by another domestically based company	*Offshore outsourcing* Company uses services supplied by an unaffiliated foreign based company

Fig. 3 Overview of a company's outsourcing options, based on Vietor et al. (2008, p. 12)

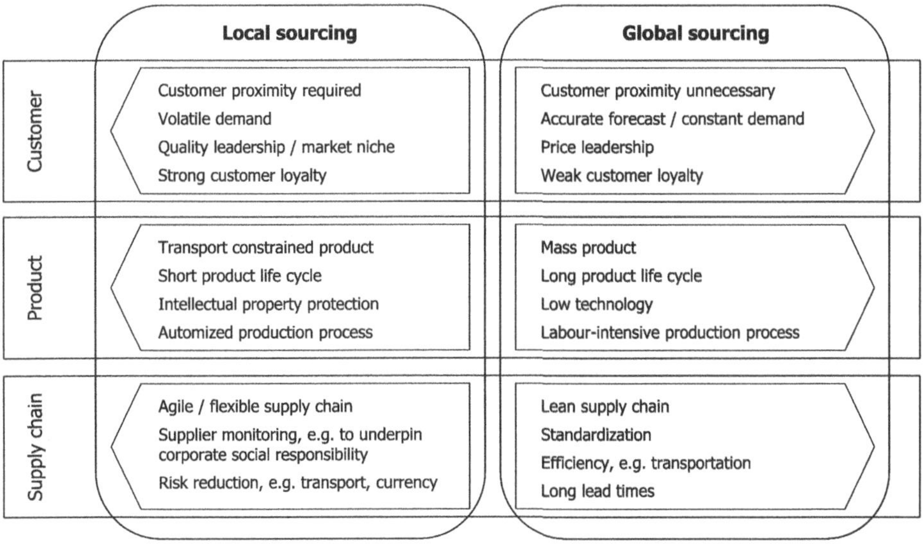

	Local sourcing	**Global sourcing**
Customer	Customer proximity required Volatile demand Quality leadership / market niche Strong customer loyalty	Customer proximity unnecessary Accurate forecast / constant demand Price leadership Weak customer loyalty
Product	Transport constrained product Short product life cycle Intellectual property protection Automized production process	Mass product Long product life cycle Low technology Labour-intensive production process
Supply chain	Agile / flexible supply chain Supplier monitoring, e.g. to underpin corporate social responsibility Risk reduction, e.g. transport, currency	Lean supply chain Standardization Efficiency, e.g. transportation Long lead times

Fig. 4 Sourcing location decision criteria

Taking these factors into consideration, it is no surprise that one hot topic in global supply management is whether and where sourcing locations are moving. As described in the following section, there is strong indication for a decline in global sourcing and an increase in regional sourcing (Ellram et al. 2013; Peter and Rathgeber 2017), see also Table 3.

Table 3 Drivers of global sourcing location decisions based on Ellram et al. (2013)

Cost-related factors	· Rising cost of fuel and associated transportation costs (Fishman 2012) · Rising cost of labour in low-cost countries (Fishman 2012; Rein 2012) · Real and anticipated volatility in currency valuation (Culp 2012)
Supply-related factors	· Growing concern toward environmental issues (Fine 2013; Mueller et al. 2011) · The fast response time and leaner supply chain associated with locating manufacturing closer to the end customer/consumer (Williamson 2012) · Perception of quicker recovery in the case of supply chain disruption (Fishman 2012; Williamson 2012)

2 Sourcing Strategies and Trends

2.1 Sourcing Environment

Improved transport and means of communication as well as decreasing trade barriers have created global supply chains over the past 50 years that were primarily trimmed for efficiency through cost savings. Significant cost savings could be achieved (Perlitz 2004; Schmid 2013) through standardization (e.g. 40-foot containers) and the proximity to production factors (e.g. wage cost difference between Asia and Western Europe). These global flows of goods and materials led to a wide range of affordable products in the western hemisphere and to a positive economic and technological development in the eastern hemisphere—especially in China. The rise of the Chinese market turned out to be twofold: the Chinese market is considered to be an attractive procurement market as well as an attractive sales market. For a long time this seemed to be an endless success story, from which Germany as an export nation benefited significantly for instance.

However, recent economic and technological developments suggest a trend reversal and even a paradigm shift. The longstanding economic boom in the coastal regions of China, led prices and wages to rise sharply, so that the long-term competitive advantage of low wages is being decimated. In addition, the strong technological progress, e.g. in computing power, sensor technology, networking, data storage and manufacturing processes, opens up new production possibilities for manufacturing companies based in Europe, which are often referred to as "Industry 4.0" (Ziemke et al. 2016).

Disruptive technological developments pose a risk for established companies and industries, while at the same time opening opportunities for new companies and industries, if they manage to offer increased customer benefits along with flexibility and speed. The photo and music industry are impressive warning examples of how long-standing market leaders can be displaced in a relatively short period of time. Taking these warning examples into consideration, the question currently arises how other industries manage their strategic and technological transformation. For example the automotive industry is subject to change by new mobility concepts. Understandably both automobile manufacturers and their suppliers are looking for sustainable business models and strategies. In contrast to the mentioned example of the photo and music industry, much longer value and supply chains would be affected in other industries, such as the automotive industry.

An important keyword in this context is the term "Industry 4.0", which although it originated in production relates to the entire value chain. Markus Schäfer, board member of Daimler AG and chief procurement officer (CPO) of Mercedes Benz Cars, understands the term Industry 4.0 as

> *"the digitization of the entire value chain—from design and development to production and sales and service [...] digitalization offers the opportunity to customize our products to meet individual needs and to make production more efficient and flexible"* (Buschmann 2016).

An implementation of the "Industry 4.0" concept along the entire value chain would therefore offer the opportunity to reduce the "time-to-market" at short notice and more flexibility to customer requirements and market fluctuations. This is particularly necessary in industries that are characterized by short innovation cycles, high product variety and high competitive pressure.

2.2   Paradigm Shift in Sourcing

With falling trade barriers (e.g. due to the worldwide spread and expansion of free trade zones) and sinking transfer barriers (e.g. through better transport and communication technologies) global supply chains with a clear focus on cost efficiency emerged at the end of the last century.

Due to the proximity to production factors (especially labour) considerable cost savings were achieved—especially as a result of increasing standardization, e.g. through the introduction of containers or the spread of the English language in business communication—and a global flow of material was established. In addition, the volume-induced fixed-costs per unit degression (Economies of Scale) and the concentration on core competencies through outsourcing (Quinn and Hilmer 1994) fuelled the trend of global trade.

However, practitioners and academics quickly recognized two major disadvantages of global supply chains: On the one hand, the risk of interruption of supply (Manuj and Mentzer 2008; Tang 2006; Wagner and Bode 2006); on the other hand, the inflexibility of global, cost-oriented supply chains due to long delivery times (lead time) and lack of adaptability (responsiveness) with increasing product variance (customization) and volume fluctuations (volatility) (Stevenson and Spring 2007; Vickery et al. 1999). Not surprisingly, practitioners and academics put an effort into supply chain management optimization for creating and securing competitive advantages (Li et al. 2006). As a

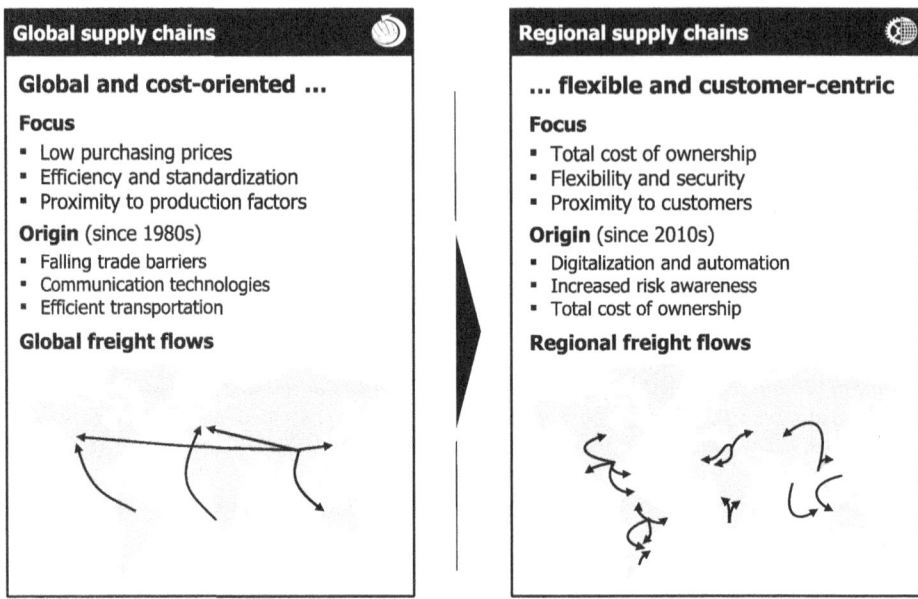

Fig. 5 Paradigm shift in supply chain management based on Peter and Rathgeber (2017, p. 184)

result, supply chain management has shifted from lean to agile and flexible (Christopher and Towill 2001). The focus shifted with increasing competitive pressure from quality and costs to availability and delivery time (Christopher and Towill 2000). Figure 5 shows the paradigm shift in supply chain management and sourcing.

3   Implications for Buyers

3.1   Enhancing Supply Chain Agility

To transform relatively inflexible global supply chains into agile supply chains, the customer needs to be put at the centre of every activity within supply chain management activity. In order to achieve this goal, three levers are given priority in corporate supply management practice:

- End-to-end process optimization of all value-added activities achieves a trade-off between efficiency and flexibility. To ensure the supply of the right raw materials at the right time at the right place in the right quality and quantity at optimal cost, supply chain management is the key to operational performance. To ensure this, the information and material flow of sales and procurement markets must be optimized (Wagner 2009; Wagner and Eggert 2016). The advancements of digitalization play a key role in this context to ease information flows between all parties involved.

- Industry 4.0/digitization offers, as described, the opportunity not only to harmonize all stages of the value chain, but also to radically optimize it. Individual technologies of the fourth industrial revolution, such as 3-D printing and advances in automation reinforce the trend towards regionalized added value.
- Regionalized value creation not only offers protection against exchange rate fluctuations and political risks, but also reduces transport costs and delivery time. This reduces capital commitment costs and enables a more flexible response to increasingly individualized and fluctuating customer requirements. This reduces risk and costs and tends to increase revenues. This trend could contribute to the realization of the vision of a transnational company of Bartlett and Ghoshal (Bartlett and Ghoshal 1986, 1989).

The authors of this chapter assume that global supply chains are changing as regional value-added networks and thus also regional supply chains gain in importance. This trend assessment is in line with current economic studies (Credit Suisse Research Institute 2015; Standard Chartered Bank Global Research 2015), and substantially accelerated by the current COVID-19 pandemic.

3.2   Transformation Challenges

The change from global supply chains to regional, customer-centric supply networks brings major strategic, technological and organizational challenges for companies. The transformation to a customer-oriented supply network is initially a strategic challenge. Thus, the new value and supply chain design goes far beyond continuous (minor) improvement and therefore requires, in addition to sufficient financial resources, also the willingness as well as the ability to make fundamental changes. In order to make transformation efforts profitable, companies must first understand the needs and preferences of their key customers. It is therefore of particular importance to place customer benefit at the centre of the planning and implementation steps. Thereby it is first necessary to establish regional value-added networks, in order to get closer to the customer in terms of space.

To do this, the companies must also develop regional competence and at the same time combine regional characteristics with global efficiency gains in a meaningful way. The sociologist Roland Robertson coined the term "glocalization" in this context (Robertson 1998). The television market is a vivid example that plays a certain pioneering role. To avoid costly quota flops, the program providers buy successful game shows or casting formats abroad, which can then be adapted according to linguistic and national characteristics.

The transformation also requires substantial technological changes, which enable stronger customer orientation, a local production footprint and faster throughput times. Categorical requirements to achieve these goals are:

- **Big-data analysis competence** for the generation of "Action-oriented Customer Insights" (Kiron et al. 2012), which are developed in specialist departments (e.g. Research & development, product management, marketing) quickly and easily operationalized
- Competences in the field of **automation and manufacturing technology**, without which a (partial) relocation of production sites would not be cost-effective, would be possible
- **Digital skills** to digitize selected steps along the value chain and thereby substantially accelerate the end-to-end process

The identification of relevant corporate competencies and skills should be systematically developed along the value chain.

Finally, an end-to-end transformation is associated with a number of organizational challenges. A new type of market strategy requires both a review of the organizational structures as well as a fundamental adjustment of all value-adding processes. It is also essential to create and adequately fill new roles in this context, while other positions will lose importance in the new setup. In the end, necessary organizational and operational changes are indispensable, including the adjustment of the corporate culture to the new way of working. This is particularly important, given that the success rates of cultural change projects range, depending on the study, between 19% (Smith 2003) and 30% (Burnes and Jackson 2011).

Case study: The supply chain speed initiative at adidas AG

Particularly in industries facing major disruption, companies have started to embark on a journey of transformation. The fashion industry is a prominent example where a clear "case for change" is evident, and where vertically-integrated fast fashion companies are pushing incumbents like sportswear leader adidas to embrace new approaches along the entire supply chain. The case of the adidas speed initiative is described below.

In 2015 adidas' five-year strategy outlined its vision to be the first fast moving sporting goods company in the world. To live up to this promise adidas had to transform its supply-chain end-to-end—from collection building to the delivery to stores. adidas set out to challenge the status quo of doing business in the fashion industry in different strategic initiatives. Adidas opened, jointly with various industry partners, a so called "speedfactory" in rural Bavaria with the intention to shorten lead-times—a courageous move in an industry where almost the entire manufacturing is based in low cost countries.

Moreover, adidas invested a range of technological and procedural capabilities along its supply chain. Adidas developed a digital material toolbox in the field of fabric and material management with 750 different material and fabric variants which designers could draw upon in their creations. Thus, material and fabric variants were reduced by more than 50%. Adidas negotiated material stock holding with tier-2 suppliers for the remaining materials in order to guarantee a 30-day lead-time for all products made from these materials—a pace only very few competitors match in this industry.

When looking at the state of the company today, it appears that adidas has profoundly benefited from the scale of change initiated in 2015. Not all initiatives worked out as planned—adidas closed its German "speedfactory" in 2019, with the intention to leverage the acquired know-how in Asia. However, the boldness to formulate a grand vision and to substantiate it with a set of promising technological and procedural initiatives, seem to have paid off: adidas almost quadrupled its market capitalization from September 2015 to September 2020 and increased its revenues from 16.9bn € in 2015 to 23.6bn€ in 2019. Thus, adidas serves as a prime example on how to master transformational challenges in difficult market environments. ◄

Exercise 8-A

A company produces highly accurate pieces used in mechanical watches. It produces high-end metal pieces as well as pieces made out of plastic. The company is based in France and supplies customers all over the globe—with a major share of high-end watch manufacturers in Switzerland.

Consider the raw materials and technologies used for manufacturing the pieces (metal punching and plastic forming) as well as the quality demands of customers on accuracy and durability of the pieces. Discuss which risks this company might have with regards to its own supply chain.

Exercise 8-B

Discuss the major drivers in the shift from global to regional supply chains. Moreover, discuss transformation challenges from global to regional supply chains.

References

Aljian, G. (1984). *Purchasing handbook: Standard reference book on purchasing, policies, practices, procedures, contracts and forms*. New York: McGraw-Hill.

Arnold, U. (2000). New dimensions of outsourcing: A combination of transaction cost economics and the core competencies concept. *European Journal of Purchasing and Supply Management, 6*(1), 23–29.

Bartlett, C. A., & Ghoshal, S. (1986). Tap your subsidiaries for global reach. *Harvard Business Review, 64,* 87–94.

Bartlett, C. A., & Ghoshal, S. (1989). *Managing across borders: The transnational solution.* Boston: Harvard Business School Press.

BME, Bundesverband Materialwirtschaft, Einkauf und Logistik e.V. 2020. *Grundlagen des Einkaufs,* https://www.koinno-bmwi.de/fileadmin/user_upload/publikationen/Grundlagen_des_ Einkaufs.pdf [12 September 2020].

Burnes, B., & Jackson, P. (2011). Success and failure in organizational change: An exploration of the role of values. *Journal of Change Management, 11*(2), 133–162.

Buschmann, J. (2016). Spitzentechnologie für die Mercedes-Benz-Produktion, *Frankfurter Allgemeine Sonntagszeitung: Sonderveröffentlichung, 1,* May 22.

Christopher, M. (1992). *Logistics & supply chain management.* London: Pitmans.

Christopher, M., & Towill, D. (2000). Supply chain migration from lean and functional to agile and customized. *Supply Chain Management: An International Journal, 5*(4), 206–213.

Christopher, M., & Towill, D. (2001). An integrated model for the design of agile supply chains. *International Journal of Physical Distribution & Logistics Management, 31*(4), 235–246.

Credit Suisse Research Institute. (2015). *The end of globalization or a more multipolar world?* https://www.credit-suisse.com/ch/de/search.html?cs-gs-field=The%20End%20of%20 Globalization%20or%20a%20more%20Multipolar%20World&cs-site=cs [19 September 2020].

Culp, S. (2012). *Supply chain risk a hidden liability for many companies.* Forbes. https://www. forbes.com/sites/steveculp/2012/10/08/supply-chain-risk-a-hidden-liability-for-manycompa-nies/ [14 September 2020].

Ellram, L. M., Tate, W. L., & Petersen, K. J. (2013). Offshoring and reshoring: An update on the manufacturing location decision. *Journal of Supply Chain Management, 49*(2), 14–22.

Fine, C. (2013). Intelli-sourcing to replace off-shoring as supply chain transparency increases. *Journal of Supply Chain Management, 49*(2), 6–7.

Fishman, C. 2012. The insourcing boom. *The Atlantic.* Retrieved from https://www.theatlantic. com/magazine/archive/2012/12/the-insourcingboom/309166/# [16 September 2020].

Giunipero, L., Handfield, R., & Eltantawy, R. (2006). Supply management's evolution: Key skill sets for the supply manager of the future. *International Journal of Operations & Production Management, 26*(7), 822–844.

Hendricks, K. B., & Singhal, V. R. (2003). The effect of supply chain glitches on shareholder wealth. *Journal of Operations Management, 21*(5), 501–522.

Hendricks, K. B., & Singhal, V. R. (2005). Association between supply chain glitches and operating performance. *Management Science, 51*(5), 695–711.

Johnson, P., Leenders, M., & Fearon, H. (1998). Evolving roles and responsibilities of purchasing organizations. *International Journal of Purchasing and Materials Management, 3*(4), 2–11.

Kannan, V. R., & Tan, K. C. (2002). Supplier selection and assessment: Their impact on business performance. *Journal of Supply Chain Management, 38*(4), 11–21.

Kiron, D., Shockley, R., Kruschwitz, N., Finch, G., & Haydock, M. (2012). Analytics: The widening divide. *MIT Sloan Management Review, 53*(2), 1–22.

Lei, D., & Hitt, M. A. (1995). Strategic restructuring and outsourcing: The effect of mergers and acquisitions and LBOs on building firm skills and capabilities. *Journal of Management, 21*(5), 835–859.

Manuj, I., & Mentzer, J. T. (2008). Global supply chain risk management strategies. *International Journal of Physical Distribution and Logistics Management, 38*(3), 192–223.

Mason-Jones, R., Naylor, J. B., & Towill, D. (2000). Engineering in the leagile supply chain. *International Journal of Agile Management Systems, 2*(1), 54–61.

Melnyk, S. A., & Stanton, D. J. (2017). The customer-centric supply chain. *Supply Chain Management Review, 20*(12), 28–39.

Monczka, R., Handfield, R., Giunipero, L., & Patterson, J. (2009). *Purchasing and supply chain management.* Mason: Cengage Learning.

Mueller, J., Dagmar, A., Hautz, J., Hutter, K., Matzler, K., & Raich, M. (2011). Differences in corporate environmentalism: A comparative analysis of leading U.S. and German companies. *European Journal of International Management, 5*(2), 122–148.

Perlitz, M. (2004). *Internationales management* (5th ed.). Stuttgart: UTB.

Peter, M., & Rathgeber, P. (2017). Lieferketten der nächsten Generation. In C. Bode, R. Bogaschewsky, M. Eßig, R. Lasch, & W. Stölzle (Eds.), *Supply management research* (pp. 181–193). Wiesbaden: Springer.

Porter, M. E. (1994). The Role of location in competition. *Journal of the Economics of Business, 1*(1), 35–40.

Quinn, J. B., & Hilmer, F. G. (1994). Strategic outsourcing. *MIT Sloan Management Review, 35*(4), 43–55.

Radovilsky, Z., & Hegde, V. (2012). Trends in supply chain management job requirements: A longitudinal study. *Journal of Supply Chain and Operations Management, 10*(1), 168–181.

Razzaque, M. A., & Sheng, C. C. (1998). Outsourcing of logistics functions: A literature survey. *International Journal of Physical Distribution and Logistics Management, 28*(2), 89–107.

Rein, S. (2012). *The end of cheap China: Economic and cultural trends that will disrupt the world.* Hoboken: Wiley.

Robertson, R. (1998). Glokalisierung: Homogenität und Heterogenität in Raum und Zeit. In U. Beck (Ed.), *Perspektiven der Weltgesellschaft* (pp. 192–220). Frankfurt a. M.: Suhrkamp.

Schmid, S. (2013). *Strategien der Internationalisierung* (3rd ed.). München: de Gruyter.

Smith, M. E. (2003). Changing an organisation's culture: Correlates of success and failure. *Leadership & Organization Development Journal, 24*(5), 249–261.

Sheffi, Y., & Rice, J. B. (2005). A supply chain view of the resilient enterprise. *MIT Sloan Management Review, 47*(1), 41–48.

Standard Chartered Bank Global Research. (2015). *Global supply chains: New directions.* https://www.sc.com/BeyondBorders/wp-content/uploads/2015/05/2015-05-28-BeyondBorders-Report-Global-supply-chains-New-directions.pdf [17 September 2020].

Stevenson, M., & Spring, M. (2007). Flexibility from a supply chain perspective: Definition and review. *International Journal of Operations and Production Management, 27*(7), 685–713.

Tang, C. S. (2006). Perspectives in supply chain risk management. *International Journal of Production Economics, 103*(2), 451–488.

Van Weele, A. (2014). *Purchasing and supply chain management.* Hampshire: Cengage Learning EMEA.

Vietor, R. H. K., Rivkin, J. W., & Seminerio, J. (2008). The offshoring of America. *Harvard Business School Case, 708–030,* 1–23.

Vickery, S., Calantone, R., & Dröge, C. (1999). Supply chain flexibility: An empirical study. *Journal of Supply Chain Management, 35*(3), 16–24.

Wagner, S. M. (2009). Supplier traits for better customer firm innovation performance. *Industrial Marketing Management, 39,* 1139–1149.

Wagner, S. M., & Bode, C. (2006). An empirical investigation into supply chain vulnerability. *Journal of Purchasing and Supply Management, 12*(6), 301–312.

Wagner, S. M., & Eggert, A. (2016). Co-management of purchasing and marketing: Why, when and how. *Industrial Marketing Management, 52,* 27–36.

Williamson, J. (2012). *Growing supply chain disruption encourages re-shoring*. https://www.man-ufacturingdigital.com/people_skills/growing-supplychain-disruption-encourages-re-shoring [16 September 2020].

Ziemke, A., Stöckel, T., & Thomsen, L. (2016). *Produktion 4.0: neue Wege für die Automobilindustrie*. Pattensen: Media-Manufaktur.

Zsidisin, G. A. (2003). Managerial perceptions of supply risk. *Journal of Supply Chain Management, 39*(1), 14–25.

Zsidisin, G. A., & Wagner, S. M. (2010). Do perceptions become reality? The moderating role of supply chain resiliency on disruption occurrence. *Journal of Business Logistics, 31*(2), 1–20.

Establishing Local Business Units

Ludwig Martin

1 From Strategy to Local Presence

Companies aim to grow. International markets are natural areas for the expansions of companies and their products. The life of a business unit abroad can be differentiated into four main phases: the decision phase, the establishment phase, the operations phase, as well as the close-down or relinquish phase. While previous chapters have predominantly dealt with matters concerning the first phase, the second phase (establishment) is the focus of this contribution.

The first phase (decision phase) sets the foundation for the subsequent phases of the life of a business unit abroad. Market assessments as well as managerial and operational matters require consideration in order to derive a suitable approach for entering a market abroad. Engaging in a foreign market and expanding a company's footprint through its product or through a business presence entails careful consideration. Companies develop strategies towards sustaining their business as well as typically growing their business. The general growth patterns of companies vary. In the neoclassical economists' view, markets are about supply and demand. Similarly, companies go into markets with perceived demand for their products. However, other factors play a role too. The Uppsala Model (Johanson and Vahlne 1977) is an often referred to theoretical model for the internationalization process of firms. This model takes more than just supply and demand into consideration and looks at how firms develop their involvement in markets abroad. The Uppsala model addresses "organic growth" referring to market and firm knowledge as important determinants in an internationalization process. Johanson and Vahlne have

L. Martin (✉)
Pforzheim University, Pforzheim, Germany
e-mail: ludwig.martin@hs-pforzheim.de

L. Martin (ed.), *International Business Development*,
https://doi.org/10.1007/978-3-658-33221-1_9

developed their original model further (cf. Johanson and Vahlne 2009). The roles of networks and trust are included in this update; the base model is, however, not altered. Coattailing, often observed in project-based industries (Malhotra and Hinings 2010), is one form of using networks for internationalization. Malhotra and Hinings (2010) present a more differentiated model of internationalization. Their model considers the type of organization. They argue that not all types of organizations (mass production, disaggregated production, project-based) act in the same way on their path to internationalization. Born global companies may well have different development paths than many of the existing firms operating abroad. Here, the Uppsala Model may not fit well either. This shows the limitations of general models such as the Uppsala Model.

Yet, for most models, knowing the target market and its environment, or actors in its ecosystem (see Chapter "Ecosystem Evaluations in Business Development") is a significant factor in the successful establishment of business abroad. Hence, market assessments are part of the considerations for future growth of companies. Decisions are made for or against internationalization, or for or against specific target locations through the assessment of markets, the assessment of the potential of products and the company's own abilities and resources (confer Chapter "Assessing International Markets"). Such entries into markets abroad can take various forms, and an overall approach needs to be taken by companies—all depending on the targeted markets.

Approaches to entering foreign markets can be categorized into three main forms: Export of goods, contractual relations with third-parties, or (Foreign) Direct Investments (FDI). Exports will typically bind fewer resources than FDIs. However, the level of control with regards to the operations as well as the product itself may well be the opposite, e.g.: A pure export of a product does not allow the producer to determine the final customer or the use of the product; however, only few resources will be committed in such straightforward export activity. Conversely, the degree of control increases with the amount of investment.

Further variations exist within these three forms of entering foreign markets. Each approach needs to be assessed in terms of the market environment, host country regulations, existing networks, desired level of control of the product's final use and destination, and resources required to enter a market in its various modes. For instance, setting up an export contract with a local agent may be straightforward: The product gets produced in the home country, is shipped to the destination, taxes and customs are paid and a third party buys the product. This third party then takes over the process of selling the product, with or without further services attached, and independently from the originator of the product. In this case, the level of control of what the product will be used for will be fairly low, yet the required resources to enter a new market with that product are also low, as they are restricted to the shipment only. Each of the approaches hence needs to be

Table 1 Modes of entry

Export	Contractual relationships	FDI
• Direct	• Licencing	• Acquisition
• Agency	• Contracted manufacturing	• Brownfield
	• Franchising	• Greenfield

assessed on their suitability for a market entry and needs to consider the product itself. Table 1 lists the various modes of entry. Two further aspects have to be considered:

- Not every mode of entry, which might have worked well in one destination, will be the ideal mode of entry for all other destinations. This is often due to external factors, such as regulations in the country of choice.
- The modes of entry are not mutually exclusive. In reality, many of the modes of entry are difficult to distinguish from each other and/or are even hybrids of others; e.g. brownfield developments and acquisitions share many similarities, as an existing facility is acquired first in a brownfield development—however, typically without staff, management or processes.

The various modes of entry are briefly described here:

Direct export: The product is produced in a home market. Orders for the product are placed by customers abroad and the product is shipped to the customer. The company interacts directly with its customers.

Agency export: An agent abroad, typically a third party entity, is the interface for the customers in this market. The producer delivers its products to the agent, who handles all local matters abroad.

Licencing: The right to use or even produce a product is given to an entity abroad (licensee). The entity abroad pays an agreed amount for this licence to the licensor (originator of the product or patent). Often the licensee is given the right to sell or use the product under their own label.

Contracted manufacturing: An entity abroad is given a contract to produce / manufacture a product on behalf of the company. The originator of the product or an agent will retain the privilege to interact with customers. It is a form of outsourcing.

Franchising: A further grade of development of a licencing agreement. The franchisee (company abroad) will receive the rights to produce, use and sell the franchisor's product or patent. Further the franchisee will have to use a business model determined and supported by the franchisor. The original brand of the company is replicated abroad through the franchisee.

Acquisition: A company buys a company abroad. This is typically the case where similar products are already being produced in a market abroad by another company. Hence the production facilities as well as supply chain and sales channels are interesting to companies going international. Often staff is retained.

Brownfield investment: Facilities of a company abroad are acquired. The company acquiring such a facility is often interested in the property and facilities of the company abroad, allowing the company to change the existing facility to its needs or simply staff it and start its business activities.

Greenfield investment: An entire new facility is built up by a company entering the country. This is often literally done on a green field, built from scratch. After completion the company will staff the facility and start its business activities.

A further addition to such modes of entry to markets abroad is offshoring. However, this is less of a market entry with a product, but rather describes the circumstance when companies take part of their company to another country. This can be part of the production or the administration. The reasons for offshoring are typically cost saving considerations (e.g. lower wages in host country) or access to particular skill sets.

2   Considerations for Setting up a Local Presence

The mode of entry selected will determine the need for the type of a local presence. The form of such a presence can be driven by various factors, and these will differ in the same way the type of organization will differ. As some firms simply require a local office to coordinate their sales activities, others may build up entire production lines in a green field type of development. Despite the need for a local presence differing from case to case, some common considerations need to be made for the presence abroad:

- Management structures
- Relationship to main company and structuring of operations
- Staffing
- Financing operations abroad

2.1   Establishing Management Structures

Stemming from observations made in his studies, Perlmutter (1969) describes, in his early work on this topic, three strands of company approaches used by multinational companies (MNCs) in managing their subsidiaries abroad. These were ethnocentrism, geocentrism as well as polycentrism; labelled the EPG profiles of companies. Perlmutter (1969) identified these EPG profiles as mind-sets within the headquarters of MNCs. In a later addition (Wind et al. 1973) regiocentrism was added, and labelled the EPRG framework. This adjustment to the original model possibly mirrored some of the developments of the time. The basis for this work was the question of the evolutionary process companies go through as they develop into MNCs. Even recommendations on how to grow into regiocentric or geocentric MNCs—perceived to hold the potential to be more successful—were given (Perlmutter and Heenan 1974). The four profiles are:

Ethnocentric companies rely on home country nationals as key employees. They are seen as more capable, fit to do the job and reliable. The head office, with its culture and belief system, is in charge.

Polycentric companies believe that each country should be run by a national of that country. A high level of confidence that the host country nationals will fit best to their environment and hence will be most profitable overall is the paradigm here.

Regiocentric companies are structured around regions (multiple countries) and teams to run these regions may be composed of staff with different nationalities, yet working on greater regional markets. This approach can be found in companies who service various (close by) markets from one regional hub.

Geocentric companies are characterized through a global approach. Neither the headquarters nor a subsidiary are seen as superior to others. Joint management of the global efforts is the aim of these companies. Staff and executives may come from any country; the mindset is global.

While at an early stage the EPRG model was used to analyse and label companies as well as aiming at growing them into regiocentric or even geocentric MNCs, the later use of the EPRG somehow changed. The recognition that growing into a regiocentric or geocentric MNC might not be advantageous to all types of companies might have emerged. The strength of the EPRG framework is within its descriptive character of the various set-ups. The basic observation of these four types of companies and which approach shapes these companies is of great importance to international management scholars. At the time when developing a market entry strategy, the insights into the different profiles of companies can assist in shaping suitable approaches. Furthermore, the understanding of the different profiles of companies can also be helpful for setting up structures when entering a market.

The differentiation on such a theoretical level can best be understood when including the principal-agent dilemma in this context. Essays of Jensen and Meckling (1976) and Ross (1973) on the theory of principal-agent relations laid the base for the Agency Theory (Eisenhardt 1989). In short, this theory describes the imbalance between principal (e.g. main company) and its agent (e.g. subsidiary or import agent) in terms of knowledge in the field. Applied to internationalization, this imbalance can be seen as an advantage to the agent. The advantage of having more (market) insights can be used by the agent, which in turn might not be congruent with the liking or aim of the principal. However, principals, or main companies, are fully aware of this dilemma and put counter-measures in place (which parallel the mindset in ethnocentric MNCs). These may include organizational-structural decisions, as well as control measures for operations abroad. It must be noted that an imbalance of (market) knowledge towards the agent may well be advantageous to the entire company; and managers of the main company may be well advised to take advantage of this, too (which parallels the mindset in polycentric

MNCs). Not all imbalance is exploited by the agent to the disadvantage of the main company. However, the art of structuring the development of an international presence is in balancing various considerations and considering future developments, too. While the EPRG Model may serve as a theoretical foundation for understanding different organizational structures, the principal-agent model may serve well to better understand the implications of the different options. Overall hybrid organizational designs, in which the EPRG approaches are intelligently combined, may be good examples for managing MNCs and can be observed in companies (Perlmutter 1996); for instance, an ethnocentric financial management unit paired with a geocentric product development unit may be beneficial to companies.

2.2   Relation to Main Company and Structuring Operations

Companies are well advised to keep in mind the financial and statutory aspects of the outcome of any organizational design additional to organizational considerations. The legal relationship of the main company and the operation abroad needs good consideration. The legal relationship is of importance in many ways. Control, involvement in decision making, use of resources and many more matters need to be legally clarified to shape the relationship between main company and the operation abroad. The type of relationship is of particular importance for tax matters of firms too, as taxation of the profits of companies are highly dependent on the place of value-adding. Further, the flow of capital as well as risk allocation are to be considered. Generally, some basic constructs for companies acting on an international level can be depicted, see Fig. 1.

The overall international business may be handled by one of the existing departments of a company. Such a set-up is labelled Type A in Fig. 1. This type of organizational structure is closely linked to an ethnocentric approach. The international ventures have an appendix-like relationship to the main company, as product development, financial control, and production will often be concentrated at the main company level. With the entry of the company into another market, in some cases a holding company may be used to buffer and to manage the actual international exposure.

Organizational structures such as Type B (Fig. 1) offer more independence for the international ventures. The main company, for its home market, as well as the international venture maintain full organizational structures with all required divisions. Ideally, the efforts in the similar divisions abroad and at home are managed closely to avoid duplication of work; however, a degree of independence is designed into such a set-up. A company with such a structure may show traces of polycentricism—depending on the control measures put in place by the head office.

Many companies are structured around their products or product ranges (Type C in Fig. 1). The product groups are the common denominator for all global activities. The structure of such companies is set around the product first and less so around the markets. The importance of the product and its originator, typically situated at the main

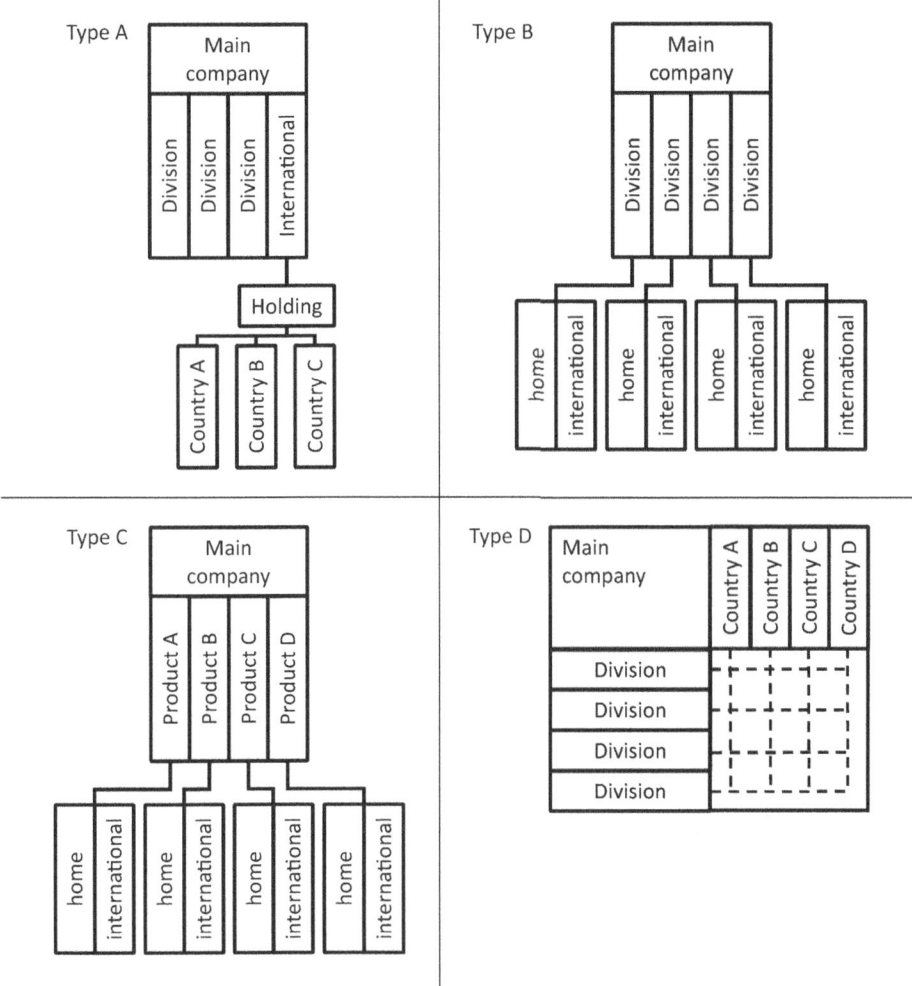

Fig. 1 Typology on structuring international companies

company, is high in this integrated organizational structure. The product centre takes control of the success of the product worldwide and will coordinate all efforts; yet relying on the international venture to play their part—somehow resembling a polycentric approach too.

A matrix structure, compare Type D in Fig. 1, can often be found. Cross-communication from particular divisions to countries and vice versa is common. A truly joint effort with low hierarchies is the aim in such structures. The work of the ventures in other countries as well as the work of the divisions are set in this 2-dimentional matrix, allowing for the company and their various parts to interact freely and use resources as required. A major drawback of such a structure is, however, the lack of the overall control of the efforts; communication among all parties becomes key to the success of companies structured in such a manner. Such structures may be a suitable setting for a truly geocentric company. Additionally, it is possible to add a third dimension (product) in such structures; management thereof, however, becomes even more cumbersome and a strong company culture, lived by all, is essential for the success of companies structured in such a manner.

Many other constellations on how the international business is encapsulated and embedded in a company's existing structure are possible. The shown types of structures are, however, commonly found. The art of managing such operations abroad successfully are, however, not within the formal structure, but more so in the lines of control and the establishment of communication channels. Often the directors of main companies are also in the steering committee or board of directors of the companies abroad. The bond between individual business units and also the control and common strategic outlook are set to be in place through these person-based mechanisms. At the main company level the decision on who to entrust with the oversight of the units abroad is a critical decision to be made. Often the heads of the international division have to fill the roles of directors of the companies abroad; the Chief Executive Officer or Managing Director may even take on this role in companies where internationalization is considered to be a top priority.

2.3   Staffing

Type A structures with international subsidiaries are common in the first step of establishing an international presence. Establishment and oversight over such units appears to be straightforward. However, no matter which type of structure is followed, the matter of staffing newly established business units abroad is a key question. Generally, two options of appointing staff exist:

- Home company sends staff to international subsidiary (expatriate)
- Home company appoints host country staff to international subsidiary (local)

The former option may also include the sub-option to send a third-party national, neither from the home country nor from the host country, to such a post. This may be particularly interesting for MNCs who already have a wide base of experienced staff ready to go elsewhere. Furthermore, the expected duration for the need for such staff needs to be assessed (see Fig. 2).

The selection for the best suited option is bound to many factors. The overall strategic outlook and own perception of the main company (see EPRG Model) is an important underlying factor for the appointment. Many authors on this topic cite the importance

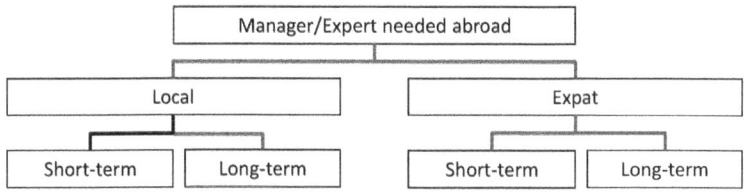

Fig. 2 Options on filling posts abroad

of knowledge transfer and the opportunities to enhance this through the correct staffing (e.g. Szulanski 1996). Language has been identified by some scholars as a key ingredient for knowledge transfer. Hence, staff with a particular command of a common language appears to be advantageous to foster knowledge transfer. However, the opposite can be the case too: when staff use their own language competence as gatekeepers for communication between main company and subsidiary (Welch and Welch 2008); playing out the principal-agency dilemma.

A further factor to consider is the cost of employment. Depending on the direction of placing expatriates, for staff sent to foreign country, a premium is often added to the staffing costs. The salary level of expatriates is often benchmarked towards the purchasing power of the employee's salary at home (Bonache and Zárraga-Oberty 2017). When high income countries send staff abroad to low or middle income countries, the wage level of the high income country is typically used as the benchmark for expatriates, nevertheless, a perceived salary drop may not be accepted by staff being sent abroad. Additionally, an allowance for expatriates may be added. In cases where companies from low/middle income countries send staff to high income countries, the direct cost of appointing an expatriate vs appointing a staff member from the host country may balance out. The additional benefits to expatriate staff, such as flights to the home country, family programmes and other costs, need to be added where applicable. This can at times increase the normal salary of an employee by a factor of as high as 2 to 3 (Black and Gregersen 1999); sending staff abroad is expensive and hence needs careful consideration. A host country-based salary for expatriates, remunerating the actual performance and not origin may hold better value (McNulty 2016).

Using local or rather host country nationals (HCN) or expatriating staff abroad has both its advantages and disadvantages; some of these advantages and disadvantages are in direct negative correlation. Using local staff in establishing a presence abroad has the main advantage that staff from the country abroad will not struggle with cultural differences in the host country. The cultural fit of any employee is an often-cited cause for a lack of performance of ventures abroad and their managers (Davies et al. 2019). HCN will not have this difficulty. However, cultural distance of HCNs to the main company has been found to be an important factor when judging the performance of subsidiaries abroad (Colakoglu and Caligiuri 2008). This is closely linked to the often mentioned need to transfer knowledge across the globe; cultural distance appears to reduce the rate or quality of such knowledge transfer. HCN will have their own network in the local industry; combining previous work experience and local networks to the benefit of the new employer. In particular, in cases where a company aims to bring new products or services to a market, a good knowledge and understanding of the local market may be beneficial. The employment of HCNs may enhance the local acceptance of companies entering new markets too.

However, the appointment of expatriates may hold other advantages. Staff who has been employed at the company before will bring the company culture into the new venture abroad; this is of particular interest where companies aim to attain a common company culture globally. In these cases the expatriate's role is perceived to be the mentor for local staff to develop into true employees of the company. Possibly more importantly the appointment of an expatriate further has the advantage of already having an established network within the company. Knowing the who-is-who at the head office can assist a new venture abroad in reducing the burden of establishing something new. The expat is trusted by the head office and the inner workings of the head office are known to the expat. Along with this a commonly cited reason to appoint an expat for a venture abroad is the familiarity with the product or service rendered by the firm. A new employee and new staff from abroad, will have to first undergo inductions and a learning curve with regards to company and products. An overview of some main considerations is given in Table 2.

There are, however, further external factors to consider that may or may not guide the company in the appointment of staff abroad: The availability of staff. In many circumstances staff, and in particular skilled staff, are difficult to find. This is true for internal expat appointments, as well as finding staff abroad. Difference in education levels, lack of university graduates and a booming home economy with a small pool of labour may force a company to appoint staff, which at times does not appear to be the ideal solution.

Any of these options have another layer too: The duration of such an appointment. When setting up operations abroad an approach might be to only send experts for short stays abroad, assisting the operations in the host country to set-up and ramp up the operations. Technical expertise may only be required at the beginning when for

Table 2 Considerations on host country national vs expatriate

Host country national	Expatriate
• Often lower overall cost of employment	• Often higher cost of employment
• Existing host country network	• Cultural proximity to main company
• Cultural proximity to host country/market	• Existing network within company
• Cultural distance to main company	• (Product) knowledge and its transfer to host market
• Local acceptance of company	• Cultural distance to host country/staff

instance installing machinery and setting up assembly lines. Short-term staff appointed for this task may be used to transfer knowledge to local staff in the host country; aiming at empowering the latter in taking over the operations. In some instances, however, and often in companies with more ethnocentric views, managers are sent abroad on a long-term basis. Using the deep knowledge of (main) company culture, processes and thinking is often cited here as the main reason to appoint an expat on a long-term basis. Long-term is understood as durations between 2 and 5 years of working and residing abroad.

The Organization of Economic Co-operation and Development (OECD) and its member states have further developed agreements and taxation standards for foreign nationals working abroad in order to avoid double taxation on their income. The place of residence, source of the income (host company vs. main company) and duration of stay are important determinants for taxation. The "183 days per year" rule is often used to determine the tax base for staff. Below 183 days per year working abroad and not formally residing there is considered a short-term assignment; the tax base is often deemed to be abroad with assignments longer than 183 days in a tax year. It must be noted that, just as for company tax, much effort is currently underway by a host of international organizations to simplify and align different systems globally in the area of taxation. Double tax agreements between countries may further determine the tax base of individuals, just as it is the case for companies. Hence the duration and type of expatriate appointment has direct implications for the individuals. Some thorough considerations and investigations on newest rules, regulations as well as bi-lateral agreements are important in order to avoid some of the common traps here.

Lastly, when employing expatriates abroad, the question of repatriation is often overlooked. Two matters need close consideration prior to sending staff abroad: Firstly, the potential expectations of expatriates at the time of their return "home" might have; secondly, salary levels for returning expatriates. In many industry sectors expatriation appointments are seen as a step up on the career ladder. Returning expatriates have the expectations that upon their return they will be in a more advanced position compared to the time they have left home. However, the reality shows that such advanced positions may not be available at the time of their return, which may translate into well-trained and experienced returning expatriates resigning due to a lack of growth opportunities within the company and feeling demoted (Black and Gregersen 1999; Goodman 2019). The other factor to consider is the expected remuneration after returning to the main company. The premiums paid by companies to send expatriates away often allows them to live at a higher living standard abroad than what they are accustomed to at home. This premium is, however, taken away again upon their return, and returning expatriates often return back to a similar remuneration level as prior to their posting. This perceived step back has long been a reason for some conflicts within a company with returning expatriates (Black and Gregersen 1999).

2.4   Financial Management of Operations Abroad

The legal structure of setting up a presence abroad will determine many aspects of its existence. This is also true for financing such operations. Initial capital to start the operations abroad is required in many cases and the task in capitalizing such an operation cannot be underestimated. As with any investment the rate of returns will be considered and will be part of prior phases of taking a company or product abroad. The required level of capitalization depends on the nature of business and required presence abroad. Typically, companies are formed in the host country to work as an independent entity in this country; initial capital is required. While the formal capital required in order to be registered in a respective company register varies from host country to host country and with the form of legal entity to be formed, the actual investment, often labelled the foreign direct investment, shall be the focus here.

A brief look at dealing with subsidiaries abroad in terms of accounting systems and standards is in order. Various laws are passed by such countries regulating business for countries and its governments to maintain an overview and order within their economic sector. Laws and regulations on accounting standards are part of this. While existing accounting rules are often similar when comparing countries, differences in country-specific interpretations and applications of set rules may exist. Further obligations on business owners stemming from regulations regulating businesses differ. Accounting rules enable shareholders to compare and judge investments on equal terms. The balance sheet and profit-loss calculations can be kept current and accurate through the efforts of accounting officers of companies. A more global approach is, however, needed when engaging on international markets and owning subsidiaries abroad. Differences in accounting rules in different countries can lead to differences in balance sheets, in particular inter alia due to currency exchange rates. For this reason many governments aim to adopt and change their own laws and regulations to be in line with international standards. The International Finance Reporting Standard (IFRS) is the leading standard here (cf. Kirsch 2017).

Financing operations abroad needs to be carefully planned. Companies typically have a set of priorities which solid financial management needs to aim at. These priorities may be:

- Profitability, own investments need to pay off.
- Liquidity, ability to pay ongoing operations.
- Risk optimization, taking manageable risks and avoiding others.

These priorities are valid for the main company as well as for subsidiaries. And a difference in the host country management to the main company's management may be experienced when interpreting these priorities. Factors influencing these interpretations on how to financially manage an operation abroad can be distinguished between internal and external factors:

Internal factors are factors from within the company. This may at a first level be the main company or the subsidiary abroad. Factors include the organizational design and willingness to give a subsidiary financial independence, risk sharing agreements across countries as well as requirements by the main company on forwarding profits to the main company.

External factors are factors beyond the immediate control of the main company or subsidiary abroad. These include *inter alia*: country risks, currency exchange rates (FX) and fluctuations, inflation levels, and taxation of profits.

The task for ideal financial management of operations abroad coupled with the management of the global firm is to balance all considerations. Some companies strive to use the same template for any new operation abroad as used before elsewhere. This helps in setting up a standard system across all subsidiaries, seamlessly connecting to the system of the main company. Other companies act more opportunistically and try to find the best fit for the situation in the new host country itself. When growing operations abroad, the main company will then have to work in an intelligent manner with differently structured entities abroad.

2.4.1 Capitalization of operations abroad

The capital required to set-up companies may stem from own resources (equity) or may be borrowed capital (debt). The ratio of debt to equity within a company is an important financial indicator. Many companies aim to leverage the gains made through borrowed capital through a smart use of their own capital. Further the debt-equity ratio is simple to employ when looking at country risks and investments. Country risks may be of a political, economic, social, technical, environmental or legal (PESTEL) nature. Of particular interest in terms of capital are typically still political, economic and legal risks. Social as well as environmental risks are, however, becoming more and more dominant factors to consider when entering markets abroad (see also Chap. 12). Nationalization of assets through governments, political instability, fast economic downturn and currency exchange fluctuations, and further restrictions on transfers of funds (profits) of subsidiaries to the main company are typical country risks considered here. To invest own capital in risky host countries may not be advisable, hence a high debt-equity ratio may be a desired state for a subsidiary abroad. Where country risks are regarded low a lower debt-equity ratio might be in order; it may be advisable to only invest minimal equity. The use of debt finance may be interesting in countries with a country risk deemed to be low, depending on the financial leverage potentially achievable. Figure 3 indicates a broad band of desirable options. Specific considerations regarding country, company and product, however, need to be added before deciding on a final investment strategy. It must further be considered that finance institutions lending to companies will aim to reduce their exposure too. To achieve this, the main companies need to provide sureties to the lender in many cases. Subsidiaries may not be deemed credit worthy when lenders evaluate them on their own. Subsidiaries with low equity levels will hence struggle to borrow capital on their own—particularly in high risk environments.

Fig. 3 Structuring capital
investment considering country
risk

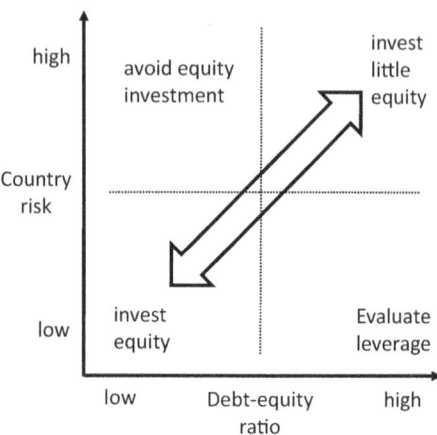

Table 3 Sources of financing for subsidiary abroad

	Internal	External
Main company	• Transfer of funds to subsidiary (available surplus / cash flow) as equity • Loan to subsidiary (interest bearing) • Cross-transfer of surplus of other subsidiaries within group	• Transfer of funds (main company raising debt)
Subsidiary	From within (cash flow)	• Issuing of shares • Additional shareholder/Joint Venture • Debt finance

When companies are seen in their entirety (main company and subsidiaries) a different view is prevalent in comparison to a subsidiary view only. Local differences in the capital markets, currency exchange effects and (tax) legal differences in home and host country need to be assessed. Generally, financing of operations abroad can be managed through internal sources or external sources (see Table 3). Internal sources may be from within the main company or its affiliates/subsidiaries in the wider group of companies, or from within the subsidiary itself.

The basic options for internal financing are: Transfer of funds from main company to the subsidiary. The main company may use available financial resources out of its cash flow and transfer these to the subsidiary. This may be as cash injection increasing equity, or it may be transferred on a loan basis (interest bearing). In cases where a group of companies exists, the group might take financial surpluses from within out of the cash flow from one subsidiary to assist another. Subsidiaries may further be in the position to finance their own operation out of their own cash flow—this is likely not the case at early stages of their existence.

External financing of operations abroad can be based on debt made by the main company (often debt raised in the home market and currency), as well as raising debt by the subsidiary in the host country, based on the currency of the host market. Both sources of financing will bear interest. Further options on external financing are the issue of shares of the subsidiary, or taking on additional shareholders, also in the form of Joint Ventures. The latter two options, however, may have a direct impact on the sovereignty of the main company or its management abroad as new shareholders will gain rights to steer the operations of the subsidiary.

The flow of funds globally is regulated by many national rules set by central banks. Hence a close look at rules of perspective host countries on transferring funds is advisable. Some countries require the proof of business licences or similar documentation for the transfer of funds; this is partially due to good governance programmes with regards to money laundering and/or corruption. This is an additional step in mastering setting up a presence abroad.

2.4.2 FX Fluctuation—Hedging Cash-Flow

Of particular interest in companies working across national borders and across currencies are the impacts of currency exchange fluctuations, a risk part of the transaction exposures. This is particularly important and clear when looking at the case of subsidiaries set up for the purpose of acting as sales agents in a host country. The main company will send its products to the subsidiary, who in turn sells these to the host country's market. Two main scenarios are possible here.

- Scenario A: The main company will invoice the subsidiary in its home currency (HC) and the subsidiary will sell in the foreign currency (FC).
- Scenario B: The main company will invoice the subsidiary in FC and the subsidiary will sell the product in FC.

In scenario A the risks related to currency exchange is with the subsidiary abroad. In scenario B the currency exchange risk is with the main company—it produced initially in HC but receives FC. This transaction exposure can be lowered by hedging through forwards or the purchase of options. The selection of the best instrument is highly dependent on the currencies and the fluctuation of exchange rates themselves. A currency exchange rate set in the future can be fixed today through forwards. This enables the main company to lower its transaction exposure, in particular when a drop in exchange rate is expected. However, these financial instruments also come at a cost. Direct costs, such as fees, as well as opportunity costs are fairly simple to determine. Further, in case of forwards, an asymmetric loss or non-gain on an upside development of the currency can be calculated too.

2.4.3 Securing Financial Base—Hedging Investments

Investment in subsidiaries abroad brings an economic exposure to the main company. In cases of greenfield or brownfield investments projects are often financed by the main company with the aim to receive returns. If the financing of the investment has been secured in HC, the returns are to be expected in HC too. Should, however, the exchange rate of the FC drop, this would imply that a subsidiary may not be able to achieve the expected return in HC anymore, despite the FC returns being stable. The subsidiary may have to increase its returns to make up for the lack of currency performance. Hence companies are advised to carefully evaluate the various options in currency use. For instance, debt financing in FC of parts or whole operations abroad lowers such economic exposure.

When investments abroad are due, a hedging strategy based on currency swaps can bear benefits too. Companies engage in currency swaps out of two reasons: lowering exchange rate exposure and aiming at better loan terms (i.e. lower interest rate). The basic concept of a currency swap is that two companies in two different countries loan each other funds for investments in the respective target country.

When companies invest abroad and seek a loan from a local bank there, a risk premium is often levied by the banks of the (target) country. This is partially due to a lack of track record of new companies in the host country. However, such risk premiums are not charged from local. Hence if a constellation can be found in which two companies seek to invest in the other country, each company can raise the loan at home and lend this to the new-entrant. Both parties can hence experience savings in interest payments. Further exchange rate fluctuations are less relevant since the repayment of a loan is based on terms in the host country, and therefore the profits of an investment are basically uncoupled from exchange rate fluctuations. Financial institutions, in particular banks acting globally, often act as brokers and intermediaries in such hedging efforts.

At the end of the agreement's term the initial loan amounts are swapped back again and both companies will be able to enjoy their investments abroad—financed using lower rates. A simplified illustration of such a hedging scenario using a currency swap is shown in Fig. 4.

3 Summary

Going abroad is a huge step for many companies in their evolution. The first steps are taken in making the final decision to take the leap through concise planning and assessments of the new targeted market as well as the validation of their own product's properties and advantages. The actual setting up of supply chains as well as marketing channels will be based on the initial considerations. The actual establishing of local business units or subsidiaries, however, requires further considerations.

The form of local presence can take various shapes. Depending on the required level of engagement in a host country, the market outlook, the product of the company,

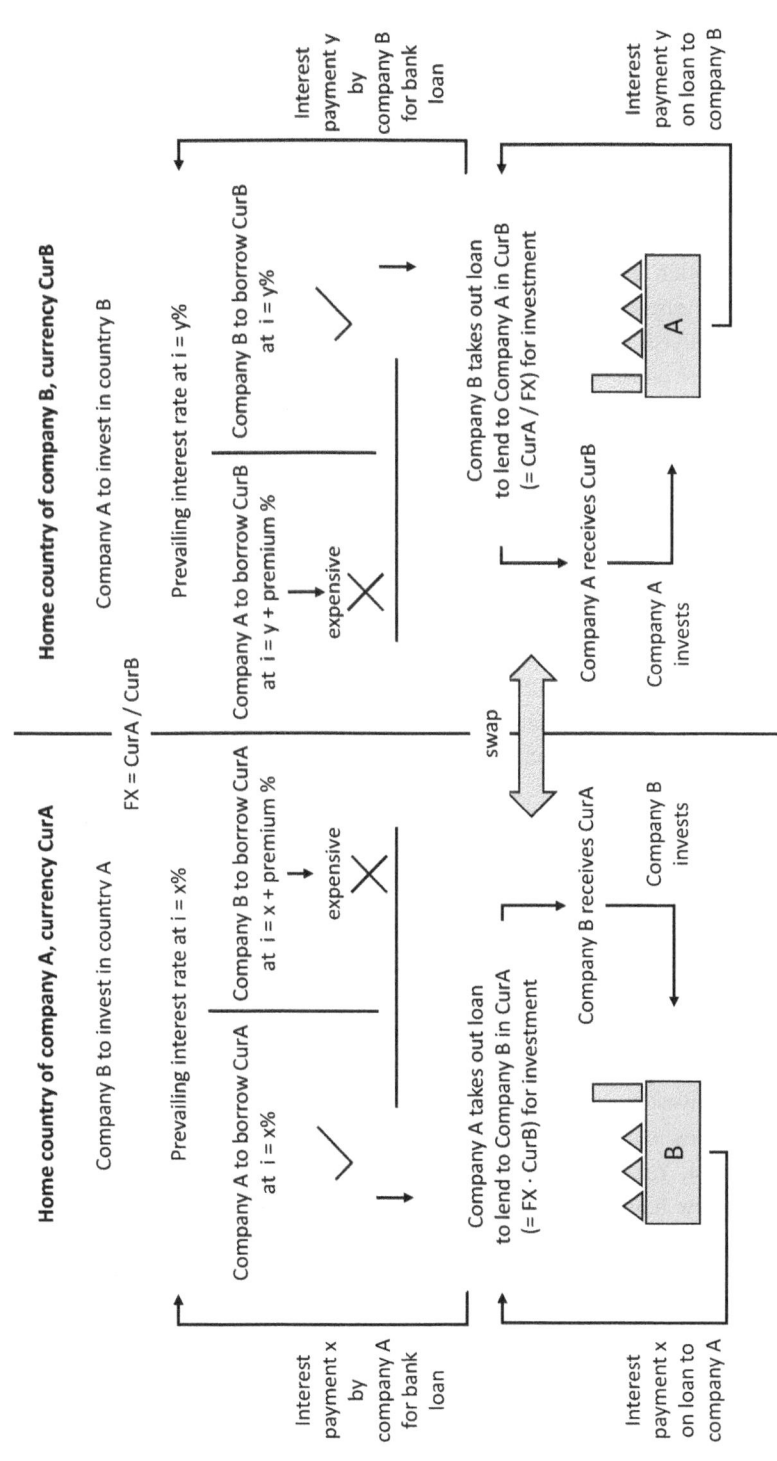

Fig. 4 Currency swap—simplified model

technical requirements as well as value chains within the company, investments in host countries can range from simple sales outlets to full new production facilities. However, some common considerations need to be made at the start of any of these developments.

Set in the overall strategy and outlook of companies the organizational structure of a new subsidiary needs to be established. Various options exist, and are often closely linked to the company culture and own perception. While it is possible to clearly differentiate between theoretical models of company designs as well as formal structures; hybrid solutions often exist too. Companies with a structure modelled around their products, might be structured ethnocentrically in one division yet follow a geocentric approach in other divisions. Companies often work opportunistically and assess the current needs and future outlooks to find suitable solutions.

Companies deal with staffing of new subsidiaries abroad in the same manner. While in many cases a particular pattern is to be followed—stemming from the overall company strategy—other options in filling key management or technical posts abroad open up and may be considered too. Generally, staff may be host country nationals or expatriates. The nature of the job to be done abroad, the expected duration thereof, the availability of staff are key determinants on the selection of the best option. In order to turn the appointment of staff into a success for the company, the human traits of the individuals need to be considered too. This does not only include the need for a good command of the host country language, but also cultural awareness of an appointee if coming from abroad. Similarly a host country national being appointed by a foreign national company will require the ability to bridge the often different approaches to managerial or technical issues arising.

Lastly the financial component of going abroad needs to be looked at. Where large initial investments are due, it is advisable to carefully investigate economic factors of the host country. Initial PESTEL analysis done may provide good first insights that have to be further deepened before committing capital to projects abroad. Where companies leave their own currency unions, transaction exposure needs to be managed. Exporting goods to a subsidiary and expecting payments by this subsidiary in one's own home currency may be short lived, if the subsidiary's foreign currency declines. Financial tools such as hedging and the use of financial options can lower such exposure.

Foreign direct investment in the form of bricks-and-mortar is welcomed by any country; however, hurdles in setting up companies abroad, from legal matters to finance control measures, exist. Yet companies around the world expand their operations, looking for markets and new homes for the products and services. Here only a snap-shot of all aspects to consider when setting up shop abroad could be discussed. The first considerations on markets, opportunities, own strengths and weaknesses, uncertainties and determinations will guide the establishment of local business units from the beginning in a practical application. Setting up a local business unit abroad may well be compared to a new entrepreneurial venture—ready for a steep learning curve.

Case study: Small and agile

QuantumHeights GmbH is a small firm from Germany. Its special interest is in African markets, this is partially due to the personal backgrounds of its directors. The company offers services in three broad portfolios: project development, environment, and research. As a small firm it maintains business units abroad: Nigeria, Mozambique and Ruanda.

A potential project was identified in Mozambique in 2015 through a network of business people as well as trade and industry representatives. A booming town with a small airport showed potential for the development of a hotel in close proximity to the airport, confirmed by an initial desktop study. QuantumHeights GmbH with its limited resources firstly established a relationship with business people in Mozambique. A young female Mozambican professional was hired to become the country representative of QuantumHeights GmbH in Mozambique; she had been identified through the wider network of one of the directors of QuantumHeights GmbH. A company was registered in Moçambique to ensure that QuantumHeights GmbH had a legal footprint in the host country as well as using this company as a buffer for any risk exposure stemming from the new venture there. Since there was no need for a company owned facility itself, the company rented an office space and post box in a services co-working space in the centre of Maputo.

An international team, partly sitting in Germany, Portugal and Mozambique was assembled for the forthcoming hotel development project. The work of the team was led through German staff in Germany, with visits to Mozambique, and the team was managed through online based communication, using standard (document sharing) platforms such as Dropbox, Skype, etc. Additional resources required in Moçambique were not hired. Individual sub-contract agreements were drawn up, mostly with a profit-sharing agreement in lieu of regular payments. This enabled QuantumHeights GmbH to use highly skilled local resources with relevant local knowledge and to save on costs for the development of the project since salary levels in the host country are lower than in Germany.

The establishment of the subsidiary in the host country was fairly simple, requiring the assistance of a local attorney. However, the initial capitalization of the subsidiary was more difficult since any transfer of funds to the host country required clearance by its national reserve bank. However, the reserve bank requires particular business permits, which are issued by district officials and only if a clear business objective can be proven to these officials. In case of project development the business project is, however, the output of the project, and hence delays in capitalization were experienced.

QuantumHeights GmbH still maintains its subsidiary in Mozambique and the local representative is still active in searching for new opportunities locally. The approach to this market is based on the established network, finding opportunities for further business. Due to its small structure it prides itself with its fast response to market needs, maintaining agility in its host countries, and low overhead costs. ◄

Exercise A

A Dutch company manufactures rotor blades for windmills. A market assessment has determined that Latin America will be a new frontier for the wind energy industry. The company thus decides to enter this market through export, supported by a local sales office and service workshop in Santiago de Chile.

Compile lists of advantages and disadvantages for using Dutch expatriates vs. local staff for the positions of Regional Manager (Latin America) and Technical Director (Latin America). Quantify costs where possible.

Exercise B

A German company produces concrete mixers. It has a subsidiary in India. Apart from producing the mixers in Germany, the mixers for some Asian markets are assembled in India and sold from there. The parts for the mixers assembled in India are shipped to India from Germany, and invoiced to the Indian subsidiary in EURO. The main markets served from India are: India (70% of machines sold), Malaysia (20% of machines sold) and Indonesia (10% of machines sold). Agency agreements are used for the Malaysian and Indonesian markets.

Discuss the impact of the fluctuation of currency exchange rates on the total result for the German company. How does it impact the Indian subsidiary? Also look at historical developments of the exchange rates.

Further: What would you recommend to the Indian company with regards to the currency used for their sales in Malaysia and Indonesia?

References

Black, J. S., & Gregersen, H. B. (1999). The right way to manage expats. *Harvard Business Review, 77*(2), 52–62.

Bonache, J., & Zárraga-Oberty, C. (2017). The traditional approach to compensating global mobility: Criticisms and alternatives. *The International Journal of Human Resource Management, 28*(1), 149–169.

Colakoglu, S., & Caligiuri, P. (2008). Cultural distance, expatriate staffing and subsidiary performance: The case of US subsidiaries of multinational corporations. *The International Journal of Human Resource Management, 19*(2), 223–239.

Davies, S. E., Stoermer, S., & Froese, F. J. (2019). When the going gets tough: The influence of expatriate resilience and perceived organizational inclusion climate on work adjustment and turnover intentions. *The International Journal of Human Resource Management, 30*(8), 1393–1417.

Eisenhardt, K. M. (1989). Agency theory: An assessment and review. *Academy of Management Review, 14*(1), 57–74.

Goodman, N. R. (2019). Expat Exodus. *Talent Development, 73*(11), 50–55.

Jensen, M. C., & Meckling, W. H. (1976). Theory of the firm: Managerial behavior, agency costs and ownership structure. *Journal of Financial Economics, 3*(4), 305–360.

Johanson, J., & Vahlne, J.-E. (1977). The internationalization process of the firm – A model of knowledge development and increasing foreign market commitments. *Journal of International Business Studies, 8*, 23–32.

Johanson, J., & Vahlne, J.-E. (2009). The Uppsala internationalization process model revisited: From liability of foreignness to liability of outsidership. *Journal of International Business Studies, 40*(9), 1411–1431.

Kirsch, H. (2017). *Einführung in die internationale Rechnungslegung nach IFRS* (11th ed.). Herne: NWB.

Malhotra, N., & Hinings, C. R. (2010). An organizational model for understanding internationalization processes. *Journal of International Business Studies, 41*, 330–349.

McNulty, Y. (2016). Why expatriate compensation will change how we think about global talent management. In Y. Guo, H. G. Rammal, & P. J. Dowling (Eds.), *Global talent management and staffing in MNEs* (pp. 125–150). Bingley: Emerald.

Perlmutter, H. V. (1969). The tortuous evolution of the multinational corporation. *Columbia Journal of World Business, 4*(1), 9–18.

Perlmutter, H. V., & Heenan, D. A. (1974). How multinational should your top managers be? *Harvard Business Review, 52*(6), 121–132.

Ross, S. A. (1973). The economic theory of agency: The principal's problem. *American Economic Review, 63*(2), 134–139.

Szulanski, G. (1996). Exploring internal stickiness: Impediments to the transfer of best practice within the firm. *Strategic Management Journal, 17*(2), 27–43.

Welch, D. E., & Welch, L. S. (2008). The importance of language in international knowledge transfer. *Management International Review, 48*(3), 339–360.

Wind, Y., Douglas, S. P., & Perlmutter, H. V. (1973). Guidelines for developing international marketing strategies. *Journal of Marketing, 37*(2), 12–23.

B-To-B Sales Approaches

Hector Gomez Macfarland

1 B-To-B Sales Overview

B-to-B sales is one of the main concepts that needs to be reviewed in order to find suitable approaches to entering new markets. B-to-B sales is defined as the process that one business, the *supplier*, follows to provide an *industrial product*, to another business, the *customer*, in exchange for money, the product price. The types of industrial products are:

- materials (raw),
- parts or components,
- subassemblies,
- capital items/assets such as equipment/installations, buildings, sophisticated software.
- supply items such as paints, soaps, oils and greases, pencils, stationery, and paper, as well as
- services like accounting, legal, and marketing research and others.

The industrial products can be classified by the level of customer involvement in the buying process. There are two levels of involvement, High and Low:

- High Involvement Products are those products that represent high risk/high price for the customer, are mission-critical for the customer's core business, and are complex and sometimes hard to understand

H. Gomez Macfarland (✉)
Huston Tillotson University, Austin, TX, USA
e-mail: hgmacfarland@htu.edu

L. Martin (ed.), *International Business Development*,
https://doi.org/10.1007/978-3-658-33221-1_10

- Low Involvement Products are those products whose purchase do not represent a risk, are of low price, are non-mission critical, and are very simple to understand.

Furthermore, there are different types of customers, who have different purchasing orientations and purchasing practices. Business customers are generally classified as follows:

- for profit organisations, including:
  original equipment manufacturers (OEMs),
  users: manufacturing firms (of consumer or industrial products) and service firms,
  business distributors, or dealers;
- government customers: such as the department of telecommunication, defence, and others;
- public and private institutions such as hospitals, schools, and universities;
- other non-profit organisations.

Regardless of the country the supplier is selling his product in, there should always be an exchange of value between the supplier and the customer (Kotler et al. 2016; Zauner et al. 2015), where the value from the customer's perspective, the customer perceived value (CPV), is the positive difference between the customer's perception of the benefits that product provides after trying it, which must be equal to or larger than the expectations generated by the benefits promised by the supplier, and the perceived cost of getting the product, usually the price that was paid for it. The value from the supplier's perspective is the relationship with the customer and the stream of revenues/profits that come from it.

When the customer perceives value, the customer's behavioural outcomes, such as purchase intention and satisfaction with the supplier and his product, will be impacted positively, such as more purchases, as suggested by Eggert and Ulaga (2002). The conceptual model showing CPV is shown in Fig. 1.

The CPV can further be represented with the following mathematical model (1):

$$\text{Value (CPV)} = \text{Perceived Benefits (b)} - \text{Cost (c)} \qquad (1)$$

There are different types of benefits that a customer usually expects when purchasing a product, proposed by Walker (2012) and shown in Table 1, that can be considered when a CPV analysis is done.

The CPV model suggests that if a sales executive overpromises and underdelivers (Expectation > Perceptions) in order to get a sale, there will not be any perceived value. Therefore, the following sales will be difficult to get from the same customer, even if it is another product. A successful relationship will not be created with that customer.

On the contrary, if a sales executive manages the prospect's expectations correctly, communicates the right product value proposition concerning the price offered, and the customer perceives more benefits than expected (less promised and overdeliver) customer trust will be gained. Customer trust is the condition that exists when the customer

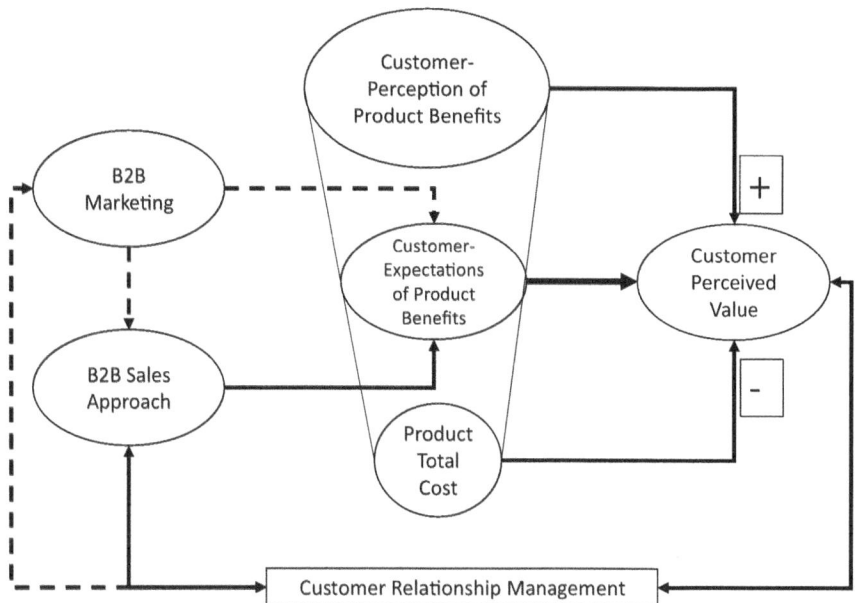

Fig. 1 Customer's perceived value model

Table 1 Customer's expected benefits

Increasing or Improving Key Indicators, such as:	Reduction of Key Costs, such as:
Profitability	Downtime
Productivity	Maintenance costs
Throughput	Operating expenses
Efficiency	The cost of financing
Market share	Product damage
Consumer awareness	Inventory costs
Safety	Labour costs
Job satisfaction	The cost of capital equipment
Response time	

has confidence in a supplier's reliability and integrity. This trust gained will help create a strong and long-term relationship with them, and the chances to grow sales faster in the future will increase.

The CPV model also suggests that marketing plays an important role in defining customer expectations, especially through marketing communication. This also sets certain expectations depending on the message transmitted. Therefore, it is important to make sure that sales and other marketing strategies are aligned.

1.1   B-To-B Sales Driving Factors

Two important factors will drive a supplier's sales and how the supplier approaches the customers, thus, a review of these factors is relevant, to frame the strategic thinking of a sales manager. These factors are:

- the Product Life Cycle (PLC) and
- Customer Buying Behaviour (CBB).

1.1.1 The Product Life Cycle

The Product Life Cycle (PLC) is the process of four recognizable stages that a product goes through, as defined by Levitt (1965):

> *"Stage 1. Market Development. This is when a new product is first brought to market before there is a proven demand for it, and often before it has been fully proved technically in all respects. Sales are low and creep along slowly.*
>
> *Stage 2. Market Growth. Demand begins to accelerate, and the size of the total market expands rapidly. It might also be called the "Take off Stage."*
>
> *Stage 3. Market Maturity. Demand levels off and grows, for the most part, only at the replacement rate.* (Non-significant sales growth)
>
> *Stage 4. Market Decline. The product begins to lose consumer appeal and sales drift downward, such as when buggy whips lost out with the advent of automobiles and when silk lost out to nylon."* (Sales decrease)

The duration of the product life cycle is impacted by the following three factors, according to Dean (1976):

- Market technical maturity, indicated by the declining rate of product development, increasing standardization among brands and increasing the stability of manufacturing processes and knowledge about them.
- Market acceptance, indicated by the customer acceptance of the basic product idea, by the widespread belief that most manufacturers' products will perform satisfactorily and by enough familiarity and sophistication to permit customers to compare brands competently and,
- Competitive maturity, indicated by increased stability of market share and price structures.

Although Dean's research is oriented to consumer products, the three factors also apply to the B-TO-B product life cycle. Each stage will require a specific sales approach that will be reviewed later in this chapter.

1.1.2 The customer's Buying Process and Behaviour

Understanding the customer buying process is the task of the supplier's sales and marketing departments. This understanding will help define a more effective sales approach.

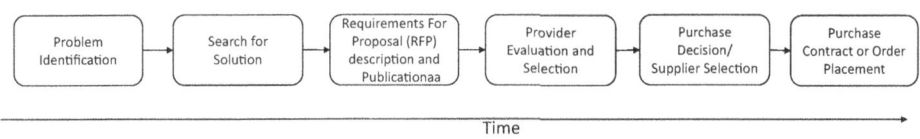

Fig. 2 The B-to-B customer's buying process

The customer's buying practices depend on the nature of business and its size and the technical complexity of the products purchased, as well as the degree of centralization of the purchase. Therefore, different buying processes could be defined. Research studies suggest that today's B-to-B customer take the following steps to purchase a solution (also shown in Fig. 2):

Problem identification and search
Today, customers need fewer sales executives' presence. According to a Gartner research report (2020), when B-to-B customers consider a purchase, they spend only 17% of that time meeting with potential suppliers. When customers compare multiple suppliers, the amount of time spent with a sales executive is maybe only 5% or 6% as they dedicate more time to identifying and understanding their "pain" and web searching for product reviews, Google search for potential suppliers' websites, discussion forums participation, and attendance to trade shows and other industry events where they can learn more about existing suppliers and their solutions, as well as use of social media especially LinkedIn and YouTube videos.

After searching for a solution, if interested, customers will contact the supplier(s) first, not the other way around. Contacting customers is getting harder for the sales executive, especially at the beginning of the sales process, if the supplier has no experience working with them.

Request for Proposal (RFP) definition and publication (or submitted to specific suppliers)
After collecting information and discussing it with the cross-functional purchasing team, that includes top-level executives and other internal influencers or advisors, a list of detailed requirements of the needed solution is defined and included in a request for proposal (RFP), including the request for a formal quote, that is submitted to the preselected suppliers.

Sometimes, the RFP is divided into two stages: 1) The Request for Information (RFI), where only the list of requirements is included but not a formal quote proposal is requested, just an estimated price. This is done when the customer is unsure if there is a market solution that could satisfy the requirements. 2) The request for quote (RFQ) is submitted only to the suppliers responding to the RFI, which comply with the majority or all requirements.

Supplier evaluation and selection

As a next step, the purchasing team reviews the suppliers' proposals. As today's purchasing team is larger and multidisciplinary, more scrutiny takes place in the evaluation. According to Demand Gen Report's 2016 B-to-B Customer's Survey (Anon, 2016), more than 60% of B-to-B customers responded that they are spending more time conducting a more detailed return on investment (ROI) analysis and building strong business cases before making a purchase. In the same research report, it is mentioned that 4 criteria are used by customers to choose a supplier:

> *"The timeline of a supplier's response to inquiries, during the purchase process when required. For example, the customer may require a demo of the solution (virtual or on site) before defining the RFP demonstrated a stronger knowledge of the solution area and the business landscape demonstrated a stronger knowledge of customer's company and its needs provided content that made it easier to show ROI and/or build a business case for the purchase."*

Purchase order or purchase contract placement

The last stage in the purchasing process is when the customer places the purchase order (P.O.) or the winning supplier's purchase contract. Sometimes, the customer will require other meetings with the winning supplier before placing the purchase contract, reviewing it, and making sure that it is understood. Also, sometimes, the contract is not negotiable. This happens mainly with government organisations or large multinational companies.

The customer's purchase decision process and behaviour are influenced by many factors that should be understood by the supplier when defining the sales approach. Various researchers have provided comprehensive models to explain customer buying behaviour, such as:

- The Sheth's model (Sheth, 1973). This model shows the background of individuals involved in the purchase decision, such as education, orientation and lifestyle, organisational size, orientation, and degree of centralisation, as the main factors that influence buying behaviour.
- The Webster and Wind model (Webster & Wind, 1972). This model considers four sets of factors: environment such as technology/innovation and culture, organisational and personal factors, as the main influence of the buying decision.
- Choffray and Lilien Model (Choffray & Lilien, 1980). This model suggest that marketing variables will influence purchasing decisions.

All these models can be summarised in one model shown in Fig. 3.

1.2   The B-To-B Sales Process

After having a deep understanding of the PLC and the customer buying process and behaviour and the factors affecting them, suppliers should define and follow a sales

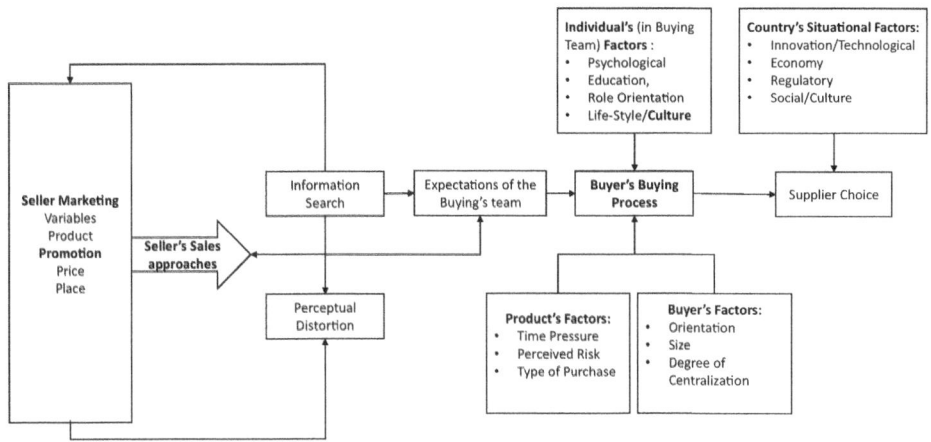

Figure Based on Models

Fig. 3 Augmented organizational buying behaviour model based on the Sheth's, The Webster and Wind, and Choffray and Lilien models

process and approach. Some researchers have suggested that companies with a realistic set of stages, known as the sales process, that is clear and easy to understand by the group of sales executives, known as salesforce, and having each of these executives dedicating three hours a month to managing such process, could increase sales by 18% versus companies not having that (Jordan & Kelly, 2015).

Although different practitioners and researchers define the process with more or fewer stages, in general, a B-to-B sales process will include the stages shown in Fig. 4.

1.2.1 B-To-B Sales Leads Generation Approaches

The B-to-B sales process starts when the sales leads' information, which are the companies or organisations that are part of the supplier's target market, is generated. Sales lead generation is one of the marketing department's responsibilities, although sometimes, it is an activity that the sales department does. Therefore, marketing managers must align with sales managers to ensure that high-quality sales leads (organisations more likely to be converted into customers) are obtained. The more quality sales leads are generated, the more opportunities there are to close sales.

High-quality sales leads generation must be one of the objectives of a business marketing plan, making sure that when leads are generated, a combination of the following lead's information is included: target organisation's demographics or firmographics such as location (s), size, business performance; geographic indicators and buying behaviour, as well as point(s) of contact information and demographics, within the target firm. These key pieces of information will allow better market segmentation (Brennan et al. 2010). Customer detailed profiling will increase the likelihood of closing a sale more

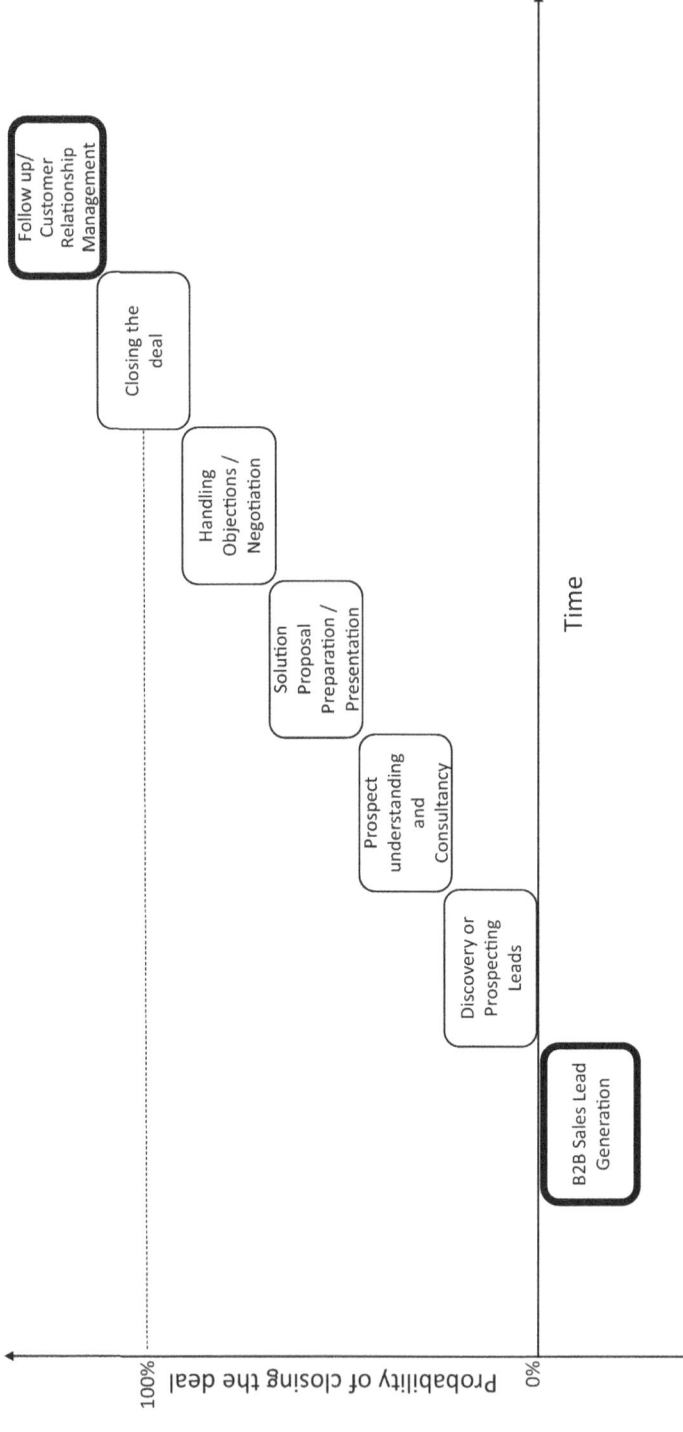

Fig. 4 B-to-B sales process

efficiently the first time. There are two approaches to get sales leads: Outbound and Inbound.

Outbound

The outbound approach is a method of finding potential customers by having the salesperson or marketer initiate the first interaction by sending out a message to potential leads, without knowing whether the leads are interested in your product. This method encompasses the first two stages of the sales process, leads generation, and prospecting. To execute this approach, you need to follow three steps:

- Get reliable potential customer point of contact (POC) information: It is important to get a full name, position, email, and phone number. This information can be purchased from companies such as Global B-to-B Contacts.
- Research: Before the first contact, it is important to research as much information as possible about the target organisation and the POC. This will help you have a better approach.
- Make contact: This first approach to a potential customer can be made by:
  Unsolicited email or LinkedIn communication, if the POC has a profile on that platform (This is discussed in detailed in Chapter "Digital Communication in B-To-B Sales", Digital communication in B-to-B).
  Cold calling.
  Well known sales executive.

Although the outbound approach is an option for sales lead generation, only 18% of marketers and sales managers think this practice provides the highest-quality sales leads (Hubspot 2020). This strategy may be a good approach for sales of low involvement products. However, when trying to make large sales of a large complex and expensive technological product, outbound practice does not generate the expected results and is considered the worst part of the salespeople's job. This situation can be explained by the cold calling statistics, which show a negative trend with fewer than 2% of the calls resulting in high-quality prospects, or by the unsolicited email outreach and LinkedIn Message having similar statistics as cold calling.

There are other factors limiting the outbound approach, such as stricter regulations in some countries or regions of the world. For example, under the new European General Data Protection Regulation, salespeople cannot use personal data (like email addresses or phone numbers) unless that person has consented to be contacted. This means no more contacting the sale lead without that person opting into receiving your messages.

However, one outbound approach works very effectively, hiring well-known people in the target market, as sales executives. These executives often have an extensive potential customer network that they could contact through a cold, or maybe "warm" call. The success response rate of this type of call is high.

Inbound

The inbound approach is a method of targeting sales leads through an effective communication campaign, nowadays, mainly through the internet. This communication strategy aims to make the sales lead initiate the first interaction with the customer.

The inbound approach will evolve through the PLC. During the market development stage, the target market does not know your brand, product, or even your company when your company is new in the market. Sometimes, during this stage, the product (i.e. customer high involvement industrial product such as large complex equipment or technology) is still in the prototype stage. Therefore, it is crucial to find a customer that is willing to try it, get their feedback, and finalise an off-the-shelf product. But, how is it possible to get sales leads that can potentially be a product testing bed or the new product's first customer?

- With the support of a company's sales channel. The sales channels are often related to some key potential customers that are leaders in the industry, locally and internationally.
- With an intense marketing communication department's support, by creating brand product awareness to generate visitors to the company's website or other online media, and persuade them for a call to action. LinkedIn "live streaming" and webinars, trade shows, and Google Ads are some ways to create awareness.

During the Growth Phase, continuing the market communication strategy defined in the developing stage and creating an authority blog or website with relevant content for your target market and positioning the product and company as the leader, is recommendable.

In the maturity stage, launching direct-response online campaigns or a direct customized offer to loyal customers, should be considered.

When the product is in a declining stage, the salesforce should introduce a new product taking advantage of the relationship with existing clients. A transition message using a direct online communication strategy such as an invitation email to a new product webinar on LinkedIn or other webinar platforms, should be implemented to support the salesforce.

1.2.2 B-To-B Sales Lead Prospecting

Sales leads prospecting is the process of identifying potential strategic customers, strategic prospects. Separating strategic customers from others is important. Strategic customers can potentially represent a valuable business partner for the supplier, and help improve supplier reputation and serve as a good reference, or as an exemplar of a success in a case study. According to Kotler et al. (2016) a strategic customer is:

"a customer whose current and potential value to us is high and to whom our (potential) value is significant as well. It is a customer who makes us change and who is willing and committed to change with us."

For example, for a supplier trying to enter the United States aerospace market to sell high involvement products, the US Airforce can be a strategic prospect. This military organisation is a leader of the entire industry in many countries. This potential strategic customer is innovative, seeking a change to improve the process to accomplish its mission more efficiently and effectively. This potential customer may be willing to give referrals within the same or other government organisation and improve the supplier's reputation and brand positioning.

The criteria for identifying strategic prospects of high-end products are:

- supplier potential sales growth within the strategic prospect,
- strategic prospect's:
  innovation orientation
  level of new technology acceptance rate, and
  business growth rate

2 B-To-B Sales Approaches

The understanding of the rest of the sales process stages, from product proposal to closing, will be accomplished by reviewing the main three sales approaches. These are explained in brief.

2.1 Transactional Sales Approach

Transactional selling consists of helping customers buy the product, usually low involvement (i.e., merchandise), they have decided to buy based on their own research, often online, and very likely, based on previous experience with the same type of product. The objective of this approach is "converting of products and services into cash flow." The product presentation and objections/negotiation stages of the sales process are often omitted. If a presentation is needed, it will be a product-based presentation, not based on customers' needs, as these customers know their own needs and what they are looking for and are often ready to buy.

This approach can be complemented by an ecommerce strategy, especially when targeting the Asian and North American Market. For example, according to Statista report (2019):

> "the gross merchandise volume (GMV) of B-to-B e-commerce transactions in Asia is projected to amount to 9.8 trillion U.S. dollars, accounting for the majority of B-to-B e-commerce GMV worldwide. North America is set to rank second with 1.4 trillion B-to-B e-commerce gross merchandise sales."

2.2   Solution Selling Approach

This approach focuses on identifying the customer's needs and then defining a solution in the form of a product or service (or a combination of both) to meet those needs. This is a customer's needs-based approach, not product 'features and benefits.'

This approach does not require going deep in the understanding beyond the potential customer's need. This approach requires a presentation of the solution and, sometimes, negotiation and objection management. It also requires a sale of the potential outcome of the proposed solution. This is a common factor with what is required for the transformational sale approach.

Solution selling can be used for both high and low involvement product sales.

2.3   Transformational Sales Approach

The transformational sales approach, also called consultative (Adamson et al. 2012) or relational approach (Inks et al. 2019), can be defined as the process of selling value (Hanan, 2004) to strategic customers. The success of this approach is based on the supplier's ability to collaborate with the customer and define a solution that will transform the customer's current business process. Demonstrating evidence of the value of the solution being defined, facilitates the process of customer transformation. An attractive return on investment based on the mathematical model [1], is a good evidence. When value is proven to the customer, suppliers increase the probability to improve their own margins in return, as they could have the opportunity to increase price, reduce selling expenses, or both.

Although it has been around for more than 50 years, the transformational sales approach has gained more traction in recent years, among researchers and practitioners of B-to-B sales.

Once the strategic prospects have been defined, the transformational approach process continues with the following stages:

- Prospect understanding and consulting: Once the sales lead becomes a prospect, it is important to continue communication, introducing the rest of the people supporting the sales effort, such engineers or technicians, to start providing a real consulting experience. At this point, the sales team needs to be perceived by the prospect as a consulting team. To do consulting, the following actions need to be taken along the way of the prospect's purchase process:
  Prospect Evangelisation: It is the process of sharing the main technology trends in the industry with the prospect and how they are benefiting from it and its pros and cons. This demonstrates knowledge and authority on the topic.
  Partnership Creation: It is the process of collaborating with the prospect as a partner, not just a customer, to co-create a solution discussing with the prospect, different

alternatives of taking advantage of the existing and emerging technology around the world (not only the supplier's technology) for their specific business processes (Steenburgh & Ahearne, 2018). The sales team should also focus upon the joint discovery of value innovation opportunities and explore the concept of customer business transformation and distinguish eight 'business-altering experiences' to guide business transformation and make customers more successful in their markets. (Kotler et al. 2016).

While this process is important to identify the specific benefits, such as improvements to customers' key business indicators, they expect a solution. If possible, a visit to the prospect's location should be executed to identify the pain or need. Also, a demonstration of the possible solutions should be presented to the prospect. A visit to any of the existing supplier's customers' locations will help create more trust in the relationship. The idea is to collaborate to create a partnership. This also demonstrates knowledge and starts to generate trust.

- New paradigms definition: It is the process of collaborating with the prospect to re-evaluate the predefined pain or need and/or pushing a solution that sometimes is not aligned with the way the prospect thinks or does things, but that at the end will improve their key business indicators. This action helps increase trust and form a solid partnership relationship.
- As a next step, a customized solution proposal is developed and presented to the prospect. This solution should be precise and include timeline, conditions, requirements, and quote for the solution.

    As part of the proposal, a pilot program of the solution can be offered in this step. Running a pilot program for a limited amount of time helps the prospect and the supplier observe the solution's benefits and its implications. This can provide information to do a return on investment analysis when a formal proposal is developed and the price is defined. This pilot program has two advantages:

    Allows the prospect to identify the real benefits of the solution

    Facilitates the estimation of the return on the investment
- Negotiation may be the next step, although it should not be that intense if an estimated ROI analysis based on pilot program results is presented.
- If the customer is convinced of the proposal, the deal is closed. A purchase order is placed, or a purchase contract is submitted to the supplier, and the prospect is converted into a customer of the solution.

2.4   B-To-B Sales Approaches by PLC Stages: A Suggested Model

There is not only one sales approach model that satisfies all management styles or supplier profiles. Preliminary research was conducted with the objective to find common ground for the sales approach path along the PLC stages from a practitioners' perspective by interviewing business to business international companies' consultants and top executives from industries such as high technology, packaging, food and skincare manufacturing, and financial services.

The results of the preliminary research are reflected in Fig. 5.

The participants concluded the following:

In the developing stage, selling value should be the centre of the sales approach. This will require having a deep understanding of:

- the customer business model, as well as an evangelisation process about the product. This is imperative in order to define a specific product or transformational/consultative centred solution.
- the culture and profile of both the organization and individuals involved in the purchase process are necessary to create more effective communication between the supplier and the customer. This is consistent with Seith's integrative model, which shows customer behaviour, and individuals and organization backgrounds as factors that impact the purchase process.
- the level of the country's innovation is also important to identify, as it would give a better understanding of customer purchase behaviour, as the higher the country's innovation index, the higher the adoption of new solutions.
- The transactional approach can also be considered for some low involvement products.

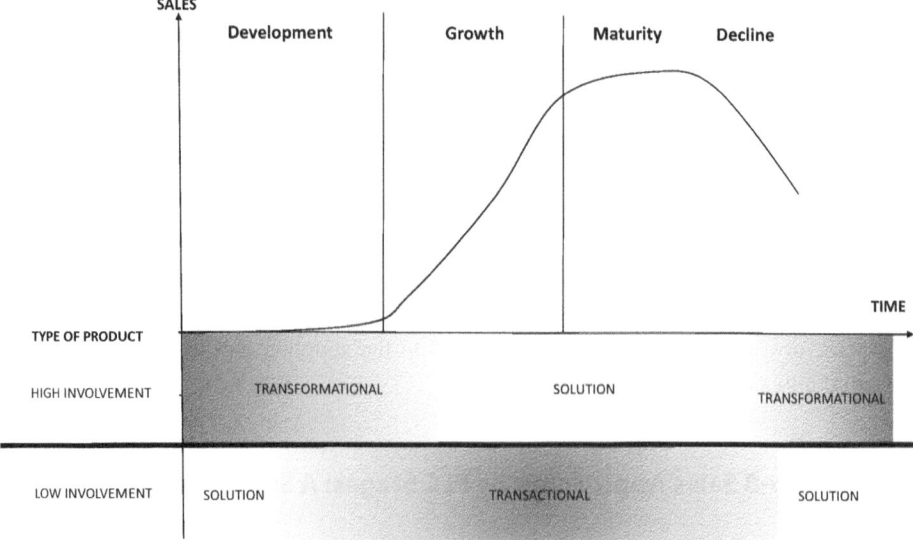

Fig. 5 Practitioners' B-to-B sales approaches suggested model

In the growing stage

- a more transactional approach is needed for low-involvement products, as the customer will be more educated on the product benefits and supplier solutions. A solution approach will also be needed in this stage for some other customers.
- In this stage, the transactional approach for low involvement products can be supported by an e-commerce strategy.
- The transformational approach should prevail for high involvement products, but only for strategic potential customers. A solution selling approach should be executed for non-strategic ones. First, customers' success stories with proved value in the developing stage will have a positive impact on the transformational approach, as the trust in supplier positioning will grow, and new customers will still seek the transformational perspective of the supplier.

In the maturity stage

- the transactional approach for low involvement product should continue with more emphasis on the e-commerce strategy.
- The solution approach is ideal for high involvement products. Although the customer still needs a proven ROI, understanding the solutions' success stories from the same or other suppliers will be enough to decide the purchase.

In the decline stage

- the approaches suggested in the maturity stage will continue in this stage. However, the customers' relationship should leverage the transformational approach for the high involvement product lift or new product selling, and a solution selling for low involvement.

2.5 Customer Relationship Management

The last stage in the B-to-B sales process is the "follow up" stage, which manages the relationship with the B-to-B customer (B-to-B CRM) after the sales are closed. However, the relationship's creation starts when the sales executive makes the first approach with the sales lead.

This CRM process is more than just a follow-up; it is a business philosophy in which the customers become the core focus of the solution supplier operation.

The customer relationship management philosophy is determinant for customer success sustainability with the solution, ensuring a positive customer experience, product adoption, and ongoing communication.

The business culture mainly determines the B-to-B CRM success. This topic will be touched upon in Chapter "Cross-Cultural Strategizing for Successful Customer Relationship Management".

Case study: A transformational approach example

Background: OHEL Technologies, LLC. is a small growing business founded by Mexicans at the end of 2018. It is targeting the US Market and countries in the European Union.

In July 2019, after a Google search for a possible solution for automatic item/tool controls solution, the US Airforce based in Las Vegas, NV. found OHEL's website (www.oheltechnologies.com) and reached out to the sales department, by phone.

After 30 min of conversation about their need and organisation long term objectives, the sales executive qualified the inbound sales lead as a strategic prospect.

After sharing existing solutions information (solution picture shown in Fig. 6) with the customer, and customer sharing information with the supplier, the customer requests a visit to one of OHEL's global customers in Austin TX.

OHEL's customer located in Austin accepted the US Airforce team's visit, and its top management welcomed them, made the solution presentation, and offered a tour through their facilities.

This prospect visit helped create trust and the supplier's good reputation in two directions, towards the prospect and towards existing customer.

Fig. 6 OHEL's Automatic Tool Control Solution. (Source: Dyess AFB website)

Fig. 7 Customer using the solution

After the visit, OHEL's team visited the prospect's facilities and collaborated with different areas to learn about their processes, to make demonstrations of the existing solutions to other members of the buying decision-making team, and finally to define ideas of possible solutions to improve their existing tool control process.

As part of their buying process, and with all the learning lessons gained about technologies, innovation, and possible future changes in the process, the prospect prepared and published an RFP. After receiving proposals from other suppliers, including OHEL's, the prospect decided to award OHEL the purchase contract in June 2020. From that moment, the US Airforce base in Las Vegas became OHEL's strategic customer.

This is a similar story as OHEL's partner IDZ Technologies, which followed the same approach in 2008 to close its first sale to Dyess U.S. Airforce Base, demonstrating value. *"Dyess has purchased 11 new toolboxes since 2008 and plans to purchase 14 more in the future. These toolboxes save 25 man-hours a day, and $35 per man-hour per toolbox"* (Dyess AFB 2009). These man-hour savings generated an attractive return on investment for the customer. Figure 7 shows the customer using the solution that saved it money. ◀

Exercise A

A German company specializes in software for the management of graveyards. The software enables owners of graveyards (usually municipalities or churches) to manage the tenor, exact location, standing periods and finances of graveyards and its grave sites. The use of graveyards is typically highly regulated and may differ from country to country and even from owner to owner.

The company decides to expand its market to Denmark. Discuss the various sales approaches for such a product and what you would recommend to the company as an approach to take.

Exercise B

Discuss the difficulties a sales department for high involvement products might encounter when markets abroad are initially developed.

Exercise C

Software as Service (SaaS) in Mexico, a mini case study

In 2000, there was no SaaS product offered in the Mexican market. However, in the United States (US), the market for SaaS was starting its growing stage. So, a Telecom Company in Mexico took that trend in the US as a reference and decided to be the pioneer in its own market, Mexico, investing in developing its own SaaS platform, and finally launched the product.

The salesforce was trained on the product's features and pricing structure and sent to the field to visit the company's existing customers to start the sales process. The marketing department prepared the marketing communication message focused on product description, emphasising its benefits vs. traditional software licensing products.

The company knew that the market was in the developing stage. However, since the initial target market was a group of existing customers, the salesforce manager thought the sales process would be fast, between 2–3 months.

The results were no sales in the first year, or even after that. The company decided to stop promoting the product after 2 years and took it out of the market.

Reflective questions:

- What is the reason for that result? Please explain using the PLC concept and the factors that impact its length.
- What sales approach would you have taken to increase the chances to be successful the first time?
- What sales approach would you have taken if you had the following scenario?

The Mexican market's technical and competitive maturity has started to grow, the product is now starting its growing stage, but at lower business spending amount than the developed countries. Mexico's business market spends only 8% of the total information technology product spending on SaaS type of products vs. the United States, Canada, United Kingdom, Poland, and the Netherlands. which invest more than 12%, see also https://www.gartner.com/smarterwithgartner/cloud-adoption-where-does-your-country-rank/.

References

Adamson, B., Dixon, M., & Toman, N. (2012). The end of solution sales. *Harvard Business Review, 90*(7/8), 60–68.

Anon. (2016). *The 2016 B2B Buyer's Survey Report*. Demand Gen. https://e61c88871f1fbaa6388d-c1e3bb10b0333d7ff7aa972d61f8c669.r29.cf1.rackcdn.com/DGR_DG043_SURV_B2BBuyers_Jun_2016_Final.pdf [2 September 2020].

Brennan, R., Canning, L., & McDowell, R. (2010). *Business-to-business marketing*. London: SAGE.

Choffray, J. M., & Lilien, G. L. (1980). *Market planning for new industrial products*. New York: Wiley.

Dean, J. (1976). Pricing policies for new products. *Harvard Business Review, 54*(6), 141–153.

Dyess, A. F. B. (2009). *Toolboxes save money*. https://www.dyess.af.mil/News/Article-Display/Article/268707/toolboxes-save-money/ [30 July 2020].

Eggert, A., & Ulaga, W. (2002). Customer perceived value: A substitute for satisfaction in business markets? *Journal of Business & Industrial Marketing, 17,* 107–118.

Hanan, M. (2004). *Consultative selling: The Hanan formula for high-margin sales at high levels* (7th ed.). New York: AMACOM.

Hubspot. (2020). *Not another state of marketing report*, https://www.hubspot.com/state-of-marketing [26 September 2020].

Inks, S., Avila, R., & Talbert, G. (2019). The evolution of the sales process: Relationship selling versus the Challenger Sale. *Journal of Global Scholars of Marketing Science, 29*(1), 88–98.

Jordan, J., & Kelly, R. (2015). Companies with a sales process generate more revenue. *Harvard Business Review, 1.*

Kotler, P., Dingena, M., & Pförtsch, W. (2016). *Transformational sales. Making a difference with strategic customers*. Switzerland: Springer.

Levitt, T. (1965). Exploit the product life cycle. *Harvard Business Review, 43*(6), 81–94.

Sheth, J. N. (1973). A model of industrial buyer behavior. *Journal of Marketing, 37*(4), 50–56.

Statista. (2019). *Global B2B e-commerce gross merchandise volume (GMV) from 2013 to 2019, by region*. https://www.statista.com/statistics/705614/global-B2B-e-commerce-gmv-region/ [15 September 2020].

Steenburgh, T., & Ahearne, M. (2018). How to sell new products. *Harvard Business Review, 96*(6), 92–101.

Walker, W. (2012). *Transactional vs. consultative selling*. Material Handling Equipment Distributors Association. https://thejournal.mheda.org/2012/06/09/transactional-vs-consultative-selling/ [31 August 2020].

Webster, F. E., & Wind, Y. (1972). A general model for understanding organizational buying behavior. *The Journal of Marketing., 36*(2), 12–19.

Zauner, A., Koller, M., & Hatak, I. (2015). Customer perceived value: Conceptualisation and avenues for future research, *Cogent Psychology, 2*(1).

Digital Communication in B-To-B Sales

Henning Hinderer and Claudio Pousa

1 Communication in Sales

Successful international business development includes the identification and harvesting of potential markets. A company that wants to sell products or services in a dedicated market at first has to try to raise awareness about the company and its offerings to the targeted customer segments. Products and services may be offerings of a company as well as other artefacts such as intellectual property e.g. software code, patents or brand names. In this chapter the term product will therefore also be used in a broader sense including not just physical products but also all other forms of commercial offerings. A company with such an offering then has to convince prospective customers, in short prospects, and turn them into customers that really generate turnover. To achieve that, it is essential to communicate with these prospects, because without communication no individual and no company can ever know about the offered products or will ever buy them. E.g. a company that has developed a new robotic application and now wants to sell it to interested companies worldwide, has to figure out who could be potential customers for the solution and in which countries they are located. It has to try to get in touch with the relevant representatives of companies of the targeted market segment in order to inform them about the benefits of the new application in the appropriate way for the regions or countries the customer company is operating in. In the best case these

H. Hinderer (✉)
Pforzheim University, Pforzheim, Germany
e-mail: henning.hinderer@hs-pforzheim.de

C. Pousa
Lakehead University, Thunder Bay, Canada
e-mail: cepousa@lakeheadu.ca

© The Author(s), under exclusive license to Springer Fachmedien Wiesbaden GmbH, part of Springer Nature 2021
L. Martin (ed.), *International Business Development*,
https://doi.org/10.1007/978-3-658-33221-1_11

companies will identify a demand for the solution and buy it. They may even order maintenance and support over a certain period of time. Due to that, the concept of the marketing mix with its Four Ps, Product, Price, Place, and Promotion, can be applied. The concept proposed by McCarthy (1960) tries to explain which instruments and decisions a company has to establish and to take in order to successfully sell products on a certain market. The P which stands for promotion refers to the way the targeted market is supposed to be addressed and how marketers plan to communicate with customers.

If the products to be sold have a certain complexity and need detailed explanation or possibly even individual customization or adjustment to a customer's requirements, it is very likely that personal communication is required. Especially when prospects are not private people but companies or organizations, personal contact seems to be necessary. But also in B-to-B sales, other ways to communicate can help to create and foster relationships with customers (Lippold 2016).

Communication channels based on digital technologies have been developed alongside analogue possibilities to communicate such as oral communication, printed information or communication over traditional telephone connections. Since back in 1971 when the first email was sent and even more since the early 1990s when technologies especially based on the internet and the World Wide Web have opened up new possibilities, digital communication has become more and more important (Kotler et al. 2017; Kannan and Li 2017, p. 22). In this context the term digital marketing describes the usage of digital communication channels with the purpose of generating new leads to potential customers, of promoting the company's offerings and of increasing sales. It is also presumed that using digital technologies in sales helps to create value for customers by offering better services and solutions as well as for the firm through fostering of customer relationships or more profitable business models (Kannan and Li 2017, p. 23).

In comparison to selling products to private consumers, marketing to businesses has significantly different prerequisites. While end customers take decisions by themselves spending their own money and usually in lot sizes for individuals or small groups in order to only meet their personal demand, businesses show significantly different behaviour. An individual who wants to have a new TV set and has access to sufficient financial means can go ahead and buy it. Companies on the other hand either purchase goods as direct material to be used for the preparation of their products such as electric motors for robots if the company sells robots, or the goods are used and applied internally as indirect material in order to support the business operations such as notebooks used by the sales force to write proposals or to communicate with customers. In both cases the volumes purchasers negotiate will be notably higher than an individual will ever do. At the same time, purchasers do not act to meet their own, personal demand but the one derived from the requirements of their company. This means that they act as intermediaries who do not spend their own but their firm's money, and they source products that other people e.g. production managers or engineers will need or use. The professional purchasing process tends to be much more formal due to stronger legal or compliance related restrictions (Backhaus and Voeth 2014, p. 38).

The concept of the buying centre describes the different roles that can be identified when companies execute a professional purchasing act. Purchasing activities involve not only the purchasing agent and the internal user who requested the products and has got the specified demand, it additionally identifies decision-makers who keep control of the budgets which are about to be spent and gatekeepers who may allow or impede sales representatives to get in touch with relevant actors within a company. Other employees or even external people who might have a significant influence on the decision-making process can also be considered as parts of the buying centre (Webster and Wind 1972; Johnson et al. 2011).

Ideally, communication in B-to-B marketing reaches all participants of the buying centre in a suitable way. This is even more challenging in international contexts because additional languages or geographically widespread teams need to be addressed. Since the purchasers involved search for information online and expect to find a way to communicate using digital technologies, an appropriate communication strategy will be necessary (Lüders 2020, p. 71). An integrated approach will have to include traditional analogue as well as technologically advanced digital communication channels (Rakić and Rakić 2014). The focus of the following explanations in this chapter will lie on digital communication.

2   Goals of Communication

The top marketing priorities regarding digital communication are to develop customer relationships, to raise brand awareness, to strengthen the company's leadership position and to develop a favourable brand position. Corporate website development takes up a majority percentage of digital budgets, with email marketing campaigns, social media and the development of microsites, online video, podcasts and webinars following and accounting for almost 75% of digital budgets (Brosan 2012).

Generally speaking, goals of any business communication can be classified in three main dimensions (Eagly and Chaiken 1993):

- cognitive,
- affective and
- behavioural

The cognitive aspects of communication refer to instilling in the target audience a certain knowledge about the seller. This knowledge could be very basic, e.g., a new company or a new brand might have an initial cognitive goal of letting their audience know that the company and the brand "exist", to more advanced, e.g., letting the audience know that the company has a new product, that it is participating in a certain project or that it has developed certain capabilities or exclusive expertise.

The affective dimension refers to developing in the target audience an affective response to the seller, its products, and its brand name. Usually this affective response aims at developing brand recognition, preference and, eventually, loyalty. Sometimes, the cognitive and affective goals are achieved simultaneously. For example, by encouraging senior executives and internal consultants to participate in conversations with customers through specialized social media platforms, some companies aim at sharing some of their expertise with their audiences (cognitive goal) as well as positioning themselves, their executives and internal consultants as respected experts in their field, thus enhancing their reputation and perception of mastery and expertise (affective goal).

Finally, the behavioural dimension aims at achieving a behavioural response to the communication. While in consumer markets the typical behavioural response is to purchase the product, in B-to-B markets the response can be more complex than that. As will become clearer in the next section, in a B-to-B sales process, the purchase decision, i.e. the closing of the sale, comes after fulfilling a number of stages, and agreeing with a number of people involved in the decision-making process in the buyer's organization. In this case, the behavioural goal can be that the target audience, for example, a purchasing agent attending a trade fair, agrees to organize a presentation with the decision-makers and other people in the buying centre, to move the sales process one step forward.

In international B-to-B sales processes, given the complexity of the decision and the high stakes linked to the decision, these three goals are worked out sequentially, moving from a cognitive goal, to an affective goal, and finally a behavioural goal (in consumer markets, the order might be different). Hence that the decision-makers in the buying organization first acquire some knowledge about the selling organization, its products, services, knowledge and expertise, then they form an affective response to the seller's communication, in terms of positive attitude or preference towards the seller, and finally this turns into a positive purchasing decision which stands for the achievement of a behavioural goal.

In any case, sales in the long run always has the goal to sell products or services. However, especially in B-to-B sales people tend to be less focused on spot business but more focused on relationships with prospects and customers. Communication has the purpose to create trust and reliability and thus allows the establishment and maintenance of business relationships.

3 Communication in the B-To-B Sales Process

Traditionally, the exchanges between a seller and a buyer leading to a sale have been modelled through a number of stages depicted as a sales process. Using a sales process is useful for a common understanding in practice but also in teaching, training and for research purposes. Many different models have been used, going from four or five stages, up to seven or even nine (Futrell 2001; Moncrief and Marshall 2005). However, a five step approach seems to be appropriate with reference to the above mentioned communicational goals (see Table 1).

A key initial stage in any sales process is prospecting. Prospecting is the method that sales people use to find and identify potential new customers, or potential new business opportunities with existing customers in all possible markets to be addressed in the world. Methods can include asking for referrals, cold calling, searching in databases and others. As the contacts developed using these methods bring more "suspects" than actual "prospects", the salesperson should also use some complementary methods to screen out or qualify these leads, sorting out those that won't probably lead to new businesses (thus, consuming valuable sales time and resources) from those that actually are real prospects with needs that can be satisfied by the seller in a reasonable timeframe.

A second step in the sales process is approaching the potential customer. Through an initial sales call—and most likely, a series of follow-up meetings—the salesperson opens up the sales process with the prospect, tries to establish a base of trust and respect between both organizations, and starts identifying potential areas where his organization can add value to the buyer. It is very important in this stage to start building trust between buyer and seller because, if trust is not present, the probability of closing any business deal between both organizations is almost zero: customers simply do not do business with a company they do not trust. Establishing an early position of trust, will allow the salesperson to ask questions concerning future plans, needs and shortcomings that can become future business opportunities for the selling organization.

A third step typically considers presenting the offer, service or product to the potential buyer. Once the salesperson has identified a business opportunity with a particular buying organization, the next step is to present potential solutions that the seller can offer to solve the problem or improve the operations of the potential buyer. This step is more effectively achieved when the salesperson adopts a more conversational approach, where an initial solution can be presented, followed by questioning about how the buyer sees the proposed solution, followed by a more detailed presentation of additional details, and closing an intermediate agreement that this is the solution the buyer was looking for. Building on successive steps of presentation-questioning-presentation-agreement the seller moves the sales process towards the stage of closing.

Of course, the presentation stage is not always linear and moving in one smooth direction. At any point, objections or other obstacles may emerge, and it is important that the salesperson accepts these as part of the selling process. Often, an objection appears due to a lack of information or understanding on the part of the buyer, and if properly addressed by the salesperson, can be transformed into an opportunity to build more value for the buyer organization and build additional trust in the seller organization.

When the presentation is complete, all the objections are solved and the value that the seller will be creating for the buyer is clear for all parties, then the salesperson can advance to the fourth step: closing. If the salesperson has completed all the previous steps proficiently, closing should come as the natural conclusion of the process. If he has identified the needs of the buying organization, showed how the product can fulfil

Table 1 Five stages of the sales process in B-to-B and corresponding goals

Stage	Prospecting	Approaching	Presenting	Closing	Follow-up
General goals	Identify and qualify leads Develop prospects Establish initial contact	Establish trust and credibility Build differentiation Identify potential areas for new opportunities	Inquiry about specific needs Match offerings with needs Identify ways of creating value	Agree on a specific solution Establish mutual commitments	Deliver value Facilitate value appropriation Deepen customer relationships Gain customer preference
Communication goals	COGNITIVE (i.e. instilling in the target audience and prospects knowledge about the selling organization, its products, brands, capabilities and expertise)				
		AFFECTIVE (i.e. developing in the target audience and prospects an affective response to the selling organization, typically defined through recognition, preference, and loyalty)			
				BEHAVIOURAL (i.e. promoting in the target audience and prospects a behavioural response, typically defined through actions and decisions that move the sales process one step forward, towards the closing of the sale)	

those needs, and addressed all potential objections and doubts, then closing should be a smooth transition towards the next required steps to implement the agreed upon solution. If the buyer is not ready to close, then the salesperson has probably omitted something during the previous stage and should go back to verify that all of the buyer's concerns are addressed and covered.

Finally, once the deal is satisfactory to all parties and the sales process ends, the salesperson should follow up to guarantee that all the commitments made will be honoured by his organization and that it will deliver the value promised during the sales process.

One important aspect to consider in B-to-B sales processes is that the five-step process presented here can be applied at two levels: the individual and organizational level. At the individual level, when the salesperson meets a purchasing agent or a decisionmaker in the buyer organization, he can use this five-step process in each individual sales call, ending that particular call with a closing and a commitment to follow-up in the next weeks or in the next meeting. Similarly, when dealing with numerous decision-makers involved in a purchasing process, the salesperson can use the same broad process at an organizational level to go from the opening of the relationship up to the closing of a contract, something that might take several weeks or months and multiple interactions with multiple decision-makers.

A second important aspect to consider in B-to-B sales processes is that, closing a deal and implementing a solution is not the end of the process. In a larger picture, if the solution sold and implemented adds real value to the buying organization, this deepens the trust between both organizations. Thereby, it opens up new business opportunities, new possibilities of collaboration and thus a potential, long-term, fruitful relationship for both parties.

In the last two decades, the traditional sales process has been affected by a number of transformative factors including a more strategic role of the salesforce, the need to develop long-term relationships with customers to accelerate the business cycle and improved buyer knowledge. These aspects increase the necessity to better communicate with the customer during the whole process and therefore strengthen the use of new communications technologies.

4   Characteristics of Communication

Communication comprises the exchange of information between two or more participants. The Speech Act Theory proposed by Austin (1962) stated that communication can be composed of a set of speech acts, whereas a minimum of at least one act has to take place. As shown in Fig. 1 each act of communication needs a sender who wants to transmit a message to at least one or more receivers. In the sales process these could be represented by a seller and one or more buyers.

The receiver can be known or unknown to the sender before he or she sends the message. The message will be transferred through a communication channel and it contains

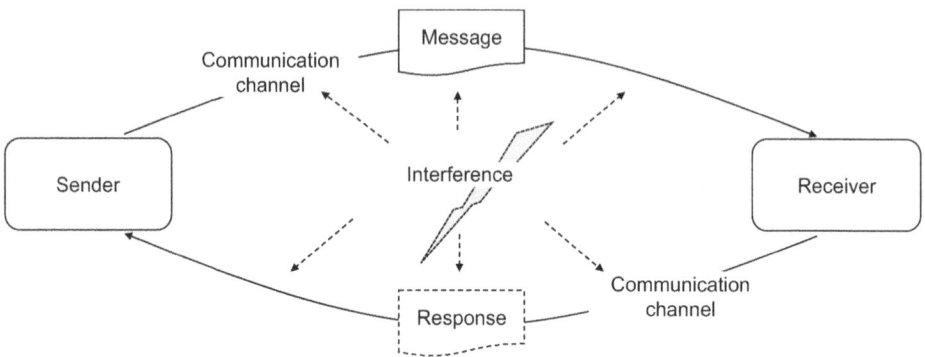

Fig. 1 Extended Schema of Communication (Shannon and Weaver 1975; Berger 2010)

the information that is supposed to be transmitted (Kotler and Keller 2016, p. 32). The transfer of a message can always be subject to interference caused by noise, an interruption of the connection or a lack of attention of the receiver. A loss of content, misunderstandings or maybe an unexpected or even no reaction might be the result. Interference can affect the sender, the channel, the message as well as the receiver. Additionally, the receiver has to understand and interpret the message in the intended way in order to induce the expected action. The receiver can answer by giving feedback to the initial message. The response is a new communication act with the same characteristics.

Communication takes place directly in a physical meeting, without any technical support e.g. when a sales representative and a prospect meet and communicate in person. If a meeting cannot take place physically communication channels can be applied. These may use digital or analogue media for the transmission of the chosen message, such as printed advertisements or billboards or the channels explained in Sect. 1.5. Beyond that, a communication instrument uses one or more communication channels to transmit the necessary messages (see Sect. 1.6).

One of the basic concepts of communication in marketing follows the idea that at first the attention of the targeted person has to be captured in order to raise interest in the given subject. The next step is to put effort into the creation of the prospect's desire which will hopefully lead to the intended action (Attention-Interest-Desire-Action or AIDA model) of the communication activity (St. Elmo Lewis 1903, p. 124). The intended actions may include purchase decisions of customers but also the registration for a newsletter or even the click on a company's website can be expected actions. The concept has been developed to the Five As in newer publications by Kotler and Keller (2016, p. 69): *Aware, Appeal, Ask, Act, Advocate.* In any case, if no attention is paid then the message or the content of the message will be ignored. E.g. a paper brochure dropped unexpectedly in the receiver's mailbox is very likely to end up in the waste bin without being read. The same happens with ads in search engines. Experienced users are used to the appearance and tend to ignore the first entries in a search result page but move on to the requested search results right away.

Table 2 Selected Attributes to characterize communication (cf. Hinderer 2005:60, extended)

	Attribute	Values	Short forms
Classifiers	Digitally supported	yes, no	y, n
	Synchrony	synchronous, asynchronous	s, a
	Feedback	yes, restricted, no	y, r, n
	Level of disclosure	one-on-one, one to many, many-to-many, one-to-public	1:1, 1:n, n:n, 1:∞
	Level of communication	user-user; user-system; system-user, system-system	u-u, u-s, s-u, s-s
Characteristics	Distance	near, distant	n, d
	Formalization	formalised, dynamic	f, d
	Duration	short, medium, long	s, m, l
	Frequency of occurrence	seldom, frequently	s, f
	Data security	low, high	l, h

An act of communication can be characterized and classified by several attributes which can help to better understand communication especially in the context of B-to-B sales (Hinderer 2005, p. 60). In the following sections, only digital communication channels which use information technology for the transmission of the message will be considered. A channel can be offline or online and communication may be private or public (Dahiya 2018) and the actions on one of the sides can be executed not only by human beings but also by automated computer systems. It can provide for one-way or two-way communication which might allow synchronous or asynchronous responses over the same channel (Kovaitė et al. 2020). On the one hand, synchronous communication expects both participants to be present at the same time and to answer, give feedback, or interact with only a very short latency. On the other hand, asynchronous communication allows a time lag between two acts of communication over the same channel. Other characteristics such as time intensity of a conversation, the complexity and grade of formalization of the subject, the size of the addressed customer group or the expected security level may be relevant too. An overview of several attributes and their possible manifestations is given in Table 2. As described by Hinderer (2005, p. 60) attributes which have a strong influence on the categorization and possible contexts of applications are considered as classifiers while more descriptive attributes are considered as characteristics.

5   Digital Media Channels for Communication

These channels can be adapted to serve the communication goals in B-to-B as well as in B-to-C sales. In recent decades numerous new media based on digital technologies have been developed. If the digital technologies or rather digital media are used for the purpose of communication either with a very dedicated or a rather unspecific target group they can be considered to be digital communication channels. Various technologies and solutions are currently at hand and can be applied in marketing. Infrastructure in most cases is based on internet technologies (TCP/IP, WWW) and thus available and accessible online (Kovaitė et al. 2020). However, the different peculiarities of the characteristics of each of these technologies open up a broad range of possible ways to communicate with the representatives of both B-to-C as well as B-to-B markets. To set up target-oriented communication strategies several communication channels can be combined to form appropriate communication instruments. To do so, an overview of the currently available digital solutions can be helpful. For further reference and for more detailed information also see Kreutzer et al. (2020), Bly (2018), Kotler and Keller (2016), Hinderer (2005).

5.1   Text, Audio and Video Communication

Electronic mail or email has been one of the first communication channels which can be considered to be digital. The sender needs to know the unique email address of the receiver to be able to send a message which may contain text and any kind of file as an attachment. Since the message is delivered and stored in the mailbox, a receiver does not have to react directly. This makes communication via email asynchronous because there may be a short or even a long period of time between two acts of communication. Emails can be addressed to one or more addressees and the list of receivers can be disclosed as a carbon copy (CC) or undisclosed as a blind carbon copy (BCC). This way communication can take place on a one-to-one as well as on a one-to-many basis.

In the beginning the transmission of voice via *telephone* started to be an analogue electrical signal. However, nowadays in most cases data transmission takes place by means of digital technologies such as ISDN (Integrated Services Digital Network) with its roots in the 1980s or VoIP (Voice over IP) where telephone conversations are provided over the internet protocol where small data packages are sent over the internet. A telephone conversation at first is a one-to-one communication which requires both participants to be present synchronously at the same time on either end of the established connection. In case an answering machine is used, the communication becomes asynchronous since the receiver of the voice message can only answer with a time lag after listening to the recorded audio signal. Computer-based automated telephone bots allow the automatic answering of calls to e.g. pre-select different customer concerns such as service requests, problem handling or contractual issues.

As soon as more than two people are involved in a call, the term *telephone* or better *audio conferencing* can be used. Each participant is connected by a separate telephone connection to the joint call. In such conferences synchronous communication from one person to a defined audience (one-to-many; 1:n) takes place where the speaker can share information with or announce news to the other participants. In case of a group discussion with disclosed participants n-to-n communication takes place. Such a group can be set up in a moderated or non-moderated form. Such conferences can be established consisting of regular telephone lines if the chosen provider allows that service or over communication platforms such as Skype, Facetime or WhatsApp.

Digital short text messages became relevant with the start of the *text message* or *Short Message Service* (SMS) which allowed the writing and sending of limited messages, in the beginning, of no more than 160 characters. The messages are written on and sent via a mobile phone. In the recent decade numerous other and newer online, internet-based text message services have appeared such as WhatsApp, Threema, Snap Chat, Telegram, or WeChat. These apps provide for extended possibilities by allowing the sending of longer text strings, emojis, pictures or even files. Since the recipient gets the message delivered into a kind of mailbox, communication takes place asynchronously. The approach of the platform Twitter is slightly different. The text messages can be made publicly available and, by adding hashtags, the messages can be found by interested recipients who actively look for information within the given context. Text messages can be sent by a person or by an IT system which might be programmed to react on predefined occasions. If the communication is initiated e.g. because a user is located in a certain region or is close to a certain point of interest communication can even be related to proximity in the near field.

Digital technologies also allow the sharing of spoken messages or music not only as complete audio files but also as data streams. Such *audio streams* can be played back as soon as the first data package is available on the receiver's device. The audio message can be provided as a live broadcast with an offset of only several seconds. Pre-recorded sequences can be used as well for streaming purposes. Audio streaming is a one-way transmission of data and information. There is no feedback of a listener possible using the same technology. The source of the audio stream can be kept private with very restricted access or it can be shared with a group and be streamed only upon personal registration. Or it can even be made public and thus be accessed by a broader, anonymous audience. Audio streaming can be used e.g. for a product explanation or a blog or "podcast".

Not only audio but also *video streaming* can be used for a one-way communication. Platforms such as YouTube, TikTok or Vimeo allow the uploading of video files which can be viewed by an audience of a predefined level of disclosure. Similar to audio streaming the message is broadcast in data packages which can be displayed as soon as the first package has arrived on the receiving device. Live streams can be used for online presentations or events which take place and require attendance at a certain point of time. Pre-recorded videos may be used for product presentations, image videos or for coverage of a prior event. If feedback or a two-way-communication is desired an additional communication channel has to be integrated. In many cases, text-based communication as described below is provided.

In a *video conference* two or more people can communicate simultaneously. All participants share a live video stream over a platform such as Skype, Facetime, Zoom,

AlphaView or again WhatsApp. Therefore, the technical requirements for a user to be able to participate, including a webcam and microphone as well as a sufficient bandwidth of the available internet connection, are comparably high. There are different levels of security and protection of privacy possible. The communication can be very dynamic. However, a designated lead or moderator of the conference may be useful. Usually video conferences are used rather in established and distant customer–supplier-relationships than in spontaneous encounters. Depending on the application and platform used, it is possible to share the content of a screen or just a section or a single window of the screen. Sometimes digital gestures such as raising hands, applause or being inactive can be used to communicate too.

Online text chats are a communication channel that allow synchronous communication from user to user as well as in groups. Users can send text-based messages while the conversation typically is displayed as a thread. In the function of a chat bot computer systems based on especially designed algorithms and recently in some cases even supported by artificial intelligence may replace human beings in certain situations as communication partner. If the communication takes place personally it can be very informal, however computer systems are still restricted to comparably formal situations of communication. If the bots are able to interpret and send responses in spoken language they can be applied as telephone bots on telephone hotlines as well.

5.2   Website-Related Communication Channels

Company owned *websites* can be public or with restricted access if a registration with login is needed. They contain mainly messages without a formal structure based on text, pictures or video sequences. The communication is directed one-way from the sender, who provides and stores the necessary data on a webserver, to the receiver, who will need a web browser on a computer or a smart device to display the information. Options to give feedback can be provided for users by adding text chat or a posting functionality such as guestbooks or forums. Information is shared asynchronously due to the necessary publication process of the data on a webserver. It can be provided for interested people who view a company's website occasionally as well as for existing customers who might look for updated information on products or services frequently. There are cases where the message is dedicated to an anonymous audience somewhere around the world or even for only very local usage, e.g. by showing the availability of tables in a restaurant or special offers in a shop.

Another option to communicate about an offering from one to many or to the public is *banner advertisements*, posted on websites of third-party providers such as magazines and news pages, industry organizations or focus group websites. In this case the selling company pays for the display of its logo or any other digital banner. If and to whom the banner is displayed on a certain site may depend on several factors. If there is no registration necessary and the website does not work with so called "cookies" to be able to recognize visitors there are few options to control the display. The banner will be shown to every visitor. The idea is then that the target group has been pre-selected due to the active choice to navigate to the given site. On the other hand, if a session or even a certain user can be identified, a more detailed user-profile can be applied to predict the interests of an individual user. This can be achieved by user data-based algorithms working behind the scenes which are supposed to select those banners and thereby marketing messages that fit best to a user's preferences and experiences so far.

To relate the targeted user group well to the actions of a user *search engine advertisements* can also be useful. On search pages such as Google, Duckduckgo or Ecosia an advertising company can choose certain key words or search terms in relation to which its ads are supposed to be displayed. Every time a user gets the ad displayed a predefined fee will be charged to the marketing company. The purpose of advertisements on search engines is that users who are searching for a certain term which also fits to the message to be sent are more likely to be interested in the message than a broader audience. Communication remains one-way and feedback is only possible by tracking the users' paths from the search engine. However, if the expected user profiles and relevant search terms are well defined, a communication close to a one-on-one situation might be achieved. Only by measuring the origin of visits on their own website can certain insights into the efficacy of the channel be drawn. Nevertheless, two-way communication with feedback from the customer can only be achieved if other channels are included in the communication setup. Regular search results are influenced by criteria which try to indicate how well a search result fits the user's request. In order to appear as far up on the list of search results as possible search engine optimization can be considered to be a tool to support the impact of information provided on a website. It means that content, wording, linking and other aspects of a website's design need to be created in a way that is appreciated by the search engines.

5.3   Social Media Activities

In contrast to private websites, where single people or organisations or companies share information, on *social media networks* numerous participants can actively contribute content, comment on the input from others, easily share the information or even recommend it to others. A user can decide to share information with only one other user or a group of mutually approved contacts or to make it public. Given that, social media platforms allow two-way communication in a very open way from one to many in groups or even to the public. *Professional social networks* such as LinkedIn or Xing mainly aim at networking in business contexts. People who have met in reality or share common professional interests can get linked to each other and share contact data. That provides for an easy way to keep in touch without having to maintain a personal address book anymore. Members can also take part in discussions or share authored information on a certain subject on their own sites or within groups of common interest. Besides basic data every participant needs to fill in his or her pre-structured profile, communication is not formalized. Functionalities to further support asynchronous communication allow postings, comments, gestures or even private text messages.

Private social networks such as Facebook, Instagram or smaller ones like Jodel or Nachbarschaft.de in Germany aim at the maintenance of personal relations and communication in private environments. Sharing of photos, videos, comments on posted content or stories as well as text chat messages are very common on different levels of disclosure. In case of an approved contact, information classified as private is shared additionally to the profile information which was posted publicly. Users can follow the activities of others, comment on these or even recommend or share them with others as well. Banner advertisements can be displayed on both kinds of platforms allowing the marketing company to address people with even more focus on certain characteristics in their profiles.

Subject based forums can be seen as a special form of websites. On such forums, users who share a common interest on specific subjects e.g. outdoor sports, renewable energies or even robotic applications in industry are registered. These users can post information, comment on new developments, ask questions or answer them. Communication usually takes place asynchronously on a one-to-many or on group level. Due to the required registration a certain level of security and privacy is provided. How often users communicate can differ from very rare interactions up to continuous participation in the online discussions. Forums can be set up independently or on social media platforms. The owner posts information, usually on blogs, on a certain subject in order to communicate with his or her followers but the setup is comparable to forums if feedback or discussions are possible.

Comparable to recommendations by word-of-mouth or by reference customers in the real world *online recommendations* can be used as a third-party communication about a company or its offerings. Users can post recommendations on both kinds of networks mentioned above as well as in forums or blogs or by text messages or email. In the case that a specific user on one of these platforms has got many "followers" and is talking about products or recommending companies the communication channel can be considered as influencer marketing. One possibility is that these people who can address and create awareness in very broad or very specific audiences, act independently and without any financial relation to the company which provides the discussed product. By sponsoring such influencers, the messages that are being spread can be managed by the selling company. However, independent recommendations are considered to be much more trustworthy since these have to be earned. If they are paid endorsements, prospects will tend to doubt the message due to the given bias of the influencer.

5.4   Online Collaboration and Other Channels

Online collaboration platforms such as Windchill, Microsoft Teams or Dropbox provide many forms of communication by sharing information and data e.g. on joint projects or development items. Most of the solutions include a filesharing functionality which allows distant collaboration on joint files and data. Without the integration of video or audio conferencing, communication is mainly asynchronous. Access to data is, in most cases, very restricted and subject to high security requirements.

Data exchange e.g. the issuing of requests for quotes (RfQ) or requests for proposals (RfP) is also the main function of *supplier portals*. They give purchasing companies the possibility to communicate requirements and expectations to a group of pre-registered and qualified suppliers. Communication and questions about details and clarification of terms and conditions can be included. Industry-oriented RfX portals usually show similar functionality, whereby these are not provided by a purchasing company but by a third party or an industry organization.

5.5   Characteristics of Digital Communication Channels

Table 3 summarizes the characteristics of the different digital communication channels. An explanation of the different criteria and their manifestations is given in Sect. 1.4. Due to the very dynamic development of digital communication it can be assumed that this snapshot of the as-is situation may change quickly. New channels will be developed and used for communication in marketing while others might become outdated and their usage will come to an end over time.

6   Digital Communication Instruments

As indicated in Table 1 the communication goal is a cognitive one at the early stages of the sales process, meaning that the selling company's efforts are aimed at educating the potential buyer on the benefits or opportunities that the company's products can offer. In a digital world, companies can combine several digital channels to set up and use communication instruments in order to achieve their individual goals. For example, they can establish a corporate website as a centralized hub where potential customers are directed to obtain more information. Many of the proactive communications campaigns in B-to-B markets, e.g. email campaigns supported by brochures distributed at an industrial trade show, or advertising published in a specific trade magazine, provide initial information about the company and its products, which is enough to entice their targets to look for more information on the website.

Table 3 Digital communication channels characterized

	Synchrony	Feedback	Level of communication	Level of disclosure	Distance	Formalization	Duration	Frequency of occurrence	Data security
Electronic mail/email	a	y	u-u	1:1	d	i	m; l	s; f	m
Mailing list	a	y	u-u	1:n	d	i	l	s; f	m
Telephone (VoIP)	s	y	u-u	1:1	d	i	s; m; l	s; f	h
Telephone bots (VoIP)	s	r	s-u	1:1	d	i	s; m	s	m
Telephone/audio conferencing	s	y	u-u	n:n	d	i	m; l	s; f	h
Short message services	a	y	u-u	1:1	n; d	i	s; m; l	s	m
Text message services	a	y	u-u; s-u	1:n	n; d	i	s; m; l	s	m
Audio streaming (livestream)	s	n	u-u	1:n	d	i	m; l	s	h
Audio streaming (pre-recorded stream)	a	n	s-u	1:n	d	i	s; m; l	s	m
Blogs	a	r	u-u	1:∞	d	i	s; m; l	f	l
Video streaming (livestream)	s	n	u-u	1:n	d	i	s; m; l	s	h
Video streaming (pre-recorded stream)	s	n	s-u	1:n	d	i	s; m; l	s	m
Screensharing with audio connection	s	y	u-u	1:1; 1:n	d	i	m; l	s; f	m
Video conferencing	s	y	u-u	n:n	d	i	l	s; f	h
Text chat (online)	s	y	u-u	1:1	d	i	s	s	m,l
Text chat (bot)	s	r	s-u	1:1	d	f	s	s	m
Websites	a	r	s-u	1:∞	d	i	s; m; l	s; f	l
Banner advertisements	a	n	s-u	1:∞	d	i	s; m	s	l

(continued)

Table 3 (continued)

	Synchrony	Feedback	Level of communication	Level of disclosure	Distance	Formalization	Duration	Frequency of occurrence	Data security
Search engine advertisements	a	n	s-u	1:∞	d	i	s; m	s; f	l
Search engine optimization	a	n	s-u	1:n	d	f	s; m; l	s; f	l
Professional social networks	a	y	u-u; s-u	1:n	d	i	m; l	s; f	l
Private social networks	a	y	u-u; s-u	1:n	d	i	l	s	l
Subject based forums	a	y	u-u	1:∞	d	i	s; m; l	f	l
Online recommendations	a	y	u-u	1:∞	d	i	s; m; l	f	l
Influencer marketing	a	r	u-u	1:∞	d	i	s; m	s	l
Influencer sponsoring	a	n	u-u	1:∞	d	i	s	s	l
Online collaboration	a	y	u-u	1:n	d	i	l	f	h
Filesharing	a	y	s-u; u-u	1:n	d	f	l	f	h
Supplier portals	a	y	u-s	1:n	d	f	m; l	f	h
RfX portals	a	y	u-s	n:n	d	f	m; l	f	h

When the potential buyers arrive at this website, there are different types of information, some developed to achieve the cognitive goal and others developed to achieve an affective communication goal. The information developed to achieve a cognitive goal refers to information about the company's products, examples and photography of installations, videos about the benefits of their products, or white papers explaining the company's experiences with different clients and industries. All these media provide the potential client with enough information to evaluate whether they could be interested in contacting the supplier to evaluate a proposal in more detail.

It is important to note that B-to-B website visitors can self-select themselves as potential customers for one or more of the products of the supplier. After watching or reading the material available at the website, they can realize that a business relationship with the supplier can potentially be beneficial and decide to contact them. In these cases, the potential customers have already gone through the first stage of the sales process (i.e., Prospecting) and the business relationship starts at the second stage.

The media presented in such a website can also be developed to achieve an affective reaction, and in some cases, there might be some overlap between the cognitive and affective goals. When the goal is to achieve an affective reaction, it means that the potential client is expected to develop positive evaluations or judgements about the supplier, its products and expertise. For example, after watching a video about other, similar installations, or reading white papers about how the advertising company solved a particular problem for another customer, the potential customer might think that the supplier is thorough, careful, reliable and knowledgeable. All of these can be considered as affective reactions to the material that a prospective customer saw. Similarly, clients' testimonials are uploaded to the website as a reference and to generate a positive affective reaction in the viewers, who might feel identified with the businesses represented by the testimonials.

The company's website can be connected to other digital platforms, like a YouTube channel, the LinkedIn accounts of managers and account executives, the company's Twitter feed or even the company's pages in private social media networks. If the supplier is using private social networks, then it is open to engage in conversations with actual or potential customers. Although some B-to-B companies perceive social media as not relevant and rather trivial for business purposes (Bernard 2016) and is an option used mainly by companies that are more advanced in the use of digital technologies, social media networks can be very useful to promote conversations with actual and potential customers. It can project an image of expertise and knowledgeability, build brand differentiation and, generally speaking, achieve both cognitive and affective goals.

Additional digital technologies for conferencing or collaboration allow the supplier to maintain virtual meetings with potential customers, share presentations and perform virtual product demonstrations. These technologies permeate the third stage of the sales process (i.e. Presentation) and are very convenient when dealing with potential international customers, whose decision-makers are scattered around different countries. These remote meetings allow the supplier to achieve:

- cognitive goals by, for example, providing information about products, services, applications or ways of implementing a solution,
- affective goals (by showing deep knowledge about the potential customer's problems and opportunities) and even
- behavioural goals (by moving the sales process forward and promoting decision-making).

In a digital world, synchronous virtual meetings can replace costly business travelling, visits to factories and facilities and crowded board rooms.

Although private social networks are being used extensively in B-to-C contexts, B-to-B marketers have been more reluctant to use these platforms for different reasons. They usually perceive them as rather irrelevant to target professional decision-makers, they perceive social media as rather frivolous and not relevant to a B-to-B environment, and they feel like they will have little control of the conversations conducted in social media around their companies, products and services. Despite this reluctance, some companies are making extensive use of social media. IBM by making extensive use of professional and private social networks, for example, addresses five key areas (Bernard 2016):

- enhance the reputation of company members in their fields of specialization;
- develop relationships with new prospects and showcase successful outcomes;
- generate demand by directing prospects and decision-makers to their website or events pages;
- public relations and press activities; and
- develop marketing insights, unveil emerging trends and identify interests.

Adopting an affective digital communications strategy that includes social media, affects the company as a whole and, demands a high level of commitment to the strategy as well as a clear vison concerning the specific role of digital media in the marketing and communications plan accordingly (Kreutzer et al. 2020). Any company participating in social media will automatically open up communication channels with actual and prospective customers, but also with its employees, other business partners, the supply chain and the business community. Showing isomorphic behaviours such as copying what others are doing, is very likely to lead to unsuccessful experiences. The company must clearly define how digital media integrates with the rest of the communication plan, which also includes the chosen analogue communication channels as well as the sequence of activities and an appropriate timeline. Furthermore the company has to devote specific and sufficient resources, e.g. people and money, to achieve its goals (Buratti et al. 2018).

Another influential activity companies can do is to add online content to promote or redirect conversations with customers or to actively participate in these conversations. To be prepared to do so companies have to train and encourage employees to use social media and participate in conversations around the company and its products, as well as train and control the social media behaviour of employees. Alongside these influential activities, they also perform a number of external marketing actions to indirectly influence the stakeholders' participation in the conversations that take place on different platforms (Huotari et al. 2015). By doing so companies who manage their appearance and presence on private social media networks well are able to maintain and enhance customer relationships even with professionals. It may also help to establish and foster the company's brands which can finally support sales but at the same time allow employer branding and thus make social media a recruiting tool (Andersson and Wickström 2017).

Research shows that, when B-to-B companies start using social media as a communications platform, they tend to publish more general content, without targeting specific stakeholders. On the contrary, as their experience with the platform increases, they tend to be more specific and publish more differentiated content aimed at specific stakeholders (Andersson and Wickström 2017).

Different instruments can be used to achieve different communication goals by targeting different audiences and stakeholders. For example, even private social networks like Facebook can be used to re-publish a company's photographs and news already used on its website, while the participation in trade fairs and other events, might be represented in a more casual way thus presenting the company in a more informal light. Professional social networks like LinkedIn can be used to show how specific products or services have solved specific problems, and also as a recruiting tool. Similarly, YouTube can be used e.g. to show videos of how to assemble products, how organizations are using and implementing the products, and for sharing other visual content to support launching new products. Blogs and websites can be used to present company information, testimonials of satisfied customers, and in-depth information about the company and its products in the form of free articles (Andersson and Wickström 2017). In other cases, companies are using YouTube as a virtual showroom presenting different products and their applications and integrating these videos on their websites too. They use Skype and other audio or video conferencing platforms to interact with customers and offer live demonstrations. Professional social networks such as LinkedIn are applied to promote a direct link with key company managers and other professionals. A mix of contacts may help to find distributors abroad, establish strategic partnerships with them, or arrange for joint participation in international trade fairs. LinkedIn or even Facebook, emails, conversations over Skype and even virtual plant visits can be instrumental in closing successful collaboration agreements (Bocconcelli et al. 2017).

An additional possibility to support the sales process and to achieve cognitive or behavioural goals is to include third party messages such as recommendations on social media platforms or by word-of-mouth taking place via other channels. It describes communication between customers who exchange experiences about a certain product, comment on it or maybe even recommend a certain solution without getting paid or having any other personal interest (Levy and Gvili 2015). However, these kinds of credentials will only be recognized by prospects as trustworthy recommendations if they are truly earned and given by non-biased customers. On the contrary there are paid references or own comments which are suspected to thus be influenced and untrustworthy (Stephen and Galak 2012).

The different communication instruments can be chosen and combined to set up a communication mix to achieve a company's marketing goals. The broad variety of media and communication channels at hand which is still continuously extending allows a very unique and customer specific approach. On the other hand, the sheer number of options makes it necessary to develop a target oriented communication strategy.

Case study: Digital communication at BEC GmbH

The company BEC GmbH, located in Reutlingen, Germany, is a young and very innovative medium-sized and at the same time very internationally engaged business working on robotic solutions in several fields of application, which use cutting edge technology. Besides industry applications such as autonomous robotic ground vehicles for plant logistics and operations support or in enhanced building technologies for new dimensions in architecture, they are always looking for new ways and fields of applications for robot-based technologies. BEC is engaged in areas of human–machine interaction where safety requirements are extremely high. They provide complex solutions for motions simulation, entertainment or even therapeutic radiology. Due to the very specialized know-how their customer base and potential market segments are very specific but present worldwide. Even as a young and still medium-sized company they have earned a good reputation in the respective industries. BEC has a strong focus on personal communication in its sales strategy. At the same time, it continuously tries to support this by using digital communication instruments. Some examples are shown in Fig. 2.

The anchor of the digital communication strategy is the BEC website. It gives detailed information about the company's offerings. The corporate strategy as well as achievements with reference customers from different countries and in research projects are explained supported by short video sequences. All that is meant to create awareness and to show that BEC is a reliable and very innovative partner in all kinds of challenging robotic applications. In order to bring customers to the website BEC works with methods for search engine optimization and also with search engine advertisements on a case-by-case basis. The website contains several ways to contact the company and an interested person may even register for the company's newsletter. BEC is present on social media on professional networks such as LinkedIn as well as on private ones like Facebook and Instagram providing audio-visual content about projects and achievements. All communication activities follow the intention to create new or to foster existing customer relationships by digital communication means wherever these customers might be located in the world. ◀

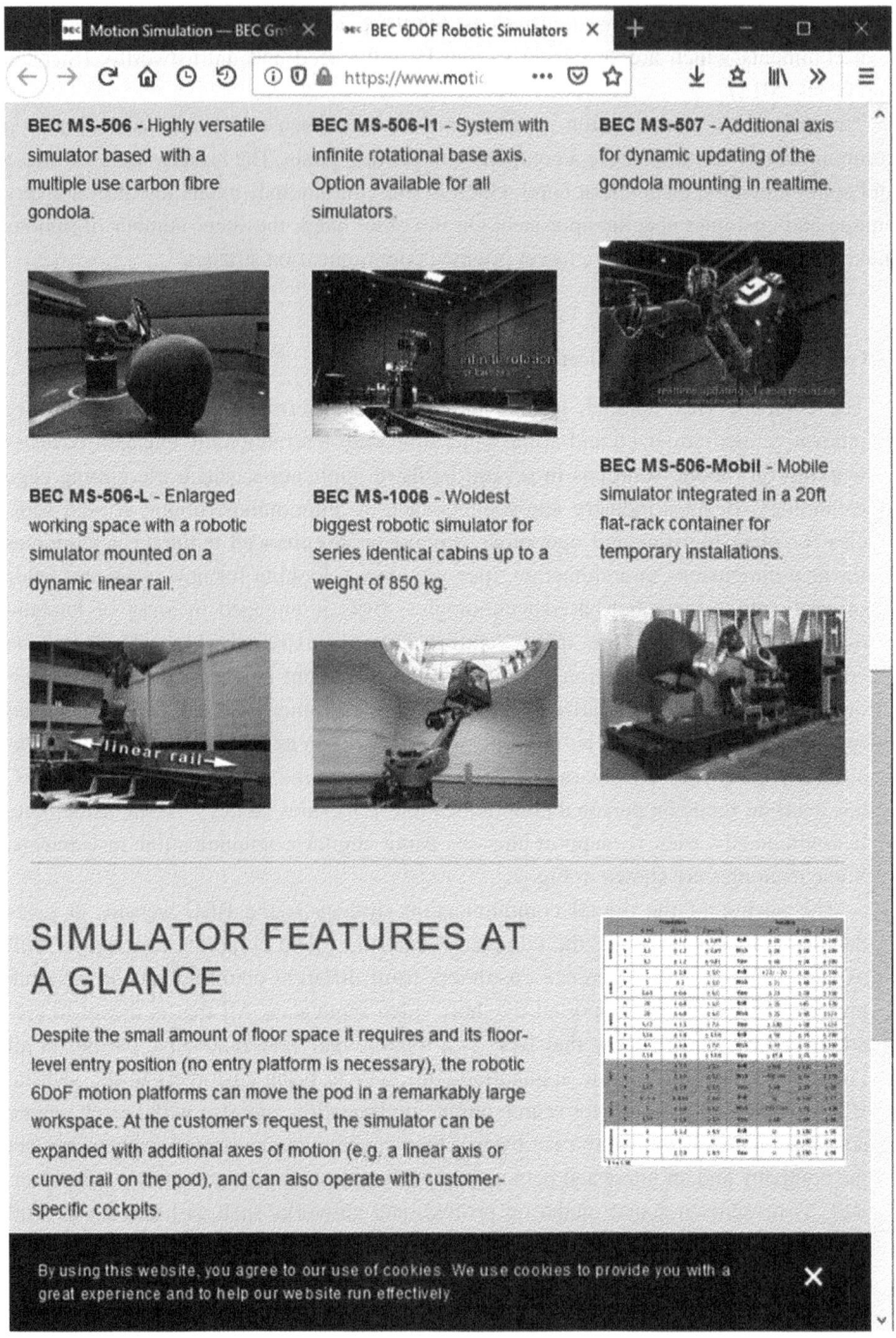

Fig. 2 Two examples of international content of the BEC GmbH website. (Source: With kind permission of © BEC GmbH (2020))

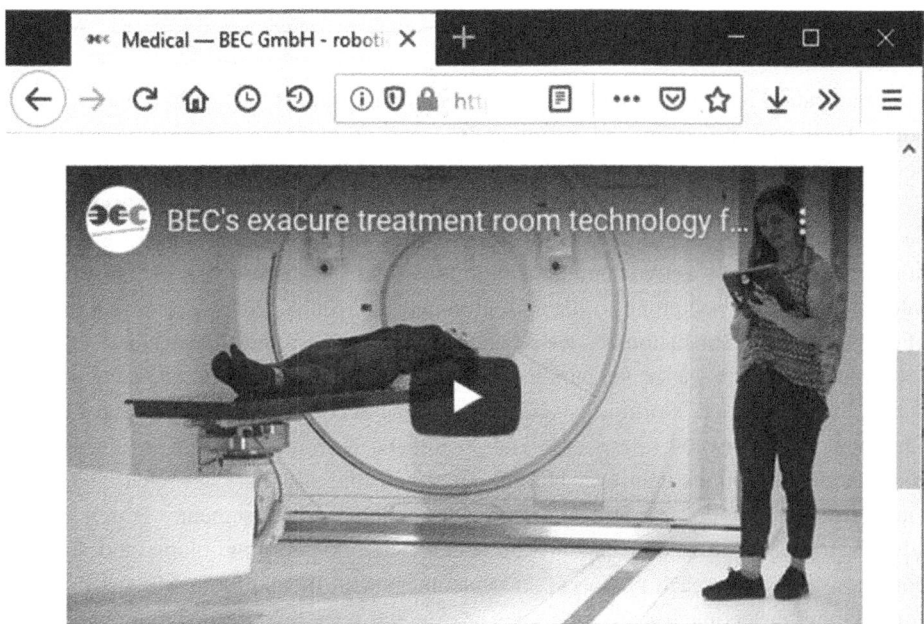

RADIOTHERAPY

The exacure system is the first stand-alone medical device that has been developed by BEC, as a certified medical device manufacturer (DIN ISO 13485) and got successfully installed at MedAustron in Wiener Neustadt.

A custom-modified industrial robot, designed and adapted for medical use, is the core of the *exacure*-system. Its most distinctive feature is the ceiling mount, which allows for movement in seven independent degrees of freedom. The robot can not only be positioned in all three dimensions and six degrees of freedom, but also be moved along the ceiling towards and from the beam nozzle in order to further improve flexibility of patient positioning. Another advantage of the ceiling-mounted system is the integrated optical tracking system: it monitors the treatment couch position 500 times per second and applies corrections in real time, if necessary, to ensure optimal treatment results.

Fig. 2 (continued)

7   Conclusion

Communication is a key activity in sales, and companies must engage in proactive communications with prospects and customers to open up business opportunities and help deliver customer value in domestic but even more in international contexts.

Traditionally, in B-to-B markets the salespeople were in charge of identifying prospects, opening up business process with them, closing the deal and nurturing the relationship. By using proactive communication tools, the salesperson was in control of the sales process from beginning to the end, although the results, such as closing a number of deals with different customers, were contingent on the customers' decisions.

In recent years, however, the number of digital communication tools available to companies have increased enormously and changed the access to information and the balance of control between salespeople and customers. Nowadays, companies have more communication options than ever before, e.g. email, message services, chat, audio and video streaming, video conferencing, websites, banner advertisements, search engine advertisements, professional and private social networks, forums, blogs, and supplier portals, available to reach prospects and customers with their offerings, but part of the control that salespeople had over the sales process has been relinquished to prospects and customers. Technology has appeared as a transformative factor in B-to-B sales, that dramatically improved buyer knowledge and at the same time helped smaller companies to actively communicate with customers worldwide.

This means that prospects and customers can look more easily than ever for their own information, share their thoughts and experiences with other customers, and probably even self-select themselves as "prospects" for a particular product from a specific supplier. While this is valuable for that particular supplier, it also means that the other suppliers will find it more difficult to open up business opportunities with these prospects (because they might have already decided that those suppliers were not the right fit). This situation only underlines the great importance of digital communications in today's global business environment. Poor planning, poor selection of media and content or poor execution of the digital communications strategy, will result in reduced competitiveness and fewer business opportunities. On the contrary, the company that understands how to integrate multiple digital platforms, unify their message across platforms and make them work internationally and synergistically with their salesforce, will be at the forefront of competitiveness and will be able to maximize their results.

Exercise A

A US American company produces waterproofing materials for roofs. Its main market is the US. An expansion into other markets, in particular Europe is envisaged.

Discuss how digital media channels can be used in preparing this market for future sales.

Exercise B

How can companies, operating in a B-to-B environment, use social media channels? And what are key requirements a company needs to meet in order to ensure that such social media presence would be successful?

Exercise C/1

You start working for a B-to-B company that only uses traditional media for their communications (e.g., participation in trade fairs, print advertising in trade journals, etc.). Management is discussing the possibility of starting to use some type of digital media and they want to hear from you what would be the advantages. What would you say are the main advantages? What arguments would you use to convince the managers?

Exercise C/2

In the same case as before, the company decides to follow your advice and move to digital media channels. Draw up a plan to start using different types of media in the short term (1–2 years) and in the medium term (3–5 years).

Exercise D

When developing and implementing a plan for using digital media communications in a B-to-B environment, how can you create synergy by using different platforms and technologies?

References

Andersson, S., & Wickström, N. (2017). Why and how are social media used in a B-to-B context, and which stakeholders are involved? *Journal of Business & Industrial Marketing, 32*(8),1098–1108.

Austin, J. L. (1962). *How to do things with words*. London: Oxford University Press.

Backhaus, K., & Voeth, M. (2014). *Industriegütermarketing*. 10th ed. München: Vahlen.

Berger, A. A. (2010). *Essentials of mass communication theory*. Thousand Oaks: Sage.

Bernard, M. (2016). The impact of social media on the B-to-B CMO. *Journal of Business & Industrial Marketing, 31*(8), 955–960.

Bly, R. W. (2018). *The digital marketing handbook: A step-by-step guide to creating websites that sell* [Online]. Irvine: Entrepreneur Press. https://ebookcentral.proquest.com/lib/gbv/detail. action?docID=5275734 [26 August 2020].

Bocconcelli, R., Cioppi, M., & Pagano, A. (2017). Social media as a resource in SMEs' sales process. *Journal of Business & Industrial Marketing, 32*(5), 693–709.

Brosan, F. (2012). Business intelligence: What works where in B-to-B digital marketing. *Journal of Direct, Data and Digital Marketing Practice, 14*(2), 154–159.

Buratti, N., Parola, F., & Satta, G. (2018). Insights on the adoption of social media marketing in B-to-B services. *the TQM Journal, 30*(5), 490–529.

Dahiya, R. (2018). A research paper on digital marketing communication and consumer buying decision process: An empirical study in the Indian passenger car market. *Journal of Global Marketing, 31*(2), 73–95.

Eagly, A. H., & Chaiken, S. (1993). *The psychology of attitudes.* Orlando, FL: Harcourt Brace Jovanovich College Publishers.

Futrell, C. (2001). *Sales Management: Teamwork, Leadership and Technology.* Mason, OH: South Western, 6th Edition.

Hinderer, H. (2005). *Eine Vorgehensweise zur Erstellung von Informationssystemen für die zwischenbetriebliche Zusammenarbeit im Vertrieb technischer Produkte.* Dissertation Stuttgart University, Heimsheim, Jost-Jetter.

Huotari, L., Ulkuniemi, P., Saraniemi, S., & Mäläskä, M. (2015). Analysis of content creation in social media by B-to-B companies. *Journal of Business & Industrial Marketing, 30*(6), 761–770.

Johnson, P. F., Leenders, M. L., & Flynn A. E. (2011). *Purchasing and supply management* (International Edition). New York, NY: Mc Graw Hill.

Kannan, P. K., & Li, H. (2017). Digital marketing: A framework, review and research agenda. *International Journal of Research in Marketing, 34,* 22–45.

Kotler, P., Kartajaya, H., & Setiawan, I. (2017). *Marketing 4.0: Moving from traditional to digital.* Hoboken, NJ: Wiley.

Kotler, P., & Keller, K. L. (2016). *Marketing management* (15th ed.). Boston: Pearson.

Kovaitė, K., Šūmakaris, P., & Stankevičienė, J. (2020). Digital communication channels in Industry 4.0 implementation. *Management, 25*(1), 171–191.

Kreutzer, R. T., Rumler, A., & Wille-Baumkauff, B. (2020). *B2B-Online-Marketing und Social Media: Handlungsempfehlungen und Best Practices* (2nd ed.). Wiesbaden: Springer.

Levy, S., & Gvili, Y. (2015). How credible is E-word of mouth across digital-marketing channels. *Journal of Advertising Research, 55*(1), 95–109.

Lippold, D. (2016). *Akquisitionsgrundlagen im B-to-B-Bereich* (2nd ed.). Wiesbaden: Springer.

Lüders, M. (2020). *Online-Informationsverhalten von Business-to-Business-Käufern.* Wiesbaden: Springer.

McCarthy, J. (1960). *Basic marketing: A managerial approach.* Richard D Irwin: Homewood.

Moncrief, W. M., & Marshall, G. W. (2005). The evolution of the seven steps of selling. *Industrial Marketing Management, 34,* 13–22.

Rakić, B., & Rakić, M. (2014). Integrated marketing communications paradigm in digital environment: The five pillars of integration. *Megatrend Review, 11*(1), 187–204.

Shannon, C. E., & Weaver, W. (1975). *The mathematical theory of communication.* Urbana: University of Illinois Press.

St. Elmo Lewis. E. (1903). Catch-line and argument. *The Book-Keeper, 15,* February.

Stephen, A. T., & Galak, J. (2012). The effects of traditional and social earned media on sales: A study of a microlending marketplace. *Journal of Marketing Research, 49,* 624–639.

Webster, F. E., & Wind, Y. (1972). A general model for understanding organizational buying behavior. *Journal of Marketing, 36*(2), 12–19.

Corporate Social Responsibility in International Supply Chains

Katharina Kilian-Yasin and Rafael Correa

1 Global Supply Chains and CSR

International trade is an old phenomenon. Evidence of ancient trade roads and sea routes dates back to earlier than the Bronze Age 3000 BC, and the Silk Road, as well as the Incense, Spice, or Amber Routes, are famous examples from very old times, too. In those days, goods in high demand that could not be produced locally with the desired quality or at all, were imported from other places, connecting continents to each other.

Early on, rulers of countries recognized that access to sought-after resources secured them wealth and power, and from the fifteenth century, some European nations systematically engaged in conquering and colonizing remote territories and stabilized their power with control over large areas and their economies with imports of goods in high demand. Colonialism, including the slave trade, set the basis for European countries', and later on, the North Americas' future economic strength, and mass supply with raw materials fuelled the beginnings of industrialized production. As an example, the industrialization of Britain`s textile production in the late eighteenth century would not have happened as it did without the exploitation of African slaves as cheap workforce to cultivate the cotton fields and work in all areas around this trade (Beckert 2015). Another example of a good in high demand securing wealth in the eighteenth century is sugar, and since

K. Kilian-Yasin (✉) · R. Correa
Pforzheim University, Pforzheim, Germany
e-mail: katharina.kilian-yasin@hs-pforzheim.de

R. Correa
e-mail: rafael.correa@hs-pforzheim.de

L. Martin (ed.), *International Business Development*,
https://doi.org/10.1007/978-3-658-33221-1_12

the second decade of the twentieth century, access to fossil fuels has become a cause of power and wars.

As one can see with these examples, the phenomenon of global supply chains is nothing new. The focus nowadays is less on enlarging the power of rulers than on satisfying consumer demands, but the connection of continents through international trade has been continuing since ancient times. However, with the development in global transportation and communication infrastructure that took place after the second half of the twentieth century, its dimensions and value grew dramatically—to a point at which the vast majority of the products consumed in Europe or North America nowadays are either produced in, or contain almost countless parts and components from places around the whole globe. The world`s largest companies have several hundreds of tier-1 suppliers and up to almost 20,000 tier-2 and below suppliers, "tier-1 to tier-n " denoting the levels in the supplier pyramid from direct to sub-suppliers (van Weele 2018). The ability to successfully manage complex supply chains across continents is of crucial importance for companies today. While in the past perceived as purely operational, supply chain management (SCM) is nowadays understood as a strategic function, comprising the sourcing activities of international purchasing and procurement (see also Chapter "Sourcing Strategies and Trends: Global Versus Local"). Orchestrating efficient international supply chains and mitigating supply chain risks are core elements of profitable overall business operations and international business development (ibid.).

Being able to source goods or services from abroad allows companies to reduce costs and focus on marketing or improving their main product and developing new products, thus making them innovative and competitive (Porter and van der Linde 1995). Global supply chains offer many advantages, such as lower costs for labour, land, material, buildings, machinery etc., and access to a larger talent pool. Internationalized production is also credited for bringing hundreds of thousands of people out of extreme poverty all around the world (OECD 2016). However, incidents of poor labour conditions, human rights violations, environmental pollution and resources depletion are the dark side of globalized trade, and the necessity of ensuring responsible practice along companies` supply chains has become an urgent issue.

The ideal of doing trade upon moral principles is also an old phenomenon. In the Middle Ages, tradespersons in Europe established the ideal of the "honourable merchant" against practices of deceit and cheating, and agreed on codes of conduct with values such as integrity, honesty and decency. The ideal lives on today; many companies nowadays explicitly refer to that traditional ideal and their responsibility to be honourable corporate citizens who contribute to the overall welfare of society. While in the past, the ideal of the honourable merchant did not address ethical responsibility towards producers in remote countries, those companies who invoke these principles today often extend them to their international supply chains.

The often-quoted classical theorist of economics from the eighteenth century, Adam Smith, is usually connected with a concept of unfettered free markets which regulate themselves to the benefit of all, because an "invisible hand" balances the self-interests of the participants in trade. What is often marginalized, is the fact that Adam Smith was also very much concerned about the purpose of trade to free societies from feudal control, violence and inherited accumulation of wealth and power. While Smith opposed barriers to free trade by unnecessary government regulation, and was also against legislation that favours interest-groups' concentrations of wealth, he saw the role of governmental regulatory frameworks in setting limits to the self-serving greed of merchants, and to enable justice and prevent steep inequality. Smith`s concern clearly was about how trade could benefit nations, and contribute to freedom, prosperity and welfare of societies as a whole, and not about how single businesses could best accumulate profit over others (Aßländer 2007).

In the 1950s, the influential free-market school around Milton Friedman took Adam Smith`s "invisible Hand" metaphor quite selectively to posit perfect market balances if businesses merely concentrate on making money, and very strongly contested any social responsibility beyond profit (Friedman 1970). This US-based approach has very much dominated business theory, practice and teaching for decades until today.

Nevertheless, as internationalization increased its pace to reach the degree of hyper-globalisation in the years before the financial crisis of 2008, and it became more and more difficult for manufacturers to oversee the conditions in their supply chains, increasing news reports about irresponsible business practice unsettled the public. Information travels fast across the globe with the speed of communication and social media, and consumers feel uncomfortable about the conditions under which some of their goods are produced. Long existing voices in business research, theory, teaching and practice, which contradict and relativize the pure dogma of unadulterated focus on profit, have gained ground. Today, the subject of corporate social responsibility (CSR) in international supply chains is present in broad public discourse, and consumers and society increasingly expect companies to source their supply upon socially responsible principles and demand supply chain transparency. Together with the challenges of environmental pollution, resource depletion and global warming, human rights in international supply chains have also reached the agendas of the most influential business leaders, as the Davos World Economic Forum of January 2020 has shown. The topic of social responsibility has become very important for international business managers, and since SCM is the core function of companies for their supply, it is a significant asset for professionals in this area to have a good understanding of CSR.

2   Understanding CSR

As seen above, the social, political and economic evolution of trade has led to a situation in which consumers expect businesses to implement CSR practices in managing not only their own domestic operations, but also their international supply chains. In the following, an overview of what CSR exactly is about and what it entails in terms of obligations for businesses and managers will be provided.

2.1   CSR and Its Constituents

A widely accepted definition of CSR was proposed in 1979 by Archie B. Carroll. According to him, CSR encompasses the economic, legal, ethical, and discretionary expectations that society has of organizations at a given point in time (Carroll 1979).

The *economic* element of this definition is usually the easiest one to grasp because intrinsic to the nature of a business: it is the foundation of a business to be profitable. The *legal* element simply emphasizes that businesses are expected to operate under the applicable legal limits and to observe whichever legal obligation they are subjected to: Paying taxes, not exploiting their employees and not emitting more pollutants than they are legally allowed to, for instance. The *ethical* element encompasses all activities that society expects from a business in the spirit of fairness and justice in areas where the letter of the law is not codified and available, but where general society feels that this would be "the right thing to do". This element is the crucial and necessary basis of CSR in a business. The *discretionary* element is expressed through additional philanthropic engagement to which a company either commits spontaneously, or upon pressure from its stakeholders. The discretionary level of CSR is necessarily based on the company`s fulfilment of its ethical responsibilities; discretionary engagement without a fundament of ethical practice must be judged as hollow window-dressing.

It follows from these four elements that businesses have to do more than simply operate within the strict limits of the law to claim that they are assuming their corporate social responsibilities. It is a significant element of this four-layer definition that a company`s CSR behaviour must correspond to the expectations of society. Such societal expectations may change considerably over time.

As implied in the introduction, the notion of socially responsible business gained traction in the second half of the twentieth century, starting out in the United States. Before this period, society did not really expect businesses to care about anything more than their economic activities, because people trusted businesses to act responsibly, according to the then existing standards. In the 1960s, however, society in the USA was undergoing major changes through the so-called civil rights movement, which brought subjects such as racial equality, women and consumers' rights and the environment into the spotlight. By then, even if companies still did not perceive their social role as today, the societal context in which they operated was changing dramatically, with new demands and expectations (Carroll and Shabana 2010).

The period between the early 1970s and the late 1980s marks more an evolution than a revolution in the level of attention that the issue of CSR received—especially by academic work that tried to better demarcate the limits of corporate responsibility towards society.

In the 1980s, the ecological environment started to appear more frequently as a topic of concern amongst consumers, and, in fact, some of the brands that are still recognized as trailblazers for environmentally and socially responsible operations were founded at this time. The fact that these businesses prospered and still exist is an unmistakable sign that consumers' CSR awareness has been steadily growing since then (Latapí Agudelo et al. 2019).

The 1990s were marked by a significant shift in the global economic scenario. The fall of the Soviet Union and the opening of markets in developing countries such as China and India, the strengthening of political treaties, unions and agreements such as those of the European Union (EU), the World Trade Organisation (WTO) and the North American Trade Agreement (NAFTA; now: USMCA), as well as technological innovation in transport and communication set the stage for the birth of globalization. Companies could now extend their supply and distribution chains to the farthest corners of the world in order to generate efficiencies with cheaper production abroad and stabilize their competitive position, or maximize their gains. On the other hand, the combination of this increasingly open global market with societies more and more aware and informed about social, economic and environmental issues, put managers in a new and challenging position. Nowadays, managers have to cater to numerous new sets of rapidly-evolving expectations from heterogeneous groups on a truly worldwide stage. Responsibly managing international supply chains in the twenty-first century has become more complex and more important than ever.

2.2 CSR and Related Concepts

To fully understand the concept of CSR, it is worthwhile clarifying its delineations in relation to other concepts that are used, with considerable freedom and sometimes interchangeably, among managers and academics alike. As the very concept of CSR evolved and became better known throughout the timeline seen above, it was naturally frequently questioned, dissected or twisted to better fit to specific context conditions or interests (Carroll 2015).

The concept of business ethics (BE), for instance, appeared in the 1980s and was frequently used to discuss the unethical behaviour of managers involved in widely publicized scandals at the time. While obviously belonging to the wider concept of CSR, the idea of BE has the advantage of, at least semantically, separating the behaviour of said individuals from that of the company as a whole.

More or less at the same time, stakeholder management (SM) appeared as an approach to take into consideration the multiple parties affecting and affected by the business and balance their interests in a fair and effective way (Freeman 1984).

Corporate citizenship (CC) is yet another framework related to CSR. In essence, it was a term adopted within the business community to try and cast companies in the role of responsible members society. A good law-abiding citizen is considerate and fair towards the other members of the social group, and he also gives back to the community. Looking closely, it corresponds to the legal, ethical and discretionary levels of the four elements of CSR mentioned above. It could be argued that the idea of CC allows managers to keep addressing the same issues as CSR while avoiding the notion of "responsibility".

In recent years, another term has come to be used almost as a synonym for CSR: sustainability. Derived from the concept of sustainable development, the concept of sustainability was quickly embraced by the business community after the 1990s. Today, it is understood that in order to run a business sustainably, companies must perform well not only financially, but also socially and environmentally. They must, in other words, strive for a positive "triple bottom line" (TBL) including the "3P" of profit/prosperity, people and planet (Elkington 2018). Sustainability has become a favoured terminology among managers not only because of its positive character and wide acceptance, but also because it tangibly defines areas of action, and maybe because it, just as CC, circumvents having to pinpoint individual managers' "responsibility".

With all these concepts, it is essential to keep in mind that none of these fully replaces or displaces CSR. Corporate Social Responsibility is still the overarching and most complete concept to guide managers of corporate operations in today's world.

3 Why Engage in CSR? —Short Terms Costs, Long-Term Benefits

From an ethical perspective, the answer to the question of "Why engage in CSR?" is obvious: companies should engage in CSR because it is the morally right thing to do. From an economic, as well as business and managerial perspective, things are not as straightforward—putting a CSR strategy in place usually causes, at least at the beginning, additional costs, which in the short term are expected to come out of the bottom line. Initial costs occur for SCM staff with CSR expertise, for training and external advisors and for adjustments in the procedures and IT-systems. Recurring costs result from employing salaried SCM staff with CSR expertise, as well as gathering and evaluating information, auditing, monitoring and developing suppliers, and reporting. Apart from the required investment, however, there are also significant benefits of shifting SCM practise to CSR, which may, if successful, offset the costs in the long term and even enhance competitiveness.

The main purpose of a business is to deliver a required good to its customers, ensuring the expected functionality and quality at an accepted price; for many decades, it has not been a necessary feature to additionally include CSR into the value of the product or service. Nowadays, however, consumers and society increasingly require social responsibility and transparency, and a growing number is ready to pay a premium for responsibly produced goods. More and more policies and regulations enforce this trend on a governmental level. Throughout the years, the list of obligations imposed on businesses in terms of their social, economic and environmental responsibilities has grown consistently and is still growing. A recent comprehensive study conducted on behalf of the European Commission aims at assessing possible pathways for a regulatory framework on a European level on companies' "appropriate due diligence throughout the supply chain" (Smit et al. 2020). The study includes an academic analysis of the costs, and also of the potential benefits of CSR. The benefits are many, among which the most tangible ones, as reported by companies and evaluated by researchers, will be listed in the following.

3.1 Financial and Stock Performance and Cost of Capital

Naturally, the first question a manager asks when considering whether to engage in CSR is: "how will this impact the financial performance of the company?" Although studies that can actually quantify how much good or bad CSR practices affect a company's bottom line are rare, there is evidence that the said relationship is a positive one. Companies with good social and environmental practices tend to perform better financially than comparable companies with worse CSR profiles, even if the magnitude of this impact varies according to the market in which they operate.

In addition, companies that invest in CSR tend to outperform others on the stock market. Their stock prices have been shown to gain more in value and display less volatility over time, especially in times of crisis. In fact, studies indicate that a good CSR profile helps prevent or mitigate drops in market value during and after times of crisis (see e.g. Schnietz and Epstein 2005; Janney and Gove 2011).

Still on purely financial benefits of implementing good CSR practices, companies with good sustainability records tend to be more attractive to investors and to experience lower costs of capital. This effect is probably associated with how the market perceives a given company in terms of reputation and risks, as will be seen in the following section.

Finally, it is important to highlight that, on the contrary, there is no evidence to indicate that engaging in CSR could have a negative impact on a company's financial performance. This means that even with the necessary initial investments, the implementation of such policies is very unlikely to hurt a company's bottom line (Smit et al. 2020).

3.2 Credibility, Brand Reputation and Risk Reduction

While authors still argue about how to directly quantify the financial benefits brought by good CSR strategies, many agree that brand reputation is a consistent indirect link between the two, and that it improves with good and well-communicated CSR practice. In fact, since reputation—or image—is a matter of perception, it has become increasingly important that companies promote their good deeds among their stakeholders. Especially in the eyes of today's consumers, more concerned than ever with ethical, social and environmental issues, a brand's reputation or image ever more depends on its performance in these areas. If a business has a credible CSR image, it will establish itself as reliable and honest, and consumers will assume its products are of higher quality than those of companies without such a reputation (McWilliams and Siegel 2001). As a result, businesses with a positive reputation should sustain higher profit levels over time (Roberts and Dowling 2002).

A carefully cultivated reputation can have the added benefit of reducing corporate risk. A company that makes a true effort to monitor and improve its CSR standards is more likely to anticipate problems and, therefore, less likely to be involved in negative incidents with international repercussions. It is also less likely to have to bear the heavy costs of litigation and reparation that follow such events. Even if putting in place and enforcing strict CSR policies along the supply chain does not guarantee full risk elimination, it should decrease its likelihood and, at the very least, offer a company the argument that it did everything within its reach to prevent it.

3.3   Operational Efficiency and Innovation

A less direct but perhaps more palpable effect of investments in CSR can be seen on a company's operational efficiency. CSR measures can lead to a more efficient use of resources and, therefore, to lower production and operational costs.

Some companies have achieved remarkable savings through CSR. One North-American company saved nearly 10 billion US dollars after investing 2 billion US dollars in resource efficiency (Whelan and Fink 2016). Another US corporation saved 300 million US dollars after reducing its greenhouse gases and water use. In addition, studies show an overwhelmingly positive correlation between solid CSR practice and operational performance, especially when regarding approaches that involve a company's workforce (ibid.). Said improvements do not need to happen "in house" to produce positive effects. With Sect. 1502 of Dodd-Frank Wall Street Reform and Consumer Protection Act of 2010 (see Sect. 4.4 of this chapter), an increased oversight duty was imposed on companies trading with so-called "conflict minerals" in their supply chains. While companies saw the monitoring of compliance with the Act as an unfair burden at first, some of the very same companies are now experiencing it as an indispensable tool for maintaining price and supply stability. Through CSR obligations, companies gained better overall knowledge and control over costs and risks throughout their supply chains.

As another benefit, companies are required to think outside the box and come up with creative solutions in order to improve their CSR performance, in a process that often yields new products, processes and business models. Hence, CSR can be an important driver of innovation in the twenty-first century.

3.4   Workforce Motivation and Attraction of Talent

In post-industrial societies, where the average level of wealth is very high, people don't just work to sustain their existence, but also to indulge in commodities, luxuries and leisure activities which make their lives comfortable and enjoyable, and which provide them with social prestige. In a society where almost everybody is saturated with consumables, travel and leisure opportunities, individuals start asking themselves "What next?"—some may be satisfied with working for even more money to buy another property abroad or investing in shares. Meanwhile, others have fundamental questions about the purpose of their work beyond material affluence. In 2012, a study found that significant portions of well-qualified university students prefer to work for socially and environmentally responsible employers, and that up to a half of them would accept salary reductions if they could contribute to social justice and environmental protection with their work (Szeltner and Zukin 2012). Staff turnover in CSR-committed companies is low in comparison to conventional companies, as loyalty and motivation to work for an employer who is "doing good" is high. The positive reputation and credible CSR commitment of a company attract future employees, and it has been found that CSR orientation of companies especially appeals to highly qualified talent, so that companies can gain competitive advantage by hiring and retaining the best qualified staff over their non-CSR-oriented competitors.

Additionally, practicing CSR along supply chains into less affluent countries improves the working conditions for local employees and workers: fair wages, decent safety and health conditions as well as caring for the local ecological environment strengthens workers and their families. This helps them to do their work well and deliver the required good reliably and with good quality.

3.5   Pre-Empting Legislation and Control

A company that is perceived as a good corporate citizen may be able to reduce the level of control and regulation it is subjected to, which gives it more freedom to operate by its own standards. This benefit of CSR is easy to understand: by its very nature, regulation is almost always reactive. This means that first a society or its legislators must identify perceived problematic or undesirable conduct to, only then, create and pass norms or laws to try to prevent or contain said behaviour. Proactively anticipating more stringent regulations allows a firm to make the necessary changes at its own pace and under the best possible circumstances (Berman et al. 1999). Companies may also avoid regulation if the government and society feel that the current legislation is enough to ensure their CSR compliance. Delaying necessary CSR measures within a company`s operations and lobbying against governmental regulation implies the risk of even higher costs when the regulation is eventually effected anyway.

4   Integrating CSR into Supply Chains—How to Make It Work

When a company has—for whichever reason or motivation—decided it wants to improve its CSR performance, the next question is how to get from intention to implementation. How can a company establish and break down strategic CSR goals into workable measures and integrate CSR into management decisions and day-to-day operations? In the area of international SCM, especially procurement and supplier relations management, crucial functions converge in which decisions affecting the overall quality of product and production, including labour standards, human rights and ecological and resource impact, are made. In the following, the steps that a company generally, and its SCM functions specifically, must take to achieve better CSR performance, will be presented.

4.1 Commitment: Integrating CSR Principles and Goals in Strategy and Leadership

The commitment of executive level management to CSR as a part of the overall company strategy is critical to its successful and credible implementation in the company's operations. It is essential to integrate CSR principles into the general strategic frameworks of a company in order to establish a balance between financial and CSR objectives already on this first level of decision-making. If, contrary to this, CSR principles are delegated to a secondary level below general strategy, there is a high risk that CSR will always be subordinated to financial and other objectives, and thereby marginalized and never successfully effected. Also, it is impracticable that distinct functions, such as those of SCM, independently establish CSR strategies detached from overall company strategy, as these would conflict with the superordinate general objectives of a non-CSR-committed company strategy. Nonetheless, input from the company`s operational units can also stimulate CSR commitment of the executive level. SCM, and specifically purchasing and supplier management is a key area to not only receive strategy directives concerning CSR and put them into practice, but also to give valuable impulses from day-to-day contact with CSR-related challenges.

Executive level commitment requires leadership of managers who understand and support the concept of CSR and possess the skills to communicate it to stakeholders both inside and outside the organization. To achieve this, companies must involve managers with CSR expertise in their executive board and/or engage in regular executive training in the areas of corporate governance, financial markets, regulation, reporting, change management, HRM, etc., all combined with CSR principles and requirements (see e.g. Epstein and Buhovac 2014, p. 45; Jang and Ardichvili 2020). Apart from managers` expertise and skills, it has been found that it significantly strengthens companies' CSR efforts when involved individuals intrinsically champion social responsibility as a personal value (Hemingway and Maclagan 2004). Consequently, the selection of morally aware and motivated leaders for executive positions, but also for other relevant company units, such as those of SCM, facilitates successful CSR implementation.

No matter if a company`s CSR commitment is inflicted by extrinsic necessity, such as societal expectations, competitive pressure, reputational issues (e.g. after a scandal) or legislation, or motivated by intrinsic moral responsibility of individuals, the CSR principles must be visibly anchored within the vision and mission of the company. Therefrom, they have to be translated into company specific goals, areas of action, policies, processes and operable performance indicators.

4.2 Implementation: Designing Systems, Structures and Processes for CSR in International SCM

Various models exist to categorize the degrees of maturity at which companies engage in CSR (see e.g. Brandenburg et al. 2018). These reach, over several ascending stages, from rejection of the concept to the very high level of utilizing CSR as a strategic impetus for overall innovative transformation of the company, or even the company`s engagement to promote CSR in the political arena beyond its own organization (Fig. 1).

Considering today`s advances in CSR research, far-developed societal awareness and the existence of many examples of company best practice, the input of this chapter on how to implement CSR in supply chains is addressed to the maturity level up from the fifth stage of "Efficient CSR integration". "Efficient CSR integration" is the stage from which professional and effective CSR-based SCM can be effected, and which is essential to ensure the embedding of CSR-targeted performance indicators of SCM into the overall company strategy and to receive executive support thereof. Furthermore, alignment is necessary to make sure that full responsibility of senior management for all CSR-relevant action and impact is assumed.

Commitment to CSR must be accompanied by all involved individuals` comprehensive understanding of its principles and relevant fields. There is international widespread consensus that the relevant fields for businesses` social responsibilities are human rights, labour standards, environmental and resources preservation, protection of workers and consumers and anti-corruption. To assess a company`s overall supply chain operations systematically, various codified sets of principles or guidelines offer guidance and orientation, the principles of the United Nations` "UN Global Compact" and the "OECD Guidelines" being the most widely internationally acknowledged (UN Global Compact 2020; OECD 2018). Depending on the specific business, a company must analyse where its operations have an impact on any aspect within these CSR-relevant fields and document which areas of action result from this analysis. The internationally adopted United

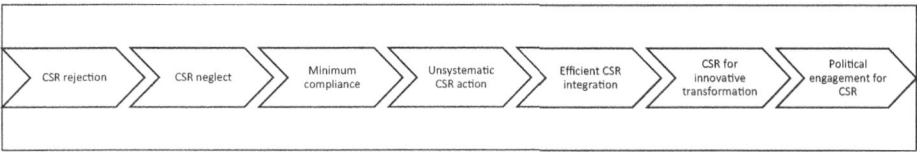

| CSR rejection | CSR neglect | Minimum compliance | Unsystematic CSR action | Efficient CSR integration | CSR for innovative transformation | Political engagement for CSR |

Fig. 1 Degrees of CSR maturity (adapted from Schneider 2012 and Marques-Mendes and Santos 2016)

Nations` seventeen Sustainable Development Goals (SDG`s) with their sub-targets and indicators can help a company to identify and formulate their own specific areas of action and targets; additionally, industry specific guidelines, initiatives and indicator frameworks exist (see Sect. 4.4 of this chapter).

In order to operationalize CSR commitment in the identified areas of action, clear responsibilities for CSR-related tasks have to be assigned and communication routines between executive management, buyers, quality managers, CSR commissioners etc. must be established. Next, applicable policies and management systems must be devised. Practically, this implies that existing SCM systems must be either supplemented with additional CSR-relevant indicators and target values, or reviewed and adapted, or re-designed for CSR from scratch. Buyers must then scope procurement processes for potential CSR risks and map operations to identify possible and actual problem areas, as well as information gaps. In case of information gaps, buyers should consult with various kinds of stakeholders to gather the necessary information to fill these gaps. Based on a prioritization of the most significant CSR risks, plans to end CSR-adverse practice must be developed, and measures to cease and prevent problematic procurement issues must be implemented. As easy as this may sound, the implementation of appropriate measures requires, besides specialized procurement expertise, a lot of general and specific geographical, political, industry, sector, product and CSR-related knowledge, experience and methodological skills so that remediation of problems and improvement of CSR impact is eventually achieved. This involves continuous stakeholder dialogue and supplier relationship management up to tier-n suppliers. Remediation measures may range from renegotiating contracts with existing suppliers, defining and including binding conditions in new contracts, offering compliance support or training to suppliers, acquiring and selecting new suppliers, and, in some cases, ending contracts with non-compliant suppliers. To ensure the effectiveness of these measures, monitoring and evaluation systems must be set up and, if necessary, regular auditing of suppliers along the whole supply chain, followed by remediation and improvement actions, must be organized. In order to generate transparency, accountability and credibility, the CSR efforts and results of the procurement function need to be communicated through reporting, stakeholder dialogue and publishing externally relevant information.

Figure 2 gives a simplified overview of the general measures that a company must take to entrench CSR in its supply chain. What may theoretically look like a neatly sequential procedure with consecutive steps, usually in company reality is an iterative and organic process of continuous learning, development and, if successful, improvement.

Along the steps illustrated above, the relevant procurement processes, tools and documents such as surveys, manuals, checklists, questionnaires, approvals and contracts must also be either adapted or designed anew to cover CSR requirements. The short case example below shows which steps and tools a company sets out with to adapt its process of supplier approval to CSR requirements for a so-called "conflict metal" in their supply chain.

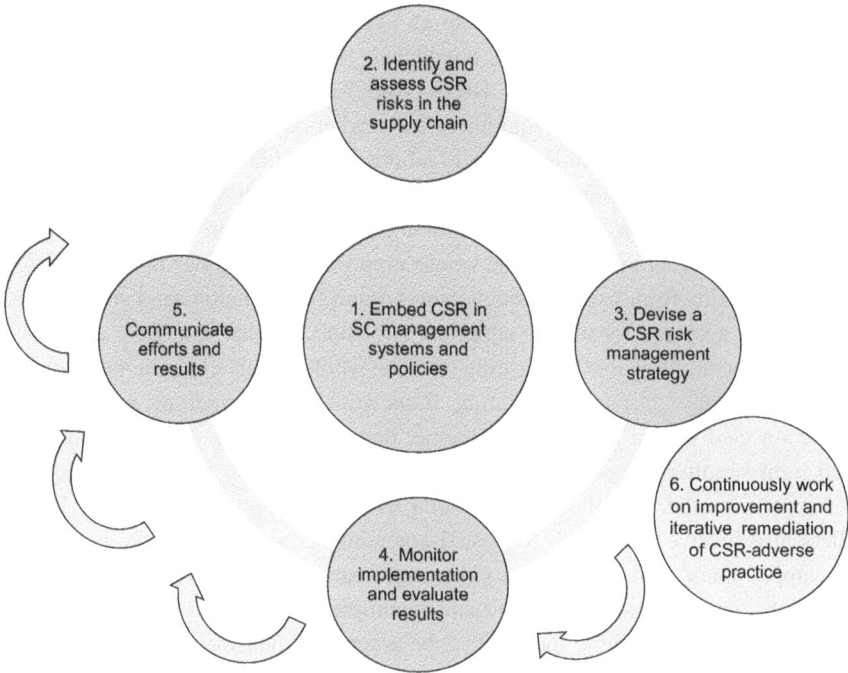

Fig. 2 Implementation of CSR in SCM practice (based on OECD 2018)

Case study 1: CSR-consistent conflict mineral supplier approval

Against the backdrop of rising awareness and knowledge about the risks of so-called "conflict materials" in production, an automotive supplier set out to improve its international supply chains with regard to CSR. This anonymized case study shows how this was done with the example of lead used in batteries.

The company followed the UN Global Compact as the overarching guideline for CSR categories, as well as selected Sustainable Development Goals (SDGs) for areas of action and criteria, and the CSR-relevant ISO standards for indicators. Additionally, the company developed a lead industry specific system of CSR indicators. It first included CSR standards in their general QM and SCM systems for tier-1 lead suppliers, and afterwards aimed at extending this to further sub-suppliers.

As a first step, the company tried to gain an overall impression of its international lead supply chain by conducting a survey with all tier-1 suppliers asking them to describe the management processes with their suppliers and how they ensured that the UN Global Compact principles were followed. They also asked whether they could confirm UN Global Compact compliance of their suppliers and demanded names and places of sub-suppliers in order to map an overview and identify potential overlaps. From the results, a risk rating was conducted, followed by recommendations and a timeline to remediate problematic issues. Additionally, yearly auditing visits with a CSR minimum check (safety equipment for workers, regular health checks, disposal of toxic waste, paid holiday leave, child labour etc.), which had previously only been conducted with tier-1 suppliers, were also established for tier-2 suppliers with the suggestion that they in turn also monitor their suppliers. Through these actions, the company is far from monitoring the whole supply chain up to tier-n, but has extended its regular audits from five lead smelters to around forty smelters and some mines. As a next step, a survey for all sub-suppliers is planned, which can serve as a basis for extending the auditing and monitoring over the whole supply chain in the future.

The company introduced a rating framework with numerous auditing criteria and connected it to a traffic light scheme, depending on the degree of compliance. Red light suppliers receive a list with conditions they have to fulfil immediately to get approval, otherwise they are excluded from the supply chain. Yellow light suppliers also receive a list with requested amendments with a deadline, but remain in the supply chain until completion. Green light candidates receive approval. The classifications are continuously updated and accompanied by a CSR risk mitigation plan. Concerning new suppliers, these are only accepted when they proactively fulfil the green light CSR requirements. The aim is to continuously improve CSR performance of all suppliers to fully eliminate CSR-adverse behaviour.

The introduction of CSR indicators into the company unit's general SCM system is not essentially different from updating existing regular QM systems, but requires specific expertise and effort. ◄

4.3   Organisation: Evolution, Innovation and Culture

A company's commitment to implement CSR in its supply chains requires, and also promotes overall organisational change towards CSR orientation. The necessity to adjust policies and alter processes is a demanding challenge, which entails a lot of work and effort and may put managers and employees who appreciate established routines under pressure. However, the pressure to change also has the potential to unleash problem solving creativity and inventiveness, ultimately leading to innovation. If a company manages to encourage and support their employees' contributions to CSR on all levels, it can cultivate a climate of organizational evolution in which individuals can grow with a sense of impacting business and society in a positive way. A successfully CSR-oriented organizational culture nurtures workforce motivation and loyalty, and enhances the company's employer reputation to attract talent, as well as earning credibility in the perception of consumers and society. The following case study illustrates how a company's CSR activities contributed to innovation and a positive organisational culture.

In the year 2015, German chocolate producer Alfred Ritter GmbH & Co. KG with its chocolate brand "Ritter Sport" presented its first Sustainability Report for the year 2014. The report covered the fields of Product Responsibility, Environmental Protection and Social Responsibility. The company`s fourth Sustainability Report is planned for publication at the beginning of the year 2021. Ritter`s first Sustainability Report documented the change from launching single CSR-related projects, which was the company`s CSR approach for the early 2000's, to embracing CSR as an integrated element of the overall company strategy (Ritter 2018).

One of Ritter`s early explicit CSR-related activities was to establish an energy management concept in order save resources and reduce emissions. This involves the idea that, until today, all operations, including those of overseas own and partnering cocoa plantations, are continuously assessed upon energy consumption, and measures for improvement are developed and implemented. The stirring process for the chocolate mass can serve as an example: After years of an existing and unquestioned stirring period and temperature, it was tested whether the same quality could not be achieved with a shorter period and/or a lower temperature. As this turned out to be the case, significant energy and cost savings could be achieved—76% of the energy could be saved, which corresponds to 900,000 kilowatt hours.

With purchasing CO_2-neutral electricity and producing an increasing portion of energy themselves through the company`s own cogeneration unit and photovoltaic panels on the plant's roofs, the company aims at reaching CO_2-neutral production by 2025.

Today, all areas of the company`s operations are managed with a regard to CSR, which starts with establishing cocoa beans and cocoa butter supply chains independent from the financial speculations and soil depleting monocultures of the conventional global cocoa beans market and production. Ritter has, over the years, managed to achieve 100% of sourcing from certified exclusive partners or own plantations, and engages in auditing and developing hazelnut and sugar suppliers, improving social standards, education and training of workers on home and overseas plants, reducing unnecessary ingredients and additives in the chocolate, and innovating packaging with regard to material efficiency and recyclability. Recent examples for CSR-driven problem solutions are the development of a cocoa beans opening machine, which reduces risks of injury compared to the traditional opening with a machete, and the replacement of a plastic sleeve on a cardboard box by a perforation and re-sealable flap, thus avoiding more than 8 tonnes of plastic per year. During the COVID-19 pandemic in 2020, the company introduced a staff rotation system with two weeks' training for a pool of employees to replace colleagues in cases of sick leave. Even though until the end of August 2020 such replacements had not yet become necessary, employees said their actual work benefitted from the practical experience in other company areas, and they appreciated the spirit of solidarity in times of crisis.

The reflex of seeking improvements in the vein of ecological and social responsibility has become a part of the company's DNA. The aim to reach CSR targets in all of the company`s operations has motivated board and employees to be inventive and has unleashed potential with innovative outcomes. ◀

4.4   Frameworks: International CSR Guidelines, Reporting Standards and Certifications

Internationally operating companies, which export their goods to other countries or import goods from other countries, have to respect the laws, regulations and standards of both home and foreign country. A system of internationally acknowledged rules, principles and standards facilitates trade and engenders transparency. With regard to CSR, there are also some widely recognized principles and standards which will be introduced in the following paragraphs.

UN Global Compact
The United Nations Global Compact is one of the foremost comprehensive voluntary guidelines on responsible business behaviour for companies. The UN Global Compact promotes ten principles in the areas of Human Rights, Labour Standards, Freedom of Association and Collective Bargaining, Environmental Protection and Anti-Corruption. The principles are derived from the Universal Declaration of Human Rights, the International Labour Organization's Declaration on Fundamental Principles and Rights at Work, the Rio Declaration on Environment and Development, and the United Nations Convention Against Corruption. The UN Global Compact supports companies to take strategic actions to advance broader societal goals, such as the Sustainable Development Goals, with an emphasis on collaboration and innovation. It does so by providing frameworks, guidelines, reports, conferences, workshops and initiating networks of professional exchange across companies (UN Global Compact 2020).

OECD Guidelines
The Guidelines of the Organization for Cooperation and Development for Multinational Enterprises ("the OECD Guidelines") complement and reinforce the UN Global Compact. The OECD guidelines are CSR-related recommendations of governments for multinational enterprises; they address the same CSR categories as the UN Global Compact. These governmental recommendations back companies' CSR efforts with credibility and guidance on practical implementation. As the OECD's core task is to support the ease of international investment, the guidelines refer in more detail and concretely to areas of implementation such as Foreign Direct Investment, taxation and competition (OECD 2018).

Sustainable Development Goals

The seventeen Sustainable Development Goals (SDGs) were adopted by all UN Member States in 2015, as part of the 2030 Agenda for Sustainable Development, which set out a 15-year plan to achieve the goals. The SDGs are a universal call to action to end poverty, protect the planet and improve the lives and prospects of everyone, everywhere. Each of the seventeen SDGs contains detailed sub-targets and indicators for achievement, adding up to 169 sub-targets and 232 indicators (SDG 2020). The comprehensive scope of the SDGs enables companies to identify which of the SDGs are of relevance to their business and offers them actionable targets and indicators.

ILO Standards

The United Nation`s International Labour Organisation brings together governments, employers and workers of 187 member States. In the Standing International Labour Conference, they develop conventions, declarations and recommendations to set labour standards, introduce policies and devise programmes that promote decent work for all women and men (ILO 2019). The ILO Centenary Declaration for the Future of Work of 2019 is the newest set of principles to which the UN general assembly agreed. It declares a "human-centred approach" as its focus and evolves around the three areas of "Increasing investment in people's capabilities, Increasing investment in the institutions of work and Increasing investment in decent and sustainable work" (ILO 2019). The declaration over-arches several binding conventions that address the fundamental principles and rights of work, which the UN member states and companies should implement in practice.

European Commission Guidelines and Directives

In 2011, the European Commission (EC) launched its "Renewed EU strategy 2011–14 for Corporate Social Responsibility", followed by an overview of progress in 2019. This strategy aims at enhancing the visibility of CSR and disseminating good practices, through the integration of CSR into education, training, and research. The EC's understanding of CSR relies on the above described international UN and OECD standards and ISO26000, enumerating the following areas: "Human rights, labour and employment practices (e.g. fair wages, education and training, diversity, gender equality, workers' health and well-being) and ecology (e.g. biodiversity, climate change, resource efficiency, life-cycle analysis and pollution prevention) as well as combating bribery and corruption" (EU-EC CSR 2020). The EC employs a mix between guidance for voluntary actions of companies and binding directives for EU member states and companies therein, which these have to translate into practice, if necessary through national legislation. Among the binding directives, the 2014 Non-Financial Reporting Directive (NFRD) requires companies with over 500 employees to disclose information on environmental protection, social responsibility and treatment of employees, respect for human rights, anti-corruption and bribery, and diversity on company boards. The EC has added these requirements to the general EU accounting directives and supports companies with practical guidelines for implementation (EU-EC NFRD 2020).

ISO Standards with CSR Relevance

The International Organization for Standardization develops and promotes worldwide proprietary, industrial, and commercial standards. There are several standards concerning CSR, which are widely used by companies. ISO 26000 "Guidance on social responsibility" is the most known, non-auditable standard, which explicitly addresses CSR in the form of a guideline with the seven following core subjects: 1) Organizational governance, 2) Human rights, 3) Labour practices, 4) Environment, 5) Fair operating practices, 6) Consumer issues, 7) Community involvement and development. The issues to tackle are substantiated in 4–8 sub-clauses for each core subject, adding up to 36 issues to be measured. Further CSR-relevant and, in these cases, auditable and certifiable ISO standards are ISO 14001 "Environmental Management Systems" and ISO 45001 "Occupational Health and Safety" (replaces the former OHSAS 18001 standard). The International Organization for Standardization declares which of the SDGs it contributes to for each ISO standard (ISO 2020).

EMAS Certification

The European Eco-Management and Audit Scheme (EMAS) is a management and reporting system. It supports companies in their environmental protection and resource efficiency efforts and makes these visible through an internationally acknowledged certification standard (EMAS 2020).

GRI Reporting Standards

The framework of the Global Reporting Initiative (GRI) is one of the oldest and internationally most known sustainability reporting standards. The GRI defines itself as an independent multi-stakeholder organization which continuously develops its voluntary reporting system through dialogue with industries, governments, non-governmental organisations, communities and workers. Its mission and vision are: "A thriving global community that lifts humanity and enhances the resources on which all life depends" and "To empower decisions that create social, environmental and economic benefits for everyone" The GRI set of reporting standards is currently the most widely used Sustainability Reporting Framework internationally (GRI 2020).

RMI, EPRM and Others

The Responsible Minerals Initiative (RMI) is a network of companies which source minerals that supports responsible sourcing of minerals from conflict-affected and high-risk areas. The RMI offers companies tools and resources to make sourcing decisions that improve regulatory compliance, among these a publicly accessible list of certified mines and smelters that process cobalt and 3TG ("Tin, Tantalum, Tungsten and Gold"). The RMI cooperates with numerous external organisations and governmental institutions, such as the European Partnership for Responsible Mining (EPRM), which supplements the EU Conflict Minerals Regulations, or the Public–Private Alliance for Responsible Minerals Trade (PPA), and several more. Together with its partners, the RMI engages in examining and testing the potential of Blockchain technology for responsible minerals supply chains, and has issued a first guideline for improved interoperability of Blockchain projects (RMI 2020).

Since its passing the US congress in 2010, Sect. 1502 of the Dodd-Frank Wall Street Reform and Consumer Protection Act has become an international quasi-standard for sourcing minerals from conflict regions. The act aimed at stopping the army and rebel groups in the Democratic Republic of Congo (DRC) from illegally using profits from the minerals trade to fund their fight. Internationally, anybody who sourced minerals from conflict regions and was directly or indirectly involved in doing trade with the USA had to comply with the Dodd-Frank regulation. In 2018, US president Donald Trump suspended many of the Dodd-Frank regulations, including Sect. 1502. After the abolition, several concerned large companies declared that they would nonetheless continue keeping up these standards because the market has developed to expect "conflict free" minerals, and because they realized that monitoring and improving CSR in their supply chains has helped them to better control quality and risks, and because it`s simply "the right thing to do" (Frankel 2017).

Further Initiatives, Certifications, Standards and Labels
As awareness for CSR is constantly rising, and companies increasingly respond to societal CSR expectations, more and more organisations, networks and initiatives appear to help companies to improve and make their efforts visible. There is a wide range of widely acknowledged and internationally recognized labels as well as national or regional ones, which work upon acknowledged standards and are reliable and transparent enough to fulfil national or transnational regulations and legislation. Such established labels are e.g. the Fair Trade certification, mainly for agricultural production, crafts and textiles, especially from developing countries, as well as the Ethical Trading Initiative (ETI), the Sustainable Apparel Coalition (SAC), the Global Organic Textile Standard (GOTS), Fair Wear, the German "Grüner Knopf" ("Green Button"), the European Eco-Label as well as the "Cradle-to-Cradle" certification in the textiles industry. Other labels have rather weak criteria or cover only a fraction of CSR standards, such as some specifically designed internal company or industry standards that merely serve the purpose of a marketing tool; such examples have the effect of "Green- or Whitewashing" with the high risk of squandering a company`s credibility. Some other companies, however, introduce internal company standards and labels and reject established ones, because they exceed the conventional standards and wish to be recognized for their even higher level of CSR performance.

4.5   Voluntary and Mandatory CSR

Nothing is as convincing and credible as a decision that originates from an intrinsic motivation. Businesses have the fundamental and legitimate aim to make a profit, but many who can afford it also have the intrinsic aim to do so in a positive manner, to cause no harm and to contribute to the common good. Such businesses have to cope with the issue that doing good may—at least temporarily—result in additional costs and effort. This implies the risk that customers or consumers don`t reward the efforts and switch to cheaper competitors who do not invest in caring for CSR in their supply chains. Given the increasing consumer interest and societal expectation for CSR, however, there is a good chance that a company that practices social responsibility with transparent supply chains can today even gain competitive advantage from this capacity and cultivate it as one of its distinct selling propositions. In such cases, companies enjoy a good reputation and credibility in the eyes of consumers and society.

On the contrary, when a company merely implements CSR standards in its supply chain to brush up its image or in order to comply with regulation or laws, consumers and society may not find this very convincing. In short: voluntarily practised CSR is preferable because it is more forcefully effected through conviction, while externally imposed CSR runs the risk of resulting in mere tokenism.

Nevertheless, beyond questions of credibility and costs, for individuals or communities who are suffering from bad labour conditions, human rights violations or environmental depletion, it does not make so much of a difference for which reason CSR-adverse behaviour is extinguished, as long as their situation gets better. Therefore, if not all companies are voluntarily ready to adapt their international SCM to CSR requirements, they must be impelled to do so by laws and regulation so that people and the environment are protected from harm. In several company examples from the past, even compulsory adjustment towards CSR-compliance eventually resulted in organisational change that turned firms into proactive CSR role models.

Both the global financial crisis that started in 2007 and the pandemic COVID-19-crisis of 2020, as well as the challenges of climate change have intensified international and national debates around how to achieve more sustainability in international supply chains. As voluntary CSR adaptation of companies in EU member states upon guidelines and directives was not sufficiently practised until the beginning of 2020, the EU commission has stated that they are planning to introduce Due Diligence Legislation for companies from a certain size for 2021. As an example, the German governing parties had included in their coalition agreement the National Action Plan for Business and Human Rights (NAP 2016), as well as the obligation for companies to ensure CSR principles throughout their supply chains with a voluntary approach. However, after two devastating CSR and Human Rights due diligence assessment surveys in four years (2018 and 2020), the commissioned ministers in 2020 started to press for mandatory legislation with a "Supply Chain Law". At the time of writing this chapter, a harsh dispute within the German government about the planned law and its CSR liability regulations, bureaucracy and costs has become so intricate, that the proposal was postponed again. Observers comment that many of the strict regulations included could have been avoided, had influential company representatives cooperated earlier instead of lobbying against the law, and had more companies proactively cared for CSR in their supply chains. The claim of critics who see the danger of German companies losing their competitiveness with a German "solo-run" of SC legislation is not fully substantiated, as important economies such as Great Britain (Modern Slavery Act, 2015), France (Loi de Devoir Vigilance, 2017) and the Netherlands (Wet Zorgplicht Kinderarbeid, 2019) already have similar legislation concerning international supply chains of companies.

There is also a considerable number of companies of all sizes, including companies of significant size both in Germany and internationally, whose representatives vividly support the introduction of CSR Due Diligence Legislation for international supply chains. They do so in a similar vein as Porter and van der Linde stated for environmental regulations in 1995—they argued that binding regulation would "level the playing field" so that companies compete under equal conditions and, on the one hand, gain a buffer for transition, but, on the other hand, are also bindingly pressured to innovate (Porter and van der Linde 1995). Many companies today see the chance in mandatory CSR legislation for international Supply Chains to "do the right thing" without running the risk of losing their competitive position to companies who do not care for CSR.

5   Summary

It is hard to predict what exactly international supply chains will like look in the future. The idea that the days of hyper-globalization will soon be over has gained strength since the financial crisis of 2008, and persists amidst the uncertainties and challenges posed by the global COVID-19 pandemic in 2020. Today, it seems safer to keep suppliers closer and more accessible at all times.

Whatever the future holds, though, past and present experiences have made a solid case for incorporating CSR into international SCM activities as a means for enhanced competitiveness and successful international business development. It has become evident that striving to ensure good social, environmental and ethical practice throughout a company`s international supply chain offers considerable and palpable benefits at comparatively moderate costs.

Through CSR, complex supply chains become more reliable in terms of quality, output and costs. They become safer for all stakeholders involved, no matter where they are in the world, simultaneously safeguarding the environment, people's health and the company`s reputation. CSR makes supply chains more sustainable, ensuring all those involved the best possible chance of a brighter future. For present and future managers, therefore, CSR should always be an indispensable element of their international business operations and partnerships.

We thank our colleagues Jürgen Volkert and Adrian Boos for insightful discussions and for sharing their expertise, which greatly assisted us in writing this chapter.

Exercise A

Discuss the potential benefits as well as probable challenges a company might experience when competing on the market with distinct social responsibility objectives.

Exercise B

A South Germany-based company specializes in Ethiopian organic coffee. It sources coffee beans in Ethiopia, roasts them in Germany and sells the roasted coffee (in the form of beans as well as ground coffee) via its online shop to restaurants, hotels and coffee shops in Germany.

Identify at least five spots in the company`s supply chain that are relevant to ensure a high level of social standards and contribute to the fulfilment of Sustainable Development Goals. Draft appropriate indicators to measure the company`s performance and discuss how the company could implement continuous improvement in these areas.

References

Alfred Ritter GmbH & Co. KG. (2018). *Fortschritts- und Nachhaltigkeitsbericht – Unser Kakao.* https://www.ritter-sport.de/export/sites/default/.galleries/downloads/Ritter_NHB_2018_DE.pdf [21 September 2020].

Aßländer, M. (2007). *Adam Smith zur Einführung*. Hamburg: Junius.

Beckert, S. (2015). *Empire of cotton: A global history.* New York: Alfred A. Knopf.

Berman, S. L., Wicks, A. C., Kotha, S., & Jones, T. S. (1999). Does stakeholder orientation matter? The relationship between stakeholder management models and firm financial performance. *The Academy of Management Journal, 42*(5), 488–506.

Brandenburg, M., Hahn, G. J., & Rebs, T. (Eds.). (2018). *Social and environmental dimensions of organizations and supply chains: Tradeoffs and synergies.* Cham: Springer.

Carroll, A. B. (1979). A three-dimensional conceptual model of corporate performance. *Academy of management review, 4*(4), 497–505.

Carroll, A. B. (2015). Corporate social responsibility: The centerpiece of competing and complementary frameworks. *Organizational Dynamics, 44,* 87–96.

Carroll, A. B., & Shabana, K. M. (2010). The business case for corporate social responsibility: A review of concepts, research and practice. *International Journal of Management Reviews, 12,* 85–105.

Elkington, J. (2018). 25 Years ago I coined the phrase "Triple Bottom Line." here's why it's time to rethink it. *Harvard Business Review Digital Articles.* https://search.ebscohost.com/login.aspx?direct=true&db=bth&AN=130449047&site=ehost-live [30 September 2020].

EMAS. (2020). European Eco-Management and Audit Scheme. https://www.emas.de/ [21 September 2020].

Epstein, M. J., & Rejc Buhovac, A. (2014). *Making sustainability work.* New York: Routledge.

EU-EC CSR. (2020). The European Commission on corporate social responsibility. https://ec.europa.eu/growth/industry/sustainability/corporate-social-responsibility_en [21 September 2020].

EU-EC NFRD. (2020). European Commission non-financial reporting directive. https://ec.europa. eu/info/business-economy-euro/company-reporting-and-auditing/company-reporting/non-finan-cial-reporting_en [21 September 2020].

Frankel, T. (2017, February 23). Why Apple and Intel don't want to see the conflict minerals rule rolled back. *The Washington Post*. https://www.washingtonpost.com/business/economy/why-apple-and-intel-dont-want-to-see-the-conflict-minerals-rule-rolled-back/2017/02/23/b027671e-f565-11e6-8d72-263470bf0401_story.html [21 September 2020].

Freeman, R. E. (1984). *Strategic management: A stakeholder approach*. Boston: Pitman.

Friedman, M. (1970). The social responsibility of business is to increase its profits. *The New York Times*, September 13: Section SM, 12.

GRI. (2020). Global Reporting Initiative. www.globalreporting.org [21 September 2020].

Hemingway, C. A., & Maclagan, P. W. (2004). Managers' personal values as drivers of corporate social responsibility. *Journal of Business Ethics, 50*, 33–44.

ILO. (2019). The ILO centenary declaration for the future of work. https://www.ilo.org/global/about-the-ilo/mission-and-objectives/centenary-declaration/lang--en/index.htm [21 September 2020].

ISO. (2020). Contribution of ISO Standards to SDG`s. https://www.iso.org/sdgs.html [21 September 2020].

Jang, S., & Ardichvili, A. (2020). Examining the link between corporate social responsibility and human resources: Implications for HRD research and practice. *Human Resource Development Review, 19*(2), 183–211.

Janney, J. J., & Gove, S. (2011). Reputation and corporate social responsibility aberrations, trends, and hypocrisy: Reactions to firm choices in the stock option backdating scandal. *Journal of Management Studies, 48*(7), 1562–1585.

Latapí Agudelo, M. A., Jóhannsdóttir, L., & Davídsdóttir, B. (2019). A literature review of the history and evolution of corporate social responsibility. *International Journal of Corporate Social Responsibility, 4*(1), 1–23.

Marques-Mendes, A., & Santos, M. J. (2016). Strategic CSR: An integrative model for analysis. *Social Responsibility Journal, 12*(2), 363–381.

McWilliams, A., & Siegel, D. (2001). Corporate social responsibility: A theory of the firm perspective. *Academy of Management Review, 26*, 117–127.

NAP. (2016). *German national action plan on business and human rights*. https://www.csr-in-deutschland.de/EN/Business-Human-Rights/About-the-NAP/National-Action-Plan/national-action-plan.html [21 September 2020].

OECD. (2016). *Development co-operation report 2016: The sustainable development goals as business opportunities. Paris, Organization for Economic Co-operation and Development (OECD)*. https://doi.org/10.1787/dcr-2016-9-en [21 September 2020].

OECD. (2018). *Due diligence guidance for responsible business conduct*. Paris: Organization for Economic Co-operation and Development (OECD).

Porter, M., & van der Linde, C. (1995). Green and competitive – Ending the stalemate. *Harvard Business Review, 73*(5), 120–134.

RMI. (2020). Responsible minerals initiative. https://www.responsiblemineralsinitiative.org/about/rmi-initiative [21 September 2020].

Roberts, P. W., & Dowling, G. R. (2002). Corporate reputation and sustained superior financial performance. *Strategic Management Journal, 23*, 1077–1093.

Schneider, A. (2012). Reifegradmodell CSR – eine Begriffsklärung und Abgrenzung. In: A. Schneider & R. Schmidpeter (Eds). *Corporate Social Responsibility. Verantwortungsvolle Unternehmensführung in Theorie und Praxis*. Berlin: Springer.

Schnietz, K. E., & Epstein, M. J. (2005). Exploring the financial value of a reputation for corporate social responsibility during a crisis. *Corporate Reputation Review, 7*(4), 327–345.

SDG. (2020). The sustainable development agenda. https://www.un.org/sustainabledevelopment/development-agenda/ [21 September 2020].

Smit, L., Bright, C., McCorquodale, R., Bauer, M., Deringer, H., Baeza-Berinbauer, D., et al. (2020). *Study on due diligence requirements through the supply chain – Final report.* Luxembourg: Publications Office of the Union.

Szeltner, M., & Zukin, C. (2012). Talent report: What workers want in 2012. Study by net impact and Rutgers University. https://www.netimpact.org/research-and-publications/talent-report-what-workers-want-in-2012 [21 September 2020].

UN Global Compact. (2020). The power of principles. https://www.unglobalcompact.org/what-is-gc/mission/principles [21 September 2020].

Van Weele, A. J. (2018). *Purchasing and supply chain management* (5th ed.). Hampshire: Cengage Learning EMEA.

Whelan, T., & Fink, C. (2016). The comprehensive business case for sustainability. *Harvard Business Review Digital Articles.* https://search.ebscohost.com/login.aspx?direct=true&db=bth&AN=120582856&site=ehost-live [30 September 2020].

Cross-Cultural Strategizing for Successful Customer Relationship Management

Jasmin Mahadevan and Tobias Reichert

Case study: Negotiations—Part 1

This chapter starts with the first part of a longitudinal case study. It describes negotiations between a German small- and medium-sized enterprise (SME) and a potential supplier of a customized technical component in China, also an SME. Both companies have been brought together by an intermediate service provider, Sino Network Solutions (pseudonym). The purpose of this case is to introduce cultural strategizing as a tool for successful CRM in an international Business-to-Business (B-to-B) context.

Sino Network solutions helps German companies to enter the Chinese market, and also helps with finding partners, suppliers and customers in a variety of B-to-B industries. It has two offices, one in a major German town, and one in Shanghai. Communication with the German customers takes place mainly remotely, via a variety of technologies, until a visit by the German customer to China is required. At this point, a consultant will join the German representative for business interactions with Chinese companies. All Chinese employees of Sino Network Consult have worked or studied in Germany for some time; they speak German at least adequately, and English fluently. All of them have a university degree in a relevant field, plus the required work experience.

J. Mahadevan (✉)
Pforzheim University, Pforzheim, Germany
e-mail: jasmin.mahadevan@hs-pforzheim.de

T. Reichert
NOVA School of Business and Economics, Lissabon, Portugal

© The Author(s), under exclusive license to Springer Fachmedien Wiesbaden GmbH, part of Springer Nature 2021
L. Martin (ed.), *International Business Development*,
https://doi.org/10.1007/978-3-658-33221-1_13

This case focuses on the following situation: The managing director of a German SME, Mr. Bernhard, has been searching the Chinese market for a supplier of a key technical component for a long time. This work has been carried out for him by a consultant from Sino Network Solutions, Mr. Wang. Mr. Wang has identified a promising supplier in China, also an SME. Mr. Bernhard has flown to China in order to inspect a prototype manufactured by the prospective supplier in order to find out whether this company would be the right partner for him in China. It is the first time that Mr. Bernhard and Mr. Wang meet in person, but they have been working together remotely for quite some time.

Mr. Bernhard and Mr. Wang have travelled by train from Shanghai to an upcoming industrial town in inner China. They arrive at the train station. The managing director of the Chinese SME, Mr. Huang, meets them there and drives them personally to the production site where a first prototype of the required technical component is about to be presented for the first time. Mr. Bernhard has sent specifications for the prototype in advance, but this is the first time that both managing directors meet in person.

About ten minutes are spent with introductions, then the technical component is presented by the general manager. Almost instantly, Mr. Bernhard says (in English): "This component does not meet specifications. Please let me talk to a technical expert." The Chinese managing director, Mr. Huang, does not react. Now, Mr. Bernhard addresses his intermediary, Mr. Wang, in English: "Mr. Wang, please tell them to call a technical expert." Mr. Wang does not answer, but instead talks to Mr. Huang in Chinese (which Mr. Bernhard does not understand). Afterwards, Mr. Wang assures Mr. Bernhard that everything is in order and that "Mr. Huang suggests that Mr. Bernhard has a rest in his hotel room, and Mr. Huang will fetch him for lunch afterwards". Mr. Bernhard is visibly annoyed and says (in German and rather sarcastically) to Mr. Wang: "Of course! Taking a rest and having lunch together will *definitely* solve this technical failure."

During lunch, the conversation never touches upon the prototype, and whenever Mr. Bernhard wants to steer it towards this direction, his intermediary, Mr. Wang, talks to Mr. Huang in rapid Chinese and translates only very little of it to Mr. Bernhard; "It would be too confusing, don't worry", he tells him.

Mr. Bernhard flies back to Germany, with the sure knowledge of a failed mission, but assured by Mr. Wang "not to worry, everything went very well, trust me". Two weeks afterwards, an improved technical component is delivered by the prospective supplier. It meets all specifications. ◄

1 Culture and Its Impact on Customer Relationship Management

Customer Relationship Management (CRM) involves all activities related to managing the relations between buyer and seller long-term and across the various stages of the Customer Life-Cycle (overview in Hippner and Wilde 2006). In B-to-B-settings, these mutually constitutive roles are represented by organizational Buying and Selling Centres (Backhaus and Voeth 2010). Within these Buying and Selling Centres, different professions and organizational functions, such as marketing, financial control, engineering and many more, are involved, each of them representing a specific aspect of the organizational buying or selling process. In the previous case, Mr. Bernhard and Mr. Wang represent the Buying Centre for the specific technical component, whereas Mr. Huang represents the Selling Centre.

Culture is part of the interactions between the two organizational entities. Culture refers to the social dimension of human beings, that is: how people behave, what they believe in, how they experience the world, and what they expect in relation to other people. Culture is formed via enculturation, that is: exposure and adaptation to a certain group. As a result of this life-long process, different groups of people develop different ways of how to behave, what to believe in, how to experience the world and what to expect from themselves and others. This means that the way in which the three protagonists of the previous case live their roles (Buyer and Seller) are not universal and objective, but shaped by their previous experiences: they are cultural. One can thus understand culture as the way in which we normally do things around here (Deal and Kennedy 2000) which is specific to a certain group of people and which differentiates them from other groups of people.

This becomes visible in the previous case: Buyer and Seller clearly have different ideas of how to proceed, and these ideas are cultural. It is also clear that Mr. Wang, as the intermediary, is the only one who can 'cross' the border between these divergent ways of doing things: He is engaged in cross-cultural management activities that are successful in bringing together both parties, even though Mr. Bernhard does not understand why his intermediary is successful in the end (Mr. Bernhard's way of doing things remains culture-centric). This case thus also exemplifies the advantage of cross-cultural CRM versus culture-centric CRM.

The first step towards successful cross-cultural CRM in B-to-B-situations is thus a thorough assessment of the relevant root causes for differences (what makes people behave differently?) and proper management of those assessed differences (how can I overcome this difference?).

1.1   Layers of Culture in B-to-B Interactions

In B-to-B settings which involve Buying and Selling Centres of different organizations, at least four social demarcation lines can influence how people behave. These are:

1) Societal or national culture: which country / society are people from?
2) Industrial cultures: which industry provides the framework for people and organizations?
3) Organizational culture: which organization (company) are people from?
4) Professional / functional culture: which job-related knowledge and skills do people use at work?

Societal and national culture refer to norms and practices specific to a certain country or society. These units can, but do not necessarily have to, overlap. For instance, French-speaking and English-speaking Canada can be considered to be two societies in one country. Also, for Germany, there are notable differences in the GLOBE study data for Germany (West) and (East). In the previous case, these units are Germany (West) and China, and one can find objective data on cultural differences for both countries.

The demarcation lines of the next layers of culture, however, are fuzzy and subject to change; therefore, there is no conclusive data available on them. Rather, practitioners need to observe the interaction itself to see which difference emerges and is rooted in which of the aforementioned layers of culture.

Industrial cultures, such as automotive, chemical engineering or bio-technology are relevant, as they often provide the legal, political, economic and other relevant boundary conditions that frame what people and organizations do. For example, a certain industry might be supported by the government or not.

Organizational cultures describe how different companies translate the aforementioned societal, national and industrial culture to create a specific spirit and ways of doing things. For instance, one might find two car manufacturers in the same country whose 'cultures' nonetheless slightly differ.

Professional and functional cultures refer to the insight that people are trained to do their job in different ways and that education also provides them with 'normal' ideas and ways of how to normally do things. For instance, a financial control expert and a mechanical engineer will look at the same selling decision differently, based on their professional knowledge. Functional culture can, but does not have to, overlap with professional culture: It refers to the job and position (= function) which a person has in an organization, and this also leads to group-specific ideas and ways of doing things Functional culture is often the smaller unit, especially in large companies (e.g. two research engineering departments developing two distinct functional cultures).

1.2   A Structured Approach to Cross-National Differences in CRM

As the previous considerations suggest, one can find multiple 'nested cultures' within each other, all of which are relevant to successful CRM in B-to-B-settings. The difficulty lies in figuring out which cultural layer becomes salient and when and how. Successful cross-cultural CRM thus requires those involved to act as "cultural detectives" (Mahadevan 2017) and to pay attention to what happens in a situation, in order to make an informed decision as to which cultural approach might be the most useful here.

In order to achieve a structured analysis it makes sense to start with the largest unit of culture, that is: national and/or societal culture, and to ask to what extent and how it manifests itself on lower levels, that is: in specific B-to-B-interactions. For instance, in the previous case study (part 1), Mr Bernhard is surprised by the fact that his Chinese counterpart seems unwilling to discuss what (to Mr Bernhard) seems to be the most urgent problem, namely the defective prototype. Rather, the Chinese managing director suggests rest and having lunch together, and in the end, Mr Bernhard is completely puzzled by the delivery of the perfect prototype: To him, this is not a 'logical' link between what has happened and how the situation turned out: It would not have been Mr Bernhard's learned way of how to normally do things in such a situation.

Here, studies on cross-cultural differences on national and societal cultures can be helpful for understanding how such divergent strategies in one and the same situation are not a personal 'nuisance' on the part of the other person but learned culture-specific strategies that, in a certain cultural context, have proven successful.

1.3   The Cultural Dimensions of Project GLOBE

The most recent and comprehensive comparative cross-cultural study on national and societal level is Project GLOBE (House et al. 2004, see also https://globeproject.com/). Comparative Cross-Cultural Management (CCM) works with so called cultural dimensions or cultural value orientations. These are universal aspects of culture which are assumed to exist in all cultures, e.g. the insight that all social groups are characterized by a differentiation of power: In order to function, social groups need to put some people in charge who then have 'more power'. What differs is only the degree to which a difference in power is considered to be fair and accepted as 'normal'. In comparative CCM terms, this dimension is referred to as 'power distance', defined by project GLOBE as *"(t)he extent to which the community accepts and endorses authority, power differences, and status privileges"* (GLOBE 2020a). In societies with higher power distance, an unequal distribution of power is more accepted than in societies with lower power distance.

Project GLOBE, which partly built upon earlier studies (e.g. Hofstede 1980, 2001), has defined nine cultural dimensions (GLOBE 2020a). The average score of 62 countries regarding these cultural dimensions is visualized in an online database (GLOBE 2020b). Cultural dimensions are depicted on the level of values (*should be*, that is: commonly held ideas of how things should be normally done) and on the level of practices (*as is*, that is: how things are normally done in practice), based on data gathered from approximately 17,000 middle managers from three industries (GLOBE 2020a).

Table 1 explains these cultural dimensions and compares the practice scores (how things are normally done) of the P.R. China and Germany (West) with each other. The practice score—and not the value score—was chosen because it is more indicative of how an activity *really* turns out in comparison to an abstract cultural 'ideal' which the value score describes.

Table 1 also depicts whether a country score is below or above the average score of all 62 GLOBE countries. This is relevant, because this provides managers with an idea of whether the underlying goals of their strategizing activities will be shared by the representative of another societal culture.

As the mean value and also the variance of the scores differ from dimension to dimension, the relative score, not the absolute score, is provided. For instance, sometimes a medium score will be "above" or "below" GLOBE average. The score of Germany (West) for in-group and institutional collectivism, for example, is "medium" in absolute terms, but, with this score, Germany (West) is well below the aggregated average score of all GLOBE countries. Humane orientation is a notable dimension, because Germany (West) scores the lowest on this dimension regarding practice in relation to all other GLOBE country scores. This suggests a cultural 'extreme' point and a potential cultural 'blind-spot' when it comes to strategizing. Further details, and also a helpful visualization of these scores, the bandwidth of all GLOBE country scores, the relation between a country and the GLOBE average as well as the absolute country scores in numeric terms can be found at: https://globeproject.com/results?page_id=country#country.

1.4   Learning: Comparative CCM Insights on the Case Study (Part 1)

As Table 1 of the previous section suggests, the GLOBE database enables a relative comparison of two or more countries in relation to a certain cultural dimension, with ensuing considerations of how one's counterpart from another country might behave, and which strategies and actions they might believe in. The first recommendation is to focus on those cultural dimensions for which the scores of the respective countries differ the most regarding practice.

However, cultural dimensions, if applied to a situation as hypotheses to be tested, need to be falsified or proven, and further refined 'in action'. Not all cultural dimensions can be applied to all situations. For example, both the P.R. China and Germany (West) score relatively low on gender egalitarianism which might explain why only men are acting in the previous case study (part 1). This then makes it impossible to observe gender (in-) equality in the situation.

Table 1 GLOBE cultural dimensions and comparative country scores P.R. China and Germany (West)

Dimension	Definition	Practice score	
		P.R. China	GER (West)
Performance Orientation	The degree to which a collective encourages and rewards (and should encourage and reward) group members for performance improvement and excellence	Medium (above GLOBE average)	Medium (slightly above GLOBE average)
Assertiveness	The degree to which individuals are (and should be) assertive, confrontational, and aggressive in their relationship with others	Relatively low (below GLOBE average)	Relatively high (well above GLOBE average)
Future Orientation	The extent to which individuals engage (and should engage) in future-oriented behaviours such as planning, investing in the future, and delaying gratification	Medium (slightly below GLOBE average)	Medium (above GLOBE average)
Humane Orientation	The degree to which a collective encourages and rewards (and should encourage and reward)	Medium (above GLOBE average)	Relatively low *(lowest of all GLOBE scores)*
Institutional Collectivism	The degree to which organizational and societal institutional practices encourage and reward (and should encourage and reward) collective distribution of resources and collective action	Relatively high (well above GLOBE average)	Medium (well below GLOBE average)
In-group collectivism	The degree to which individuals express (and should express) pride, loyalty, and cohesiveness in their organizations or families	High (well above GLOBE average)	Medium (well below GLOBE average)
Gender Egalitarianism	The degree to which a collective minimizes (and should minimize) gender inequality	Relatively low (below GLOBE average)	Relatively low (below GLOBE average)
Power distance	The extent to which the community accepts and endorses (and should accept and endorse) authority, power differences, and status privileges	Relatively high (slightly below GLOBE average)	Relatively high (slightly above GLOBE average)
Uncertainty Avoidance	The extent to which a society, organization, or group relies (and should rely) on social norms, rules, and procedures to alleviate unpredictability of future events. The greater the desire to avoid uncertainty, the more people seek orderliness, consistency, structure, formal procedures, and laws to cover daily situations	Relatively high (well above GLOBE average)	Relatively high (well above GLOBE average)

Source: Own, based on GLOBE (2020a, 2020b)

In this case study (part 1), it is assertiveness, in-group collectivism and humane orientation that provide the first useful links: Firstly, the ways in which Mr. Bernhard communicates (directly, explicitly and confrontationally) are representative of the relatively high German score on assertiveness (practice) and a low humane orientation in practice (lowest of all GLOBE countries). Similarly, the reaction of the Chinese manager ('let's take a break and have lunch') might be related back to the low Chinese score regarding assertiveness, as well as to a high in-group orientation score which is well-above GLOBE average. The latter, in combination with a medium and above average score on humane orientation, calls for expressing loyalty to the group and, thus, findings ways of carefully circumnavigating conflicts in public to find integrative solutions 'backstage'. Being aware of these differences, Mr. Wang, as the experienced intermediary, acknowledges this difference in style: He translates only very little, yet, still, achieves his goal of the perfect prototype while respecting group-orientation.

The next section will shed further light on how managers can develop and refine a structured and patterned approach to B-to-B interactions, and on how they can enlarge their professional repertoire beyond the limitations of a culture-centric approach and develop it towards cross-cultural strategizing.

2   A Strategizing Perspective on Cross-Cultural B-To-B Interactions

This section highlights the main elements of the strategizing perspective and applies it to cross-cultural B-to-B interactions. Specifically, it focuses on an activity-based approach to illustrate how individual and collective actions ultimately create strategy. The purpose of this section is to provide students and practitioners with new frameworks to better understand—and, thus: to better manage—potential difficulties in cross-cultural B-to-B interactions.

2.1   Strategizing: The Activity-Based Approach

The term strategizing is rooted in the *"Strategy as Practice"* (SaP) approach which advanced the study of corporate strategy in the early 2000s (see Golsorkhi et al. 2015). SaP understands strategy as something people do rather than something organizations have. This emphasis on the doing of strategy sheds light upon why people behave in certain ways in novel situations in order to reach their goals, e.g. an international or cross-cultural CRM situation (see case study, part 1). When it comes to the development and implementation of strategy, SaP also helps to bridge the existing gap between management theory and management reality concerning strategy.

The *activity-based approach* (see Jarzabkowski 2005), which is a key part of the SaP tool-kit, perceives strategy as goal-directed activity over time that is shaped by multiple actors. As an activity, strategy consists of intended and emergent, and of reciprocal and intertwined actions. These actions are often hard to identify at the individual level, yet, they make up collective strategic activity as a whole.

Strategizing means the shaping of strategy via different practices. These practices provide *legitimacy* to strategy, and, thereby, give a strategic activity the right to be pursued by the people within an organization.

There are two opposing but complementary types of strategizing. These differ 1) regarding the practices they use, 2) regarding the types of legitimacy which they wish to create, 3) regarding their nature over time, and 4) regarding the kind of knowledge which they transmit.

First, *procedural strategizing* uses formal administrative practices to provide an activity with *structural legitimacy*. Formal administrative practices are, for example, plans, projections, analyses, budgets, reviews and Key Performance Indicators (KPIs). By using this set of practices, an activity can be coordinated, controlled, monitored and also resourced. Thereby, the activity becomes embedded within routines. This means that it becomes part of the 'taken-for-granted' day-to-day business. Apart from this 'routinizing' of activities, formal administrative practices also provide diagnostic controls which shape strategic activity, by indicating which activities are favourable and which are not. Thereby, procedural strategizing reinforces the status of a certain activity (e.g. KPI systems to monitor CRM-success across cultures) as an organizational routine. Thus, activity that has structural legitimacy is persistent and stable. However, it is also prone to a phenomenon called *strategic drift* which causes an activity to 'drift' away from its original goals. For example, the KPIs devised for measuring the CRM-success in a certain country might not fit the cultural realities of this country anymore because culture has changed over time. The same might happen in an intercultural interaction during which a participant's general cultural assumptions do not match the specific cultural reality (context) encountered. This implies that strategic drift can occur based on several factors, such as time and context.

Second, *interactive strategizing* uses face-to-face interaction (direct communication) to provide an activity with *interpretative legitimacy*. The purpose of this is to create *frameworks of meaning*. These frameworks are able to influence people's actions, to convince them and to affect the way they perceive things. Thus, people who share a framework of meaning are prone to align their actions with the ideas, beliefs and visions that are illustrated within the framework. Therefore, frameworks of meaning are a valuable tool for promoting change, for example, as they allow leaders to frame certain activities as desirable. However, as it cannot be assumed that everybody holds the same interpretation of what is framed as desirable, these frameworks call for constant engagement in reconstructing and reflecting the meanings transported within them. Thus, activity that has interpretative legitimacy is highly goal-oriented, but not very durable.

Third and fourth, procedural strategizing is rather *static* and relies on practices which over time become part of a routine. This persistence encompasses a widely desired stability in the business world, and allows planning ahead as long as there are no unexpected incidents. However, if change needs to be incorporated, e.g. in cultural customer preferences, procedural strategizing is inappropriate. This implies that any cross-cultural preparation needs to involve the openness to change in order to still fit a novel situation. The formal administrative practices of procedural strategizing largely consist of *explicit knowledge* e.g. drawings and specifications of a technical component. This explicit knowledge is easy to communicate effectively because it can be easily put into words. This implies that for cross-cultural interactions procedural strategizing—e.g. relying on cultural checklists or defined customer preferences based on culture—are insufficient because they do not do the dynamics of culture justice.

Interactive strategizing relies on the creation of *frameworks of meaning*. These frameworks are *dynamic* and change over time. They are helpful for moving beyond the usual and the 'well-known', and for figuring out the 'unknown'. This means that they are very relevant in culturally unknown situations. Frameworks of meaning transmit mostly *tacit knowledge*, that is: knowledge based on experience which cannot be put into words and which emerges from a situation. This implies that previously unknown cultural frameworks of meaning, despite their importance, are neither easily comprehended nor created.

Table 2 summarizes the differences between the two types of strategizing. A link to cross-cultural B-to-B interactions is given.

Table 2 Features of the two types of strategizing

Type of strategizing	Procedural strategizing	Interactive strategizing
Legitimacy	Structural	Interpretive
Practices	Formal administrative practices (e.g. plans, projections, analyses, budgets, reviews and KPI systems)	Face-to-face interaction (direct communication)
Mechanism	Creation of frameworks of meaning	Embedding of routines
Nature over time	Static	Dynamic
Knowledge transmitted	Explicit (easy to verbalize)	Tacit (hard / impossible to verbalize)
Usefulness in cross-cultural B-to-B interactions	Insufficient	Necessary

2.2   Strategizing and Cross-Cultural B-to-B Interactions

When people prepare for business interactions abroad, such as supplier negotiations (case study, part 1), they work with mental models that help them structure a situation in advance and while it is occurring. These mental models primarily consist of tacit knowledge and can be understood as the monitoring systems for the situation, in short: as *procedural strategizing.* Mr. Bernhard wishes to talk about what is wrong with the prototype explicitly and in detail; Mr. Huang focuses on maintaining good relations by suggesting a break, and then lunch. Both do so because of certain mental models which tell them *why* their specific activity choices (talk about flaws in the prototype/take a break and lunch together) are the right activity for solving the problem. This means that both of them have learned structures in mind which they apply to the situation, similar to applying KPI-indicators to a CRM system.

However, as the GLOBE study implies, these procedural strategizing activities are culture-centric: they only make sense to other people if these other people share the same mental models. Mr. Bernhard's mental models involve high assertiveness and low humane orientation, whereas Mr. Huang's mental models involve low assertiveness, high in-group orientation and above average humane orientation. This means that their respective choices of procedural strategizing are *culture-centric*: they cannot be deciphered by the other person who is a cultural outsider, and this is why they fail to provide structural legitimacy. From Mr. Huang's perspective, Mr. Bernhard wishing to verbalize flaws is a clear breach of how the problem should be approached, and the idea that a 'break and lunch' might solve a technical problem is equally unthinkable for Mr. Bernhard. This is why the action of the other person does not make strategic sense to each of them: they can't even identify the other person's actions as *strategic,* that is: as contributing to reaching the intended goal. As a result, and during the further development of the intercultural interaction, Mr. Huang and Mr. Bernhard experience *strategic drift*: the general mental model (procedural strategizing) which each of them brought to the activity and which each of them constantly applies to the activity fails to deliver the intended results in this specific cultural context.

As a result of this strategic drift, a *strategizing gap* opens up between Mr. Huang and Mr. Bernhard: they fail to understand each other. What is missing in the case study (part 1), is a *strategizing turn*: that is the realization from the side of the two key actors (Mr. Huang / Mr. Bernhard) that they need to change their strategizing activities towards a more *dynamic interactive strategizing* which clearly goes beyond previous static procedural strategizing (i.e. their ideas of: 'we always have lunch in this situation' / 'we always verbalize the problem in this kind of situation'): they need to create new *cross-cultural frameworks of meaning* that go beyond the previously held static mental models used for procedural strategizing.

Solely Mr. Wang, as the intermediary, is able to engage in *cross-cultural strategizing*, that is in strategizing activities which are strategically effective and which can be interpreted as expedient by all.

These key elements for strategizing in B-to-B interactions and how they are perceived by managers in the situation (*in italics*) are depicted in Table 3.

A high score on certain—but not all—cultural dimensions also makes it more likely for a certain type of strategizing (procedural or interactive) to occur. For instance, throughout, Mr. Bernhard is more focused on structures, procedures, rules and schedules, than Mr. Huang who is focused on relationships, communication and the dynamic evolvement of shared meaning. Table 4 visualizes the interlinkages between GLOBE study dimensions and types of strategizing and gives recommendations to managers preparing for interactions in countries that score accordingly.

This suggests that the strategizing perspective can also be used as a tool for cross-cultural preparation: whenever there is a strong link between a high score on a certain dimension and a certain type of strategizing, this then implies a strong likelihood of the specific type of strategizing to prevail in the interaction. This link can be established for some, but not all, cultural dimensions: future orientation, gender egalitarianism and

Table 3 Strategizing in cross-cultural B-to-B interactions

Strategizing element	Explanation
Procedural strategizing	The commonly used strategies used to monitor a B-to-B interaction. Based on static and culture-specific mental models Sense of: *"How this kind of situation should normally be structured."*
Culture-centric strategizing	Strategizing activities which 'make sense' only to members of one culture. Based on static and culture-specific procedural strategizing Sense of: *"How things are normally done."*
Strategic drift	Procedural strategizing which drifts away from its original goal, namely to manage a B-to-B interaction successfully, because it is culture-centric Sense of: *"This does not work like it should normally work."*
Strategizing gap	The gap between two or more culture-centric procedural strategizing activities which have drifted away from their original goal Sense of: *"What is going on right now does not make any sense at all."*
Strategizing turn	The realization that one needs to change from procedural strategizing ('what should normally be done in this kind of situation') to strategizing outside of one's mental models, and the activity of initiating dynamic interactive strategizing to create new cross-cultural frameworks of meaning Sense of: *"It does not make sense at all, but maybe, I will try it out nonetheless."*
Cross-cultural strategizing	The successful implementation of dynamic interactive strategizing across-cultures Sense of: *"I had no idea that this could work, but now, it makes sense to all."*

Table 4 Learning: GLOBE Study dimensions, type of strategizing and recommendations for management

GLOBE Dimension	Quality of link to	Type of strategizing	Recommendations for managers
High performance Orientation	Strong	Procedural	Prepare for procedural strategizing
High Assertiveness	Probable	Procedural	Expect procedural strategizing, reflect upon the interaction
High Humane Orientation	Strong	Interactive	Prepare for interactive strategizing
High Institutional Collectivism	Probable	Procedural	Expect procedural strategizing, reflect upon the interaction
High In-group collectivism	Probable	Interactive	Expect interactive strategizing, reflect upon the interaction
High Uncertainty Avoidance	Strong	Procedural	Prepare for procedural strategizing

power distance remain neutral. The link also works in reverse, e.g. a low score on performance orientation suggests a high likelihood of interactive strategizing.

Managers can also apply these links to themselves and can thus better reflect upon which strategizing activity seems legitimate to them and why. This enables them to consciously choose alternative strategies in cross-cultural B-to-B interactions and to enlarge the scope of their CRM strategies and actions.

3 Application: The Qualities of Cross-Cultural Strategizing for Successful CRM

In this section, the combined learning from the cross-cultural and the strategizing perspective is applied. The second part of the case study describes all elements of successful cross-cultural strategizing, including the required strategic turn.

Case study: Negotiations—Part 2

The second case refers to B-to-B-negotiations, rooted in Mr. Bernhard's need of finding a sales partner in China. Negotiations are conducted between the German client, Mr. Bernhard, Sino Network Consult (represented by Mr Wang and his boss, Mr. Zhang), and representatives of a larger Chinese sales organization. The purpose of this negotiation is to secure and finalize an export partnership between the two companies, and make the Chinese company the only vendor of the German SME's products in China.

The second part of the case study, which takes place later than part 1, shows how Mr. Bernhard now starts to engage in *cross-cultural* strategizing, as opposed to his previous *culture-centric* strategizing (part 1). When doing so, he overcomes the limitations of a specifically "German" perspective.

Analysing the second part of the case study thus brings together the cross-cultural and the strategizing perspective on CRM in international B-to-B interactions. It enables the reader to apply previously gained knowledge and to deepen their learning on how to strategize cross-culturally in international B-to-B-settings and to move towards more successful CRM.

This case describes a crucial step towards successful cross-cultural strategizing during the negotiations which have already lasted for more than fifteen hours daily over a period of two days in a five-star hotel in Shanghai. As this is an extremely important deal, the German client, Mr. Bernhard, is represented by two members of Sino Network Consult, amongst them Senior Partner Mr. Zhang who has conducted pre-negotiations over the past six months. The prospective Chinese partner is represented by the managing director, Mr. Li, and three other managers. Mr. Bernhard is accompanied by his head of production and his financial control officer. Negotiations take place in German and Chinese, with Mr. Wang and Mr. Zhang translating.

At the beginning of day three, the situation is tense, numbers and figures have been presented and discussed. The Chinese side has requested more favourable conditions for the last two hours while at the same time stressing the interest in good relations and a long-term partnership. Mr. Zhang is the person to translate between the two parties, switching between Chinese and German.

Zhang: "Mr. Li thinks that all friends receive friendly conditions, which should also be the case for him!"

Bernhard: "But this is about quality and technology – not about haggling for discounts!" What am I supposed to do about this? Produce cheaply, and then our quality goes downhill ?!? – *Don't translate the last part.*"

Mr. Zhang translates the first part into Chinese, and then translates the following back to Mr. Bernhard:

Zhang: "Mr. Li offers you his friendship, and says that, if he were you, he would make it a point to honour your partnership with a discount."

Bernhard: "They have no idea what this is about. Our technical products have a certain quality. This is not about money – this is about the cost of production, and they have all the facts for *why* the costs and conditions are what they are. We are being totally transparent here. This is just bazaar behaviour when quality counts! – *Don't translate this.*"

Then, Mr. Zhang talks to Mr. Li, Mr. Li talks to his managers, then Mr. Li talks to Mr. Zhang, who talks to Mr. Wang. The whole conversation is in Chinese and therefore unclear to the German participants. Then Mr. Zhang asks Mr. Bernhard in the English language: "Our Chinese partners would like to know whether there are additional benefits for them which you could make part of the deal?".

Mr. Bernhard answers abruptly in English: "I would like to have lunch now", and the whole party goes for lunch, even though it is only 11:30 in the morning, carefully avoiding talking about business.

At an opportune time, Mr. Wang captures attention of the Chinese partners, and Mr. Zhang talks to Mr. Bernhard in German. Mr. Zhang says:

"I know that you have calculated the costs realistically, but this is not how you should see the situation: This is a risky business venture for both sides. You *have* to give Mr. Li something as a token of friendship and trust, and he will also give you such a token. Also, he will pay you back when it is time. At this point, whatever you concede, is not about numbers: It is the sign that there is personal trust and loyalty: you and Mr. Li are part of the same network now, and facts and calculations don't sustain a network when things get rough."

Epilogue: Mr. Bernhard makes concessions, but not after a long struggle (a strategy, of which Mr. Zhang has advised him as well). The negotiation ends with a favourable deal for both parties. ◀

As in the first part of the case study, both parties have carefully prepared their B-to-B interactions: activities of *procedural strategizing*. However, what they don't know at this stage is whether these preparatory activities are *culture-centric* or whether they *really* fit the cross-cultural interaction in which they are about to engage.

Things go smoothly for two days, but then both parties experience *strategic drift*, that is: a situation wherein they experience a feeling of 'this is not working as it should normally work'. The key conflict, in other terms: the strategizing gap, evolves around the question of whether Mr. Bernhard should grant Mr. Li a discount.

From a strategizing perspective, one must thus assume that this 'discount' *means* different things to Mr. Bernhard and Mr. Li: two different *frameworks of meaning* which fail to make sense to the other party during their *interactive strategizing activities*.

The *GLOBE cultural dimensions* shed light onto which framework of meaning is associated with 'price' and 'discount' on two levels. First, because of the link between GLOBE cultural dimension scores and strategizing, Mr. Bernhard is more likely to engage in procedural and Mr. Li is more likely to engage in interactive strategizing (Table 4). This implies that certain aspects of the interaction, such as 'price' might be non-negotiable to Mr. Bernhard (because they are a 'monitoring tool'), whereas, for Mr. Li, they are just one of the dynamics of interactive strategizing required to reach the intended goal.

Second, the GLOBE scores for each country are also visible in the interaction (Table 4). For Mr. Bernhard, 'price' is non-negotiable, because it is calculated in advance, based on objective standards, and devoid of any 'human factor'. This can be linked to the high German scores for assertiveness and uncertainty avoidance, and the low German scores, in comparison to the GLOBE average, for humane orientation and in-group collectivism. Also, Mr. Bernhard is focused solely on this business deal, not on social relations beyond it, which is potentially indicative of low humane orientation as well.

Conversely, for Mr. Li, 'price' is an indicator of trust and the relationship between the two parties, and, thus, also an indicator for long-term relations and the quality of a far-reaching business network. This can be linked to the high Chinese scores for humane orientation and in-group collectivism, and the above average score for future orientation. The GLOBE study scores thus imply that the framework of meaning which both parties apply to their B-to-B interactions are culture-centric in these aspects.

The task for both parties is now to recognize that they are experiencing a *strategizing gap* which will result in a failure of the negotiation if they do not change directions. As always in intercultural interactions, it is not fully foreseeable who needs to change their approach to what extent. Generally, from a strategizing perspective, strategy is the *collective* result or *individual* actions, which implies: who can change the success of strategizing in the situation, should do it.

In this case, several people initiate small individual *strategizing turns* towards a more successful and cross-cultural collective strategizing.

Mr. Bernhard is the first to initiate a small strategizing turn, by asking the intermediaries of Sino Network Consult, Mr. Wang and Mr. Zhang, <u>not</u> to translate what he says. This indicates that Mr. Bernhard is aware of a strategic drift occurring and tries to figure out how to change his strategy.

Next, the intermediaries of Sino Network Consult, Mr. Wang and Mr. Zhang, engage the Chinese partner in deeper conversation, potentially trying to *re-frame* the perspective of the German client in such a way to the Chinese partner that it will make sense to them. They are partially successful, because these actions make the Chinese partner, Mr. Li, switch from 'discount' to 'additional benefits' as the required indicator for trust and long-term relations. However, this still does not make sense to Mr. Bernhard, and, thus, a collective strategic turn has not yet been performed.

Mr. Bernhard then initiates another turn by suggesting lunch. There, he applies previous learning from experience, because he has observed how a similar situation was handled in part 1 of the case study. This suggests that he has acquired and now applies new *tacit knowledge*, as indicative of the *dynamic creation of new frameworks of meaning* which characterize interactive strategizing.

Over lunch the intermediaries of Sino Network Consult engage in further activities to bridge the strategizing gap, and Mr. Bernhard is given advice of how to proceed further, which he then implements during the next round of negotiation. Mr. Li also does his part, and, as a result of these individual acts of strategizing, new shared tacit knowledge across cultures is created, and new cross-cultural frameworks of meaning are built. In the end, not only an individual deal is struck but also a network is built: an example of *successful cross-cultural strategizing* (Table 3) which utilizes the features of both types of strategizing (Table 2) to achieve complementarities and synergies across cultures.

4   Recommendations for Students and Practitioners

Culture and strategy are not static but rather emergent and dynamic. This chapter provided details on the insight. It enables students and practitioners to analyse and, thus, better handle the interrelated dynamics of cross-cultural interactions and strategizing activities. Two cases exemplified and applied this learning. Out of this emerge the following recommendations for students and practitioners:

Successful management of cross-cultural B-to-B interactions requires both cross-cultural preparation *and* cross-cultural sense-making during the activity.

The GLOBE study cultural dimensions should be considered for cross-cultural preparation (Table 1). They depict relative cross-cultural differences which serve as first hypotheses of how the other party will interact or what, for instance, the global customer will demand.

For understanding what actually happens when people prepare and interact across cultures in order to reach their goals, a strategizing perspective, in particular, an activity-based approach, has proven to be fruitful. It involves two types of strategizing, procedural and interactive, both of which involve distinct qualities (Table 2).

High and low scores for certain GLOBE study cultural dimensions are strongly linked to the likelihood of one type of strategizing to be preferred in a certain country (Table 4). Managers should therefore consider these scores and prepare accordingly. They should also note how their own country scores for getting a better understanding of their own 'mental maps' regarding 'how to normally strategize' in a certain situation (Table 3).

The cultural dimensions of the GLOBE study only represent 'static' culture. However, culture is also a process of interaction which requires interactive cultural strategizing. Managers should therefore carefully balance cross-cultural preparation (which is an act of procedural strategizing) and a reflexive awareness in cross-cultural interactions (which are acts of interactive strategizing).

If their own cross-cultural expectations and mental models are not met in practice, managers interacting across cultures experience strategic drift. This refers to a situation when the afore set goals of the interaction cannot be met with the perceptions which managers have in mind. It is thus a key management skill to be aware when strategic drift occurs, to conclude that the preparation does not meet the situation anymore and to change the approach accordingly by introducing a strategic turn.

A strategizing gap opens up as result of strategic drift. Consecutively, people in international interactions do not 'make sense' to each other anymore because they act upon different types of strategizing, using culture-centric models. A strategizing gap is thus an indicator of strategic drift of which a manager is still unaware: it is experienced as the overwhelming feeling of something completely 'puzzling' or 'strange' happening, and also as a failure of one's own abilities. However, managers need to understand that there is learning in such a situation: it means that there is a missing link to the other persons' strategizing activities. Managers therefore need to develop the ability to cope with and handle such situations. Rather than engaging in an even stronger application of their own mental models, they should venture into the strategic gap and figure out what the situation 'means', based on the realization that there must be meaning behind it, even if they do not see it yet.

If managers venture into the strategic gap, they will learn alternative ways of strategizing. Their strategizing abilities will move beyond culture-centric mental models; they will develop a higher role-flexibility and will be more able to function in more CRM situations in B-to-B. Ultimately, this results in a higher ability to handle more situations more effectively and appropriately.

In order to close a strategizing gap, managers are required to perform a strategizing turn. In order to do that, managers need to be aware of the situation, and their own and their counterparts' actions in the situation.

Cross-cultural strategizing, as the goal and also the measurement scale for successful international B-to-B interactions, refers to the successful introduction and implementation of strategizing which makes sense across cultures. As an applied managerial skills set it involves:

1) the ability to identify strategic drift when it occurs,
2) to change own strategizing activities accordingly in order to gather yet unknown information about strategizing gaps, with the goal to close these, and
3) to thus initiate and perform (or at least: participate successfully in) a strategic turn, resulting in
4) effective and appropriate strategizing across cultures, thus bridging the previously existent strategizing divide.

5   Summary and Conclusion

This chapter provided a cross-cultural perspective on CRM, focusing on international B-to-B interactions. Culture in industry settings emerges on four relevant layered and interrelated units:

1) Societal or national culture: which country / society are people from?
2) Industrial cultures: which industry provides the framework for people and organizations?
3) Organizational culture: which organization (company) are people from?
4) Professional / functional culture: which job-related knowledge and skills do people use at work?

Comparative CCM frameworks, such as the GLOBE study describe differences across the largest of these four layers of culture. They can therefore provide a first entry point for preparing for B-to-B interactions involving representatives of certain societal and national cultures. However, because they are static representations of 'artificial' average behaviour, managers need to use them actively and dynamically, acting as 'cultural detectives' (Mahadevan 2017). Parts 1 and 2 of the case study illustrating this chapter provided examples for such a deduction.

Large-scale data do not exist for all other cultural layers. Therefore, managers cannot proceed from clear knowledge of the cross-cultural differences involved, but need to focus on the *activity,* that is: what happens in the situation, and deduce patterns of difference from there. Cultural dimensions are one, general, tool for 'puzzling with culture'; the strategizing perspective uses this tool from an activity-based dynamic viewpoint, and thus makes cross-cultural differences small and manageable in the situation across *all* layers of culture as they cumulate in activity.

Strategizing is thus a fruitful tool for structuring one's thinking in cross-cultural and international interactions. This was exemplified by applying the strategizing perspective onto two cases. Moreover, strategizing is an opportunity for anticipating the counterpart's strategy, e.g. if managers apply the strategizing perspective to the GLOBE cultural dimension score of a certain country when they prepare for B-to-B-interactions there: this provides managers with first strategies of how to approach the situation and which strategy to follow.

Cross-cultural strategizing is successful if managers recognize a widening strategizing gap ('my mental model does not fit to the situation anymore') and are able to contribute to or initiate a strategizing turn which closes the gap. This chapter provided the relevant tools for enabling these abilities in practice, resulting in concise and comprehensive recommendations for students and practitioners.

In summary, this chapter put forward the idea that successful cross-cultural CRM can be achieved via cross-cultural strategizing. It also provided the relevant elements for putting this idea into practice.

Exercise A

Your company is based in Austria and engages in infrastructure projects (waste water plants) worldwide. As an Austrian national you are tasked with representing the company in Egypt. Here a Request for Proposals (RfP) has recently been published and your company has been invited to participate in the bidding process. The award of the contract is based on an 80% price / 20% other criteria basis. The client is a large municipality. Three high-level employees, all Egyptians, represent the municipality in the RfP process. The RfP process allows for three face-to-face interactions of bidders with the client: First pitch, clarification meeting, closure meeting.

Discuss how you and your (engineering) team will prepare for each meeting in terms of understanding the context of the project and the meetings. Focus on 1) which aspects you will prepare for, 2) which are important and 'typical' situations that will require that you deviate from what you have prepared, and 3) how you will make sure that you transfer your learning from one meeting to the next.

Exercise B

Describe and discuss the term "strategic drift".

Exercise C

Discuss within a group of students when and how you have already experienced situations of "strategic drift" (e.g. student activities, student work experiences, other). Next, 1) decide on one situation, 2) describe and analyse this situation with the help of a strategizing perspective, and 3) come to a conclusion what you would do better next time.

References

Backhaus, K., & Voeth, M. (2010). *Industriegüter-Marketing* (9th ed.). München: Vahlen.
Deal, T. E., & Kennedy, A. A. (2000). *Corporate culture: The rites and rituals of corporate life* (reissued). Cambridge: Perseus.
GLOBE. (2020a). Data from the 2004 Study. https://globeproject.com/study_2004_2007?page_id=data#data [30 September 2020].
GLOBE. (2020b). Visualizations of the 2004 Study. https://globeproject.com/results?page_id=country#country [30 September 2020].
Golsorkhi, D., Rouleau, L., Seidl, D., & Vaara, E. (Eds.). (2015). *Cambridge handbook of strategy as practice* (2nd ed.). Cambridge: Cambridge University Press.
Hippner, H., & Wilde, K. D. (Eds.). (2006). *Grundlagen des CRM: Konzepte und Gestaltung* (3rd ed.). Wiesbaden: Gabler.
Hofstede, G. (1980). *Culture's consequences: International differences in work related values.* London: Sage.
Hofstede, G. (2001). *Culture's consequences: Comparing values, behaviors, institutions and organizations across nations.* London: Sage.
House, R., Hanges, P., Javidan, M., & Gupta, V. (2004). *Culture, leadership, and organizations: The GLOBE study of 62 societies.* Thousand Oaks: Sage.
Jarzabkowski, P. (2005). *Strategy as practice: An activity-based approach.* London: Sage.
Mahadevan, J. (2017). *A very short, fairly interesting and reasonably cheap book about cross-cultural management.* London: Sage.

Index

The manufacturer's authorised representative in the EU is Springer
Nature Customer Service Centre GmbH, Europaplatz 3, 69115 Heidelberg,
Germany. If you have any concerns regarding our products, please
contact ProductSafety@springernature.com

Printed and bound by CPI Group (UK) Ltd, Croydon, CR0 4YY

28/04/2026

02098489-0008